Ski the West

A Comprehensive Collection of Alpine Ski Areas of the Western USA

Brian E. Geppert

ISBN: 1546629041
ISBN-13: 978-1546629047

CONTENTS

Foreword   i

Ski Trip Planning   1

Ski Areas By The Numbers   6

Arizona   13

California   19

Colorado   71

Idaho   125

Montana   153

Nevada   177

New Mexico   185

Oregon   203

Utah   221

Washington   251

Wyoming   281

Photo Credits   297

Ski Area Contact Info   298

About the Author

FOREWORD

I decided to write this book because there are so many amazing ski areas in the Western US that you may not know about but should visit before you have used up your million turns. Certainly the Internet has plenty of information about these areas, but it is easier to flip through a single book then to scour the web for ski areas. This book is meant to show you all the possibilities and inspire your next ski trip. Life is way too short, so pack your bags and go skiing!

Thank you to all the ski areas that contributed to this effort –
I could not have made this happen without their help.

Thank you to my parents for instilling in me a love of the outdoors.
Special thanks go to Peter Lehman and Chris Meder for inspiring me to take up skiing at the age of 40.
Skiing has changed my life!

SKI TRIP PLANNING

This book will hopefully entice you to visit the ski areas listed between the covers. However, to make the most of your trip, I would like to offer some advice. This short chapter covers the basics of ski trip planning. Like most things, it all comes down to the details.

TIMING

The first thing to decide is the length of your ski trip. I am a fan of the 3-day ski trip because it lets you pack in a new adventure in a short time without using much vacation so that you can hopefully take several trips during the season. Start with picking the number of days you want to be on the hill, then add time for travel. You'll most often find that the travel time will prevent any runs on the first and potentially last day of your trip. However, that's not always the case. If you are flying, then it mostly depends on how close the ski area is to the airport.

Several locations, like Park City or Sun Valley, are within a very short drive from the airport (30-45 minutes). That can mean the difference between skiing on your travel days or not. For example, one could fly to Sun Valley on a Saturday, be on the slopes by noon so as to ski a half-day, ski Sunday and Monday, and fly home late Monday night.

I try to avoid the weekend skiing crowds as much as possible because I do not enjoy standing in lift lines. With a 3-day trip, you could use Fri/Sat/Sunday or Sat/Sun/Monday. The advantage to the latter is that you would be able to ski an almost full day on Monday (weekday lift lines) and fly home late. If your trip was Fri/Sat/Sunday then your last ski day (Sunday) is still competing with the weekend crowds and traffic.

Generic 3-Day Ski Trip:
- Saturday morning: Fly to destination
- Saturday afternoon: Night ski or ski half-day
- Sunday: Ski full day
- Monday: Ski full day (or as much as possible)
- Monday night: Fly back home

Another factor in timing is when to go. Ideally, you would pick a week that historically has a good chance of fresh snow with an established base. Mid-January through the end of March are usually safe bets. If you go any later, then you could run into Spring-skiing which is also ok but a different experience than normal skiing. The week would also not be close to a major holiday because that will drive up costs all around, increase lift lines / wait times, make parking more difficult, restaurants will be more full, etc. Try picking the weekend before or after a holiday weekend to avoid the crowds.

Avoid:
- Christmas through New Years
- Martin Luther King Jr. (MLK) birthday on the 3rd Monday of January.
- Presidents Day weekend on the 3rd Monday of February.

Once you've picked your destination, be sure to visit the ski area websites to see if they have any large events. For example, some ski areas host various ski races or events that close part of the mountain.

LODGING

If it's just two of you, a simple hotel is the easiest way to go. If you are bringing a family or have three or more, then look for a Vacation Rental by Owner (VRBO). AirBNB is also popular but I've found that most condos/houses are listed in both websites and are usually more expensive if rented through AirBNB. VRBO (which was merged with HomeAway.com) has a great website for filtering lodging based on number of rooms and amenities. For example, you can make sure the lodging has a hot tub and free WiFi. The website also allows for a map-view of the properties so that you can determine how far away it is from the slopes. Ideally, you can walk to the lift.

Make sure free parking is included and that there is sufficient parking for the number of vehicles you plan to bring. On many winter roads, that can be a challenge since shoulders are sometimes used for parking but not plowed.

TRANSPORTATION

If you are planning a road trip, then be sure to call your insurance and have them add on roadside assistance. For long trips along mountain passes, you are much more at risks for having a collision, accident, or car trouble due to extreme conditions. The best deal on car rentals is often by pre-paying or using a bidding site like PriceLine.com. Keep in mind that car rental fees/taxes are approximately half the cost, so if a vehicle is listed as $10/day, expect another $10 in fees before you place your bid.

Usually, you should plan to rent an all-wheel-drive (AWD) SUV for a ski trip that involves mountain driving. The problem is that when you reserve a vehicle, it does not specify whether the SUV is AWD. Therefore, when you pick up your vehicle, inspect it to make sure it is AWD and not a front-wheel drive SUV. In nearly all areas, AWD is sufficient for getting to the ski area. California has some odd laws requiring vehicles carry chains regardless if you have AWD, but only if the roads are very bad. (I believe the reason is that there are so many people that do not know how to drive in the snow that chains are one of the ways of keeping the collisions to a minimum.) Check California's Department of Transportation, CALTRANS for road conditions and chain requirements. Another wrinkle is that most car rental agencies do not rent chains.

How big of vehicle do you need? If it is just three of you, a mid-size SUV like a Nissan Rogue or Ford Escape is perfectly fine. I have even squeezed four people (with gear) in a Rogue but it wasn't pretty and only tolerable for a half hour of driving. If you have four people, I recommend a full-size SUV that has a 60-40 split rear seat. Fold the smaller seat down, place the ski bags next to the rear passenger and you are set. A full-size SUV will make this more comfortable. For example, the Chevy Tahoe has 79-inches of cargo length behind the 1st row of seats (it has three rows). That is enough to hold 200cm skis.

If you are planning to fly to your destination, then you'll need to determine when to purchase your airline tickets and what car to rent. October is often a good time to buy tickets since airlines often have a sale. However, examine the size of the airport you are using. If it is small, then the airplanes could also be small and thus there could be fewer seats available. In this case, book as soon as you can otherwise you run the risk of all airplanes being full the day you want to go. Airlines rarely add additional flights – they are more likely to run the same schedule year-round or for the season. Some airlines have different schedules for winter.

LIFT TICKETS

If you know where you will be skiing, you can usually save money by buying your lift ticket online in advance. If the ticket is mailed to you, be sure to give enough time to receive the lift ticket before you depart for your trip. Ideally, you would have your lift ticket in-hand when you hit the slopes so that you can avoid lift lines. It might sound trivial, but ticket lines can add another half-hour of waiting = less skiing. Also check to see if the weekday prices are cheaper because that may influence which resort you visit during your ski trip.

Be sure to check out some of the multi-resort lift ticket products. These are very helpful if you plan to ski at more than one ski area during the season. The table below shows some of the more popular passes. Prices could have changed so check the websites for current pricing. In some cases, there are limited quantities so it makes sense to purchase as soon as possible.

Product	Price	Benefits
Mountain Collective	$449	17 resorts, 2 days at each. 50% discount on lift tickets after you use the 2 days.
Ikon Pass	$999	18 resorts in the West (36 resorts mostly in North America). Two versions: Ikon Pass (unlimited) and Ikon Base Pass which typically offers 5 days at each resort. Includes a 25% discount on lift tickets for friends. New in 2018!
Epic Pass	$929	11 resorts in the West. Limited access to 65 resorts in the the world. The Epic Pass comes in a variety of forms, such as a 4-day, 7-day, or Epic-Local which offers unlimited access to a set of ski areas in a particular region.
Powder Alliance	$0	If you purchase a full season pass at one of the 19 Powder Alliance ski areas, it grants you 3-days at each of the other members of the Alliance.
Cascadia Pass	$209	3 days of skiing at Stevens Pass, Crystal Mountain, and Summit at Snoqualmie. Only an add-on product to a full season pass.
Power Pass	$749	Unlimited use at Purgatory, Hesperus, Arizona Snowbowl, Sipapu, & Pajarito Mountain. Includes 3 days at 15 other resorts.

Note: In 2018, the Ikon Pass (offered by the Alterra Mountain Company) was formed and replaced the Rocky Mountain Superpass, Cali4nia Pass, and M.A.X. Pass. It is unknown whether the Mountain Collective and Cascadia Pass will continue after the 2018-2019 season.

All season passes (including the Mountain Collective) are cheapest if you purchase in the spring of the prior season. Sometimes they will even add an additional perk for early-purchases.

If you'd prefer to buy an individual lift ticket, also check the website called Liftopia. Liftopia purchases discounted tickets for specific dates from resorts, then resells them also at a discount. You can save a lot of money using Liftopia, however Liftopia does not have lift tickets for all resorts. Look for Liftopia's gift card sale to save even more (usually once in the summer and then near Christmas).

Some ski areas will give you a free ski pass for the day of your arrival (or sometimes departure) if you show your airline boarding pass/ticket. In the past, the following ski areas have offered either free or highly discounted lift tickets when you show your boarding pass:

- California:
    o Heavenly
    o Kirkwood
    o Mammoth Mountain
    o Mt. Rose – Ski Tahoe
    o Northstar
    o Sierra-at-Tahoe
    o Squaw / Alpine Meadows
- Colorado:
    o Crested Butte
    o Steamboat
- Idaho:
    o Schweitzer
    o Sun Valley
- Montana: Whitefish
- Oregon: Mt. Bachelor
- Utah: Snowbasin
- Alaska: Alyeska

The list above is only for guidance. The program can change year-to-year so do your homework before you plan on skiing for free. (Alaska Airlines has the largest ski-for-free program.)

RESEARCHING THE TRIP

Here are a few of my favorite websites for researching ski areas. Quality varies across sites and some sites have information that others do not. Not all sites have all the ski areas either.

- OnTheSnow.com: Excellent breakdown of the resort information in an easy-to-read format. Allows for comparisons of resorts. Seems to have more guest reviews than other sites.

- Snow-Forecast.com: Most useful for weather predictions since it shows the forecast with a heat map for several elevations (at least base and peak).

- Snow-Online.com: Plenty of graphics, sometimes they get in the way but otherwise a good site with plenty of statistics and information. More for European resorts.

- SkiCentral.com: Decent resort information but not as easy to use as OnTheSnow. Does specify whether the ski area has night skiing and cross country skiing. No user reviews.

SKI AREAS BY THE NUMBERS

The table below shows all the ski area statistics. The interpretation of each category was left up to each resort, but typically "acreage" is meant to be lift-served acreage although some resorts might publish the ski-able acreage including hike-to acreage. The "% of Trails" category shows what percentage of the total runs at the ski area that are beginner (easiest), intermediate (more difficult), advanced (most difficult), and expert (most difficult - use extra caution). Keep in mind that some trails are longer/shorter than others, so the percentage can be misleading without looking at the trail map. The lift ticket price is the highest peak daily ticket price. The "HS Quad+" category is a count of the number of lifts that are high speed quads or larger, such as 6-person lifts, gondolas, trams, etc. Night skiing shows the nights that night skiing is offered, where "Ltd" means it is limited to certain nights of the season.

Three ski areas were omitted: Cottonwood Butte in Idaho (no data available), Sprout Springs in Oregon since it went up for sale in 2017, and Teton Pass (Montana) since it is closed, up for sale.

The table is sorted alphabetically, however the ski area sections are organized from largest to smallest (with some exceptions).

State	Ski Area Name	Page	Acreage	Lift Ticket Price	% of trails				Elevation (ft)			Lifts					Annual Snowfall	Night Skiing?	Established
					Beginner	Intermediate	Advanced	Expert	Base	Summit	Vertical Drop	HS Quad+	Quad	Triple	Double	Surface	inches		Year
AZ	Arizona Snowbowl	16	777	$89	37	42	21	0	9200	11500	2300	1	1	2	2	2	260	No	1938
AZ	Sunrise Park Resort	14	800	$71	40	40	20	0	9200	11100	1800	1	2	3	1	0	200	Ltd	1970
CA	Alpine Meadows	24	2400	$179	25	40	35	0	6835	8637	1802	3	0	3	5	2	450	No	1961
CA	Bear Mountain	58	198	$99	16	47	28	9	7140	8805	1665	2	1	2	3	4	100	No	1943
CA	Bear Valley	34	1680	$79	25	40	35	0	6600	8500	1900	2	0	4	2	2	370	No	1967
CA	Boreal Mountain	52	380	$64	30	55	15	0	7200	7700	500	1	2	3	1	2	400	Yes	1965
CA	China Peak	40	1400	$83	11	41	33	15	7029	8708	1678	0	1	4	2	3	300	No	1958
CA	Dodge Ridge	44	862	$72	20	40	40	0	6600	8200	1600	0	1	2	5	4	300	No	1950

State	Ski Area Name	Page	Acreage	Lift Ticket Price	Beginner	Intermediate	Advanced	Expert	Base	Summit	Vertical Drop	HS Quad+	Quad	Triple	Double	Surface	Annual Snowfall	Night Skiing?	Established
CA	Donner Ski Ranch	46	505	$69	25	50	25	0	7031	8012	750	0	1	5	2	2	396	No	1937
CA	Granlibakken	70	10	$35	100	0	0	0	6300	6750	450	0	0	0	2	2	184	No	1922
CA	Heavenly	20	4800	$165	20	45	30	5	6565	10067	3502	11	1	5	3	8	360	No	1955
CA	Homewood Mountain Resort	42	1260	$99	15	40	30	15	6230	7880	1650	1	3	3	0	4	450	No	1961
CA	June Mountain	38	1500	$129	35	45	20	0	7545	10090	2590	0	0	0	4	1	250	No	1961
CA	Kirkwood	30	2300	$86	12	30	38	20	7800	9800	2000	1	6	1	1	5	600	No	1972
CA	Mammoth Mountain	26	3500	$111	25	40	20	15	7952	11052	3100	14	6	4	4	3	400	No	1953
CA	Mountain High	54	290	$74	20	42	34	3	6600	8200	1600	2	2	5	5	3	132	Yes	1941
CA	Mt. Baldy	50	400	$69	20	40	20	20	6500	8600	2100	0	0	4	4	0	178	No	1952
CA	Mt. Shasta Ski Park	48	425	$58	20	55	25	0	5500	6890	1435	0	3	0	0	1	275	Th-Sa	1985
CA	Mt. Waterman	64	150	$50	20	20	60	0	7000	8030	1030	0	0	3	3	0	72	No	1939
CA	Northstar	28	3170	$111	16	47	37	0	6330	8610	2280	1	2	0	0	7	350	No	1972
CA	Sierra-at-Tahoe	32	2000	$104	25	50	25	0	6640	8852	2212	0	1	5	5	5	480	No	1946
CA	Snow Summit	56	240	$99	13	65	12	10	7000	8200	1200	0	4	5	5	5	100	Yes	1952
CA	Snow Valley	60	240	$74	14	46	32	7	6800	7841	1041	1	5	5	5	1	160	F,Sa	1937
CA	Soda Springs	62	200	$59	30	40	30	0	6750	7300	550	0	1	1	1	2	400	No	1936
CA	Squaw Valley	22	3600	$179	25	45	30	0	6200	9050	2850	1	9	5	5	5	450	Ltd	1949
CA	Sugar Bowl	36	1650	$109	17	45	26	12	6883	8383	1500	3	1	2	2	1	500	No	1939
CA	Tahoe Donner	66	120	$64	40	60	0	0	6750	7350	600	1	0	1	1	3	400	No	1971
CA	Yosemite Ski & Snowboard Area	68	88	$55	35	50	15	0	7200	8000	800	0	1	3	3	1	300	No	1935
CO	Arapahoe Basin	110	1331	$95	7	22	45	26	10780	13050	2530	1	1	3	3	3	350	No	1946
CO	Aspen Buttermilk	82	470	$169	35	39	21	5	7870	9900	2030	0	0	1	1	3	350	No	1946
CO	Aspen Highlands	78	1040	$169	18	30	16	36	8310	11675	3365	0	2	0	0	4	300	No	1958
CO	Aspen Mountain	80	675	$169	0	48	26	26	7945	11212	3267	1	0	3	3	0	300	No	1946

7

State	Ski Area Name	Page	Acreage	Lift Ticket Price	Beginner	Intermediate	Advanced	Expert	Base	Summit	Vertical Drop	HS Quad+	Quad	Triple	Double	Surface	Annual Snowfall	Night Skiing?	Established
CO	Aspen Snowmass	76	3332	$169	6	47	17	30	7880	12510	4406	8	2	0	3	7	300	No	1946
CO	Beaver Creek	96	1832	$219	19	43	21	17	8100	11440	3340	13	0	1	2	9	323	No	1980
CO	Breckenridge	90	2908	$201	11	31	24	34	9600	12998	3397	13	0	1	6	14	300	No	1961
CO	Cooper	120	400	$52	28	36	36	0	10500	11700	1200	0	0	1	1	2	260	No	1945
CO	Copper Mountain	92	2490	$150	13	16	43	28	9703	12313	2601	7	0	4	4	9	302	No	1972
CO	Crested Butte	106	1547	$120	26	57	14	3	9375	12162	3062	4	2	2	2	5	300	No	1961
CO	Echo Mountain	123	60	$54	10	75	10	5	10050	10650	600	0	0	1	0	1	275	Ltd	2005
CO	Eldora	114	680	$94	21	51	19	9	9200	10800	1600	0	2	2	4	3	300	No	1962
CO	Granby Ranch	118	406	$79	36	40	24	0	8202	9202	1000	0	2	1	1	1	220	Rent	1983
CO	Hesperus	122	80	$39	30	20	30	0	8100	8880	700	0	0	0	1	1	150	Holidays	1962
CO	Howelsen Hill	124	50	$25	20	30	50	0	6696	7136	440	0	0	0	1	3	150	W-Th	1915
CO	Keystone	84	3148	$165	14	29	57	0	9280	12408	3128	6	4	1	3	7	230	Yes	1970
CO	Loveland	100	1800	$71	13	41	20	26	10800	13010	2210	1	3	2	2	2	422	No	1937
CO	Monarch Mountain	112	800	$84	23	28	36	13	10790	11952	1162	0	1	0	4	3	350	No	1939
CO	Powderhorn	102	1600	$71	20	50	20	10	8200	9850	1650	1	0	0	2	2	250	No	1966
CO	Purgatory	108	1525	$89	20	45	30	5	8793	10822	2029	3	0	3	3	2	260	No	1965
CO	Silverton Mountain	98	1819	$59	0	0	0	100	10400	13487	3087	0	0	0	1	0	400	No	2002
CO	Steamboat	88	2965	$145	14	42	44	0	6900	10568	3668	7	1	6	2	5	336	Th-M	1963
CO	Sunlight Mountain Resort	116	680	$65	20	55	20	5	7885	9895	2010	0	0	1	2	0	250	No	1966
CO	Telluride	94	2000	$107	23	36	21	20	8725	13150	4425	9	1	2	2	5	309	No	1972
CO	Vail	72	5289	$219	18	29	28	25	8120	11570	3450	19	1	2	0	9	353	No	1962
CO	Winter Park	86	3081	$115	26	19	52	3	9000	12060	3060	9	0	4	6	5	353	No	1940
CO	Wolf Creek	104	1600	$70	20	35	25	20	10300	11904	1604	3	1	2	1	3	430	No	1939
ID	Bald Mountain	149	140	$20	25	40	20	15	4000	4800	860	0	0	0	0	2	100	No	1959

State	Ski Area Name	Page	Acreage	Lift Ticket Price	Beginner	Intermediate	Advanced	Expert	Base	Summit	Vertical Drop	HS Quad+	Quad	Triple	Double	Surface	Annual Snowfall	Night Skiing?	Established
ID	Bogus Basin	128	2600	$62	11	44	33	12	5790	7590	1800	3	0	1	3	1	250	Yes	1942
ID	Brundage Mountain	132	1920	$67	20	50	25	5	5882	7803	1921	1	0	3	0	0	320	No	1961
ID	Kelly Canyon	142	688	$42	35	45	20	0	5600	6600	1000	0	0	4	0	1	200	Yes	1957
ID	Little Ski Hill	150	50	$15	100	0	0	0	5195	5600	405	0	0	0	1	1	180	Tu-Sat	1937
ID	Lookout Pass	144	540	$45	20	50	20	10	4500	5650	1150	0	0	3	0	0	400	No	1935
ID	Magic Mountain	148	120	$32	25	20	20	30	6500	7240	740	0	0	1	2	2	230	No	1938
ID	Pebble Creek	138	1100	$47	12	30	29	29	6360	8560	2200	0	3	0	0	0	250	F,Sa	1949
ID	Pomerelle	146	500	$45	40	40	20	0	8000	9000	1000	0	0	1	1	1	500	Tu-Sa	1963
ID	Schweitzer Mountain	126	2900	$79	10	40	35	15	4000	6400	2400	3	1	3	2	0	300	Ltd	1963
ID	Silver Mountain	134	1600	$61	20	40	30	10	4100	6300	2200	1	1	2	1	2	340	Ltd	1968
ID	Snowhaven	151	40	$19	25	75	0	0	5200	5600	400	0	0	0	2	1	60	No	1948
ID	Soldier Mountain	136	1180	$43	20	50	10	20	5756	7177	1425	0	0	2	1	1	100	No	1947
ID	Sun Valley	130	2054	$125	36	42	20	2	5750	9150	3400	10	4	2	3	3	220	No	1936
ID	Tamarack	140	1020	$69	17	45	38	0	4900	7700	2800	2	0	0	2	2	300	No	2004
MT	Bear Paw Ski Bowl	176	80	$20	25	25	50	0	4203	5282	1079	0	0	1	1	1	140	No	1960
MT	Big Sky Resort	154	5800	$139	15	25	42	18	6800	11166	4350	6	7	6	11	3	400	No	1973
MT	Blacktail Mountain	168	1000	$42	15	65	0	20	5236	6780	1440	0	1	2	1	1	250	No	1998
MT	Bridger Bowl	158	2000	$60	18	50	25	7	6100	8700	2600	0	6	1	3	3	350	No	1955
MT	Discovery Ski Area	160	2000	$46	20	25	25	30	5770	8158	2388	0	5	2	1	1	215	No	1973
MT	Great Divide	164	1600	$48	10	45	45	0	5750	7330	1580	0	0	5	1	3	180	Fri	1941
MT	Lost Trail Powder Mountain	162	1800	$46	20	60	20	0	6400	8200	1800	0	0	5	3	1	325	No	1938
MT	Maverick Mountain	174	450	$38	30	40	30	0	6080	9000	2020	0	0	1	1	1	200	No	1936
MT	Red Lodge Mountain	166	1600	$60	18	28	35	18	7016	9416	2400	2	1	3	1	1	250	No	1960
MT	Showdown Montana	172	640	$45	30	40	30	0	6800	8200	1400	0	1	2	1	1	240	No	1936

State	Ski Area Name	Page	Acreage	Lift Ticket Price	Beginner	Intermediate	Advanced	Expert	Base	Summit	Vertical Drop	HS Quad+	Quad	Triple	Double	Surface	Annual Snowfall	Night Skiing?	Established
MT	Snowbowl	170	950	$48	20	40	40	0	5000	7600	2600	0	0	0	2	2	300	No	1961
MT	Turner Mountain	175	400	$38	10	30	60	0	3842	5952	2110	0	0	0	1	0	250	No	1961
MT	Whitefish	156	3000	$79	12	38	44	6	4464	6817	2353	3	2	6	0	3	300	F,Sa,Hol	1947
NV	Diamond Peak	180	655	$89	18	46	36	0	6700	8540	1840	1	2	0	3	1	325	No	1966
NV	Elko Snobowl	184	60	$20	8	90	1	1	6300	7000	700	0	0	0	1	1	42	No	1996
NV	Lee Canyon	182	195	$70	20	60	20	0	8510	11289	860	0	2	1	0	0	161	No	1963
NV	Mt. Rose - Ski Tahoe	178	1200	$125	20	30	40	10	8260	9700	1800	2	2	2	0	2	350	No	1964
NM	Angel Fire	192	560	$73	21	56	23	0	8600	10677	2077	2	0	3	3	2	210	F,Sa	1966
NM	Pajarito Mountain	194	300	$49	20	50	30	0	9000	10440	1440	0	1	3	1	1	163	No	1957
NM	Red River	196	290	$76	31	31	0	38	8750	10350	1600	0	1	1	3	2	214	No	1959
NM	Sandia Peak	198	200	$55	35	55	10	0	8678	10378	1700	0	0	4	0	1	125	No	1937
NM	Sipapu	200	200	$45	20	40	25	15	8200	9255	1055	0	1	0	2	3	190	No	1952
NM	Ski Apache	188	750	$46	18	55	27	0	9600	11500	1900	0	2	6	0	2	185	No	1961
NM	Ski Cloudcroft	202	74	$45	32	28	32	8	8400	9100	700	0	0	0	1	3	100	No	1963
NM	Ski Santa Fe	190	660	$75	20	40	35	5	10350	12075	1725	0	1	2	2	2	225	No	1947
NM	Taos	186	1294	$98	15	17	32	36	9207	12481	3274	0	4	3	5	3	300	No	1955
OR	Anthony Lakes	219	1100	$35	20	38	0	42	7100	8000	900	0	0	1	0	2	300	No	1963
OR	Cooper Spur	218	50	$36	40	60	0	0	3500	4000	350	0	0	0	2	1	100	Ltd	1953
OR	Hoodoo	212	806	$58	30	30	40	0	4668	5703	1035	0	3	1	1	0	450	F,Sa	1938
OR	Mt. Ashland	216	220	$49	5	20	50	25	6383	7533	1150	0	2	2	2	1	256	Ltd	1964
OR	Mt. Bachelor	204	4318	$92	15	35	30	20	5700	9065	3365	8	3	0	0	0	462	No	1958
OR	Mt. Hood Meadows	206	2150	$79	15	50	20	15	4523	7300	2777	6	0	5	5	2	430	W-Su	1968
OR	Mt. Hood Skibowl	210	960	$51	20	40	25	15	3600	5100	1500	0	0	0	4	5	300	Yes	1937
OR	Timberline	208	1415	$68	25	50	25	0	4850	8540	3960	1	0	0	0	5	550	F,Sa	1937

State	Ski Area Name	Page	Acreage	Lift Ticket Price	Beginner	Intermediate	Advanced	Expert	Base	Summit	Vertical Drop	HS Quad+	Quad	Triple	Double	Surface	Annual Snowfall	Night Skiing?	Established
OR	Warner Canyon Ski Area	220	240	$32	24	24	21	31	5700	6480	780	0	0	1	0	0	150	No	1938
OR	Willamette Pass	214	555	$60	21	45	10	24	5120	6683	1563	1	0	4	1	1	430	No	1941
UT	Alta	230	2200	$104	25	40	35	0	8530	10550	2020	2	0	2	4	1	551	No	1938
UT	Beaver Mountain	238	828	$50	35	40	25	0	7232	8860	1600	0	0	3	1	1	400	Yes	1938
UT	Brian Head Resort	240	650	$59	30	35	32	3	9600	10970	1320	1	1	6	1	0	360	F,Sa	1965
UT	Brighton	236	1050	$79	21	39	25	15	8755	10500	1745	3	1	1	1	1	500	M-Sa	1936
UT	Cherry Peak	246	300	$39	30	45	25	0	5775	7050	1265	0	1	3	1	1	322	M-Sa	2015
UT	Deer Valley	232	2026	$135	27	41	27	5	6570	9570	3000	13	1	1	0	0	300	No	1981
UT	Eagle Point	242	650	$65	20	35	45	0	9100	10600	1500	0	1	1	1	1	350	No	2010
UT	Nordic Valley	248	140	$50	30	40	30	0	5440	6400	965	0	0	1	1	1	300	M-Sa	1968
UT	Park City	224	7300	$172	9	51	30	10	6800	10000	3200	18	6	8	5	5	355	Ltd	1963
UT	Powder Mountain	222	8464	$85	25	40	25	10	6900	9422	2205	1	4	1	3	3	500	172	1972
UT	Snowbasin	226	3000	$109	11	43	24	22	6400	9350	2900	5	0	4	0	2	300	No	1940
UT	Snowbird	228	2500	$106	27	38	20	15	7760	11000	3240	4	0	0	1	1	500	F,Sa	1971
UT	Solitude	234	1200	$88	10	40	36	14	8005	10035	2030	4	0	1	1	0	500	No	1957
UT	Sundance	244	450	$70	35	45	20	0	6100	8250	2150	0	2	2	0	1	300	M,W,F,Sa	1969
WA	49 Degrees North	254	2325	$58	30	40	25	5	3932	5774	1851	0	1	0	1	1	301	Ltd	1935
WA	Bluewood	274	400	$39	25	45	30	0	4545	5670	1125	0	0	2	0	1	300	No	1979
WA	Crystal Mountain	252	2600	$80	11	54	32	3	4400	7012	3100	5	1	2	2	1	486	Yes	1962
WA	Echo Valley	277	70	$25	50	25	20	5	3000	3900	900	0	0	0	4	4	39	No	1955
WA	Hurricane Ridge	278	50	$34	12	38	25	25	4800	5500	800	0	0	0	3	3	400	No	1958
WA	Leavenworth Ski Hill	279	17	$20	50	50	0	0	1500	1700	200	0	0	0	0	2	100	Ltd	1928
WA	Loup Loup	276	300	$48	20	30	40	0	4020	5260	1240	0	1	0	2	2	150	No	1958
WA	Mission Ridge	256	2000	$69	11	53	22	14	4570	6820	2250	1	0	3	2	2	200	Ltd	1966

State	Ski Area Name	Page	Acreage	Lift Ticket Price	Beginner	Intermediate	Advanced	Expert	Base	Summit	Vertical Drop	HS Quad+	Quad	Triple	Double	Surface	Annual Snowfall	Night Skiing?	Established
WA	Mt. Baker	264	1000	$61	24	45	0	31	3589	5089	1500	0	0	0	2	2	663	No	1953
WA	Mt. Spokane	258	1425	$58	23	32	45	0	3818	5889	2000	0	0	5	1	1	300	Ltd	1932
WA	Stevens Pass	262	1125	$74	6	48	28	18	4061	5845	1800	3	0	4	3	1	460	Yes	1937
WA	The Summit at Snoqualmie - Alpental	266	818	$85	4	17	38	41	3140	5420	2280	1	0	0	3	1	428	Yes	1967
WA	The Summit at Snoqualmie - Central	268	539	$85	14	39	47	0	2840	3865	1025	2	0	1	4	2	428	Yes	1948
WA	The Summit at Snoqualmie - East	270	340	$85	20	45	35	0	2610	3710	1100	0	1	1	1	0	428	No	1967
WA	The Summit at Snoqualmie - West	272	299	$85	7	43	50	0	3000	3765	765	2	2	2	2	3	428	Yes	1933
WA	White Pass	260	1402	$66	20	60	10	10	4500	6550	2050	2	1	2	2	2	450	Ltd	1952
WY	Grand Targhee	282	2602	$85	33	37	25	5	7851	9920	2030	2	1	1	0	1	500	No	1969
WY	Hogadon Basin	296	60	$42	8	31	38	23	7400	8000	600	0	0	1	1	1	80	No	1958
WY	Jackson Hole Mountain Resort	284	2500	$144	13	34	41	12	6311	10450	4139	7	4	0	1	2	450	No	1965
WY	Meadowlark Ski Lodge	295	300	$48	30	30	20	20	8500	9500	1000	0	0	1	1	1	300	No	2010
WY	Pine Creek Ski	294	640	$45	30	35	20	15	6875	8225	1400	0	1	0	0	1	300	No	1952
WY	Sleeping Giant	292	184	$36	15	38	35	13	6619	7428	810	0	0	1	1	1	310	No	1938
WY	Snow King Mountain	286	400	$55	15	25	20	40	6237	7808	1571	0	1	1	1	1	167	M-Sa	1939
WY	Snowy Range	290	250	$45	30	40	30	0	8798	9663	990	0	0	3	1	1	245	No	1960
WY	White Pine	288	370	$48	30	33	37	0	8400	9500	1100	0	0	0	0	0	150	No	1938

Arizona

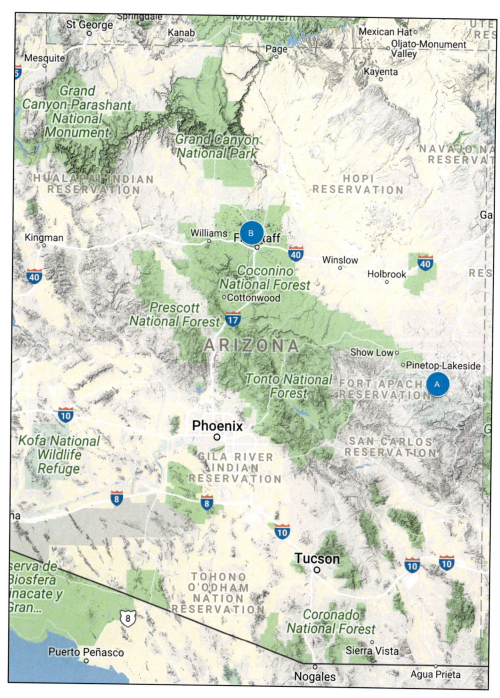

Page

A. Sunrise Park Resort..........................14

B. Arizona Snowbowl..........................16

Sunrise Ski Park

| Established: 1970 | Acres: 800 | Vertical: 1800' | Annual Snowfall: 260" |

Located in the heart of Arizona's magnificent White Mountains, Sunrise Park Resort is a recreational paradise offering a wide range of fun and excitement. In winter, their three mountains offer some of the finest skiing and snowboarding in the Western United States.

65 runs promise adventure for skiers or boarders of any level. There is also cross country ski trails, sledding, sleigh rides, and a tubing area. During the Summer, they offer scenic lift rides, mountain biking, hiking, archery, disc golf, tubing slide, air bag jump, boat rentals, and a series of 6 zip lines on Sunrise Mountain.

The Sunrise Park Lodge, located near beautiful Sunrise Lake, is available for comfortable lodging in the winter and summer seasons. The 100-room hotel offers great dining, indoor pool and whirlpool, lounge and game room. You can escape into the wilderness, ski, mountain bike, enjoy their annual festivals and fish to your heart's content.

For Snowboarders and Skiers Sunrise offers a Terrain Park. Within sight of Sunrise Day Lodge, the park features implanted wood and metal rails, boxes, and a special event area with jumps ranging from beginner to advanced.

CYCLONE MOUNTAIN (10,700')

Cyclone Mountain is home to the steepest and most challenging trails at the Resort but still leaves room for additional parking, a dedicated rental shop and a Base Area Lodge complete with bar, cafeteria and Ticket Booth.

SUNRISE MOUNTAIN (10,700')

Sunrise Mountain is home to the largest variety of trails at Sunrise Park Resort. Sunrise Mountain is also home to the largest variety of lifts and regular amenities including a rental shop, sports shop, full service ski & ride shop as well as a childcare facility and a total of 4 different places to eat.

APACHE PEAK (11,000')

Apache peak is centrally located between Sunrise and Cyclone Mountain, with a spectacular view and beautiful lodge. This Mountain is home to some of the widest and heaviest snowfall covered runs at the Resort.

Sunrise Park Resort is proudly owned and operated by the White Mountain Apache Tribe.

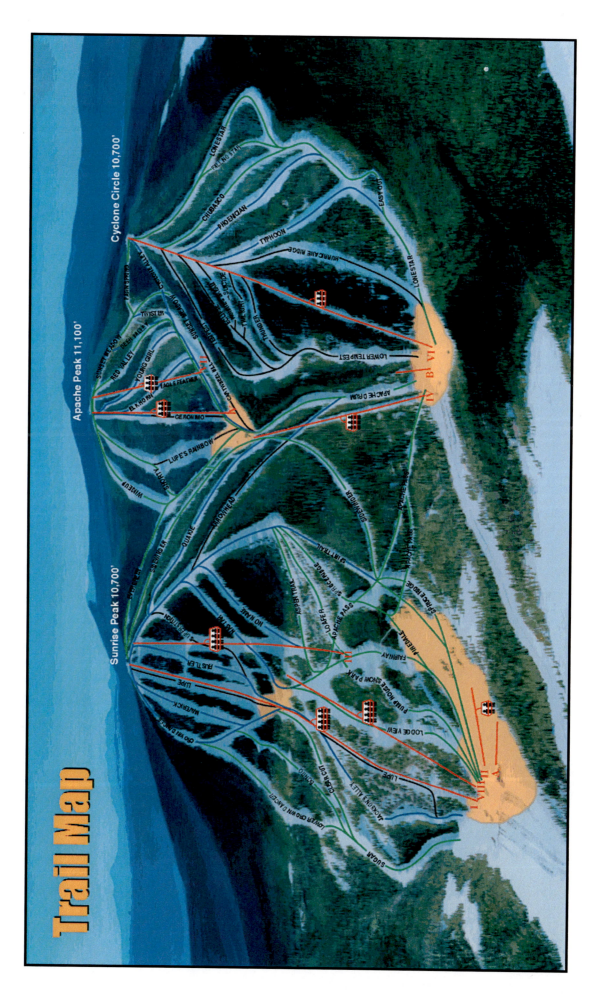

Arizona Snowbowl

Established: 1938	Acres: 777	Vertical: 2300'	Annual Snowfall: 260"

Fresh powder. Blue, sunny skies. Warm, friendly staff. All at the top of Arizona. With incredible snow and breathtaking views, Arizona Snowbowl is a haven for seasoned skiers and snowboarders, as well as first-timers.

"Snow" may not be the first word that comes to mind when you think about Arizona, but Arizona Snowbowl accumulates an average of 260 inches of snow each winter. The sun is never away for long, however, and Snowbowl is one of the best locations in the nation to ski on great snow in the warm sunshine.

With one of the best instructional programs in the west, Snowbowl is the ideal resort for families and those putting their boots in the snow for the first time. Professionally trained, bilingual instructors provide skiers and boarders of all levels a top-notch experience.

NEW LIFTS & OTHER IMPROVEMENTS

Since 2015, Snowbowl has added three new chairlifts, including a high-speed six-person lift which debuted during the 2016/2017 season. This winter (2018), the resort will open a new quad with a loading conveyor, replacing the old Hart Prairie double chairlift. The Hart Prairie beginner area features a wide-open, gentle meadow that provides beginners with a great place to learn and grow more confident on the slopes.

A new 300-seat restaurant will open this winter, doubling the dining capacity in the base area, and includes a patio and fire pit, offering a prime spot to enjoy après ski.

TERRAIN PARKS

Snowbowl's three terrain parks offer progressive features to facilitate a natural learning process: Prairie Dawg Start Park for beginners, Daydreamer Progression Park for intermediates, and Sunset Terrain Park for expert riding and freestyle skills.

GETTING THERE

Located on the majestic San Francisco Peaks at 9,200 ft. above sea level, Arizona Snowbowl lies just 14 miles outside of Flagstaff, 2 hours from Phoenix, and 70 miles from the Grand Canyon. Arizona Snowbowl offers a free shuttle service between downtown Flagstaff and the Hart Prairie Lodge at Arizona Snowbowl.

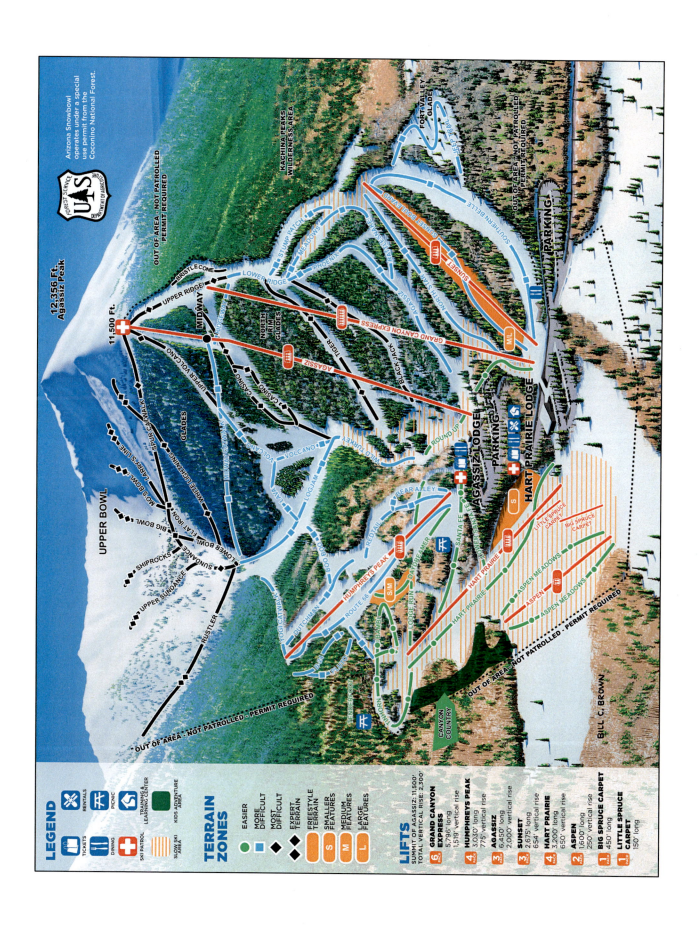

FUN FACT

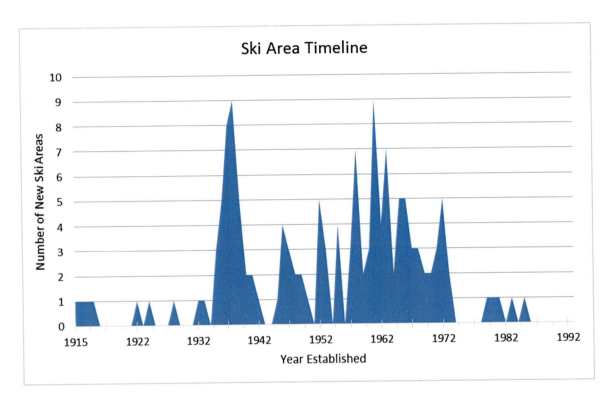

The chart above shows when all of the ski areas in this book were established. As you can see, many of these areas were started in the late 1930s when the first chairlifts began showing up. There was another boost of activity in the late 1950s into the early 1970s as skiing became more popular with big advances in equipment technology (fiberglas skis, plastic boots, better bindings, warmer clothing). Another reason for the sudden expansion was that the economy was booming. Ski areas became the next hot investment. This chart doesn't show the total number of ski areas created – just when the existing ones were established. Many more ski areas were developed but didn't stand the test of time.

California

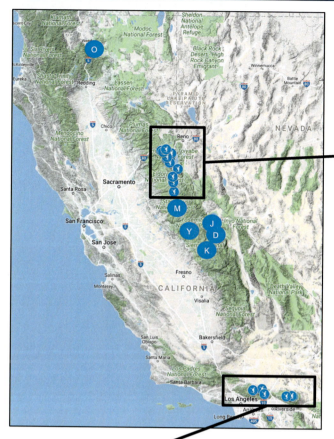

		Page
A.	Heavenly	20
B.	Squaw Valley	22
C.	Alpine Meadows	24
D.	Mammoth Mountain	26
E.	Northstar	28
F.	Kirkwood	30
G.	Sierra-at-Tahoe	32
H.	Bear Valley	34
I.	Sugar Bowl	36
J.	June Mountain	38
K.	China Peak	40
L.	Homewood Mountain Resort	42
M.	Dodge Ridge	44

		Page
N.	Donner Ski Ranch	46
O.	Mt. Shasta Ski Park	48
P.	Mt. Baldy	50
Q.	Boreal Mountain	52
R.	Mountain High	54
S.	Snow Summit	56
T.	Bear Mountain	58
U.	Snow Valley	60
V.	Soda Springs	62
W.	Mt. Waterman	64
X.	Tahoe Donner	66
Y.	Yosemite Ski & Snowboard Area	68
Z.	Granlibakken	70

Heavenly

Heavenly
LAKE TAHOE

Established: 1955	Acres: 4800	Vertical: 3502'	Annual Snowfall: 360"

Overlooking the sapphire-blue waters of Lake Tahoe, Heavenly ski resort is one of the most unique snowsports destinations on the planet. With a higher elevation and the most skiable terrain in Tahoe, you have more hidden glades to explore and groomers to rip than any Lake Tahoe resort. Beginners can get comfortable on the groomed runs while more seasoned riders can explore the back-country-like canyons, tree runs and terrain parks.

Off the slopes you'll find more activities and après ski choices than you know what to do with. Heavenly is for those who are up for first chair and are still going strong well after last call. You come here to go all in, and you worry about sleep later. Nightlife at Heavenly Mountain Resort provides a rockin' experience you won't find in any other mountain town.

Start with the Unbuckle Après Ski Party then see where the night takes you. Maybe you'll end up stacking chips at one of the South Lake Tahoe casinos, indulging in a great meal at one of the many local restaurants, grabbing a ticket to a concert or dancing at one of Tahoe's nightclubs. There's never a dull moment on this vacation.

TERRAIN PARKS
The Heavenly Mountain Resort terrain parks are some of the most-exciting, challenging, unique and well-maintained terrain parks in Lake Tahoe thanks to the tireless dedication and passion of their Terrain Park team. Whether you're a beginner or expert, they have a park that is sure to get your heart beating fast!

WINTER ACTIVITIES
There are also plenty of family-friendly events at Heavenly to choose from including tubing, ice skating, a kids ski school, the Ripperoo Parade, shows and arcades. The tubing hill is 500 feet long and has a convenient magic carpet to take you back up.

Squaw Valley

Established: 1949	Acres: 3600	Vertical: 2850'	Annual Snowfall: 450"

With access to both Squaw Valley and Alpine Meadows on the same lift ticket and season pass, skiing and riding two mountains in one day has never been so easy!

Host of the 1960 Winter Olympics, Squaw Valley is an internationally renowned resort destination, known for legendary terrain that spans 3,600 skiable acres over six mountain peaks, all accessed by 29 chairlifts. Terrain ranges from an expansive mountaintop beginner area to unrivaled expert steeps. Complete with slopeside lodging in The Village at Squaw Valley®, which bustles year round with nonstop events and over 50 bars, restaurants and boutiques, Squaw Valley has something for the entire family.

Squaw is home to the KT-22 lift, an expert's nirvana and an iconic chairlift—not just at Squaw Valley, but in the world of skiing and snowboarding. One of the best lifts in North America, KT-22 accesses 2,000 vertical feet of steeps, chutes and cliffs. It is hands-down the best expert terrain.

THE NORTH FACE® MOUNTAIN GUIDES

Take a personal mountain tour with Squaw Valley's experienced guides to discover the resorts' most coveted terrain, secret stashes and hidden groomers. The North Face Mountain Guide program gets priority lift line access and is offered daily throughout the season. These guided ski days are ideal for guests new to the mountain as well as long-time skiers and riders looking to explore the far corners of the resort.

SNOVENTURES

SnoVentures is Squaw Valley's family fun zone. Gently sloped terrain serviced by an easy-to-ride beginner lift and two surface carpets means it's perfect for beginning skiers and snowboarders. Plus, snow tubing, mini snowmobiles, a day lodge and a free shuttle from the Village make it perfect for families looking for additional activities to round out their ski vacation.

THE VILLAGE AT SQUAW VALLEY®

The Village at Squaw Valley allows you to stay in the heart of the Lake Tahoe winter action, and just steps from the slopes at Squaw Valley. With dining, shopping and activities, there's no better way to spend more time playing and less time traveling. The Village at Squaw Valley boasts standard rooms as well as studios, one, two or three bedroom units, all with access to world-class amenities and services, ensuring you'll never have to look far for anything.

Squaw Valley is part of the Ikon Pass.

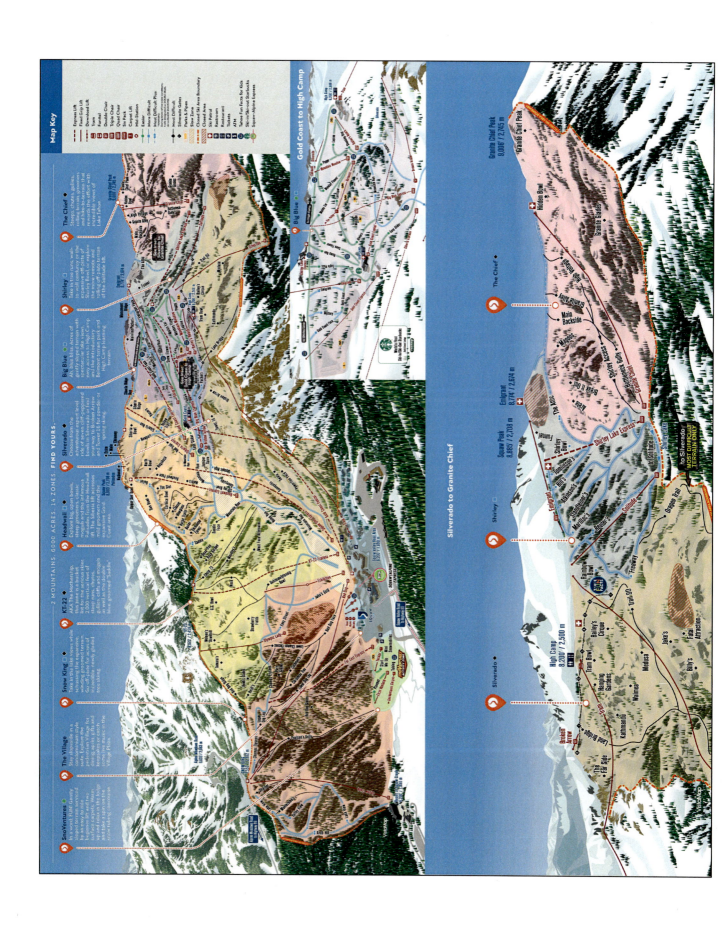

Alpine Meadows

| Established: 1961 | Acres: 2400 | Vertical: 1802' | Annual Snowfall: 450" |

Skiing Alpine Meadows and Squaw Valley in one day is now easier than ever, with both mountains on the same lift ticket and season pass!

With seven bowls and summit-to-base groomed slopes, the authentic hospitality at Alpine Meadows is a family favorite. Access to over 100 trails across 2,400 skiable acres serviced by 13 lifts makes Alpine Meadows one mountain you won't want to miss. From perfect groomers to expansive hike-to bowls, the mountain has charm and challenge, perfect for every type of skier.

At Alpine Meadows there are a number of incredible zones, making terrain decisions a good problem to have! Arguably the best terrain on the mountain, the PCT Bowls at Alpine deliver deep pow turns and full faced grins, all best experienced with a North Face Mountain Guide.

MOONLIT SNOWSHOE TOUR & DINNER

After the mountain closes and the winter moon rises, experience a snowshoe tour to the mid-mountain Chalet at Alpine Meadows. Enjoy an intimate seated dinner where you'll be served an Alps-inspired menu with dishes like potato cheese soup, chicken cordon bleu and apple strudel. This unique experience is only available for 50 guests during select dates throughout the winter.

SKI AND SNOWBOARD SCHOOL

Whatever your skill and style, get the most out of Alpine Meadows and Squaw Valley with a ski or snowboard program picked just for you. From private, beginner lessons to camps specifically designed for Women, there's a program for every ability level, designed to help you improve your skills. Group lessons, private lessons, half days and full days are all offered, giving you the ultimate flexibility.

Alpine Meadows is also part of the Ikon Pass.

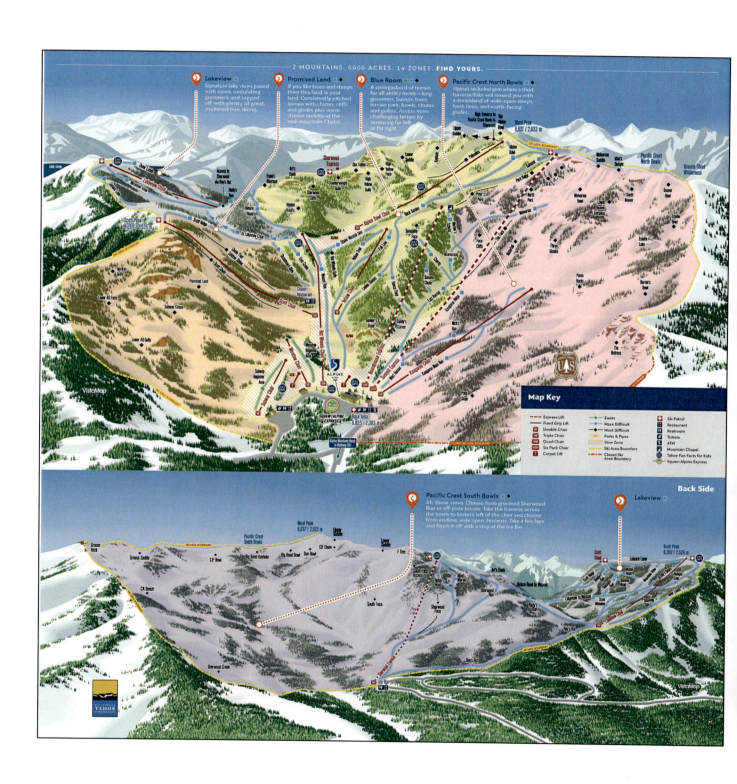

Mammoth Mountain

Established: 1953	Acres: 3500	Vertical: 3100'	Annual Snowfall: 400"

Mammoth Mountain is California's highest four-season resort and playground with a summit at 11,053 feet above sea level. With 300 days of sunshine annually, the Eastern Sierra offers infinite recreation and scenic beauty all year long. Mammoth's legendary snowfall provides a perfect winter playground, enabling Mammoth to truly claim the title of Southern California's mountain home.

Mammoth has winter activities for everyone, including: cross-country skiing, snowmobile tours, snowcat tours, and tubing. Woolly's Tube Park has six groomed lanes, a tube lift, snow play area, heated deck and snack shack.

Mammoth has it all: 3 base lodges, 10 sport shops, 12 rental/repair shops, 2 on-hill snack bars, 4 food courts/cafeterias, ski and snowboard school, race department, lockers, slopeside hotel and condominium accommodations, 5 restaurants, 7 bars, and even child care during the day. Activities around town include shopping, dining, cocktails, movie theaters, dancing and more.

Mammoth is part of the Ikon Pass.

UNBOUND TERRAIN PARKS

The Unbound Terrain Parks have led the industry in innovation, quality and design for close to 20 years. With 13 unique parks, four half pipes, 100 + jibs and up to 50 jumps on any given day covering over 100 acres of terrain, Unbound is a mecca for fun and progression. Using state-of-the-art equipment to provide a progressive environment for all levels, from beginners to a team of 10 professional athletes, the Unbound earns consistent ratings among the top parks of the world. With a longstanding commitment to athlete development, Mammoth and USSA are proud to name the Unbound Terrain Parks as the Official Training Ground for the US Freeski & Snowboarding Team.

MOUNTAIN TOURS

Get the inside scoop on what sections of the mountain are best for different conditions, and where to find specific services during a ski and snowboard tour around the mountain led by a Mammoth Mountain Host. There are even special naturalist tours as well hosted by a US Forest Service Naturalist that covers geologic history, common flora and fauna, as well as weather patterns of the region.

Northstar

| Established: 1972 | Acres: 3170 | Vertical: 2280' | Annual Snowfall: 350" |

Northstar California Resort is a multi-season destination offering effortless family adventure. The Village at Northstar features boutique shopping, elevated dining experiences, a year-round outdoor skating rink, conference centers, movie theatre, alpine-chic lodging and more. During the winter months Northstar California is home to meticulously groomed runs, award-winning terrain parks, and alpine activities including cross-country skiing, snowshoeing and tubing. Summer transforms the mountain into the largest, lift-served bike park on the West Coast alongside a network of hiking trails, the Kid Zone, and a family-friendly golf course.

EXCLUSIVE EXPERIENCES

Northstar California is home to the Burton Snowboard Academy, where snowboarders enter a realm of terrain-based learning. Little tykes learn essentials in the Ripperoo Riglet Park, while mature boarders progress on the trail, in one of the nationally-renowned progression parks or off-piste. For breaks, the private Burton Academy Lounge at Mid-Mountain offers one-on-one time with Burton-certified instructors, cocoa and fire pits.

TRADITIONS

Every winter afternoon skiers and snowboarders gather off of East Ridge Run for a complimentary glass of champagne or sparkling cider and tōst to the mountains, Lake Tahoe, and friends and family. Culinary traditions continue after ski school gets out each day, when S'mores Ambassadors descend upon the Village carrying silver platters covered in ooey-gooey chocolate, graham cracker and marshmallow treats.

NORDIC CENTER

Conveniently located at mid-mountain, the 1,400 square-foot Cross Country, Telemark and Snowshoe Center offers a warm, relaxed atmosphere including cabin-inspired indoor seating, fireplace, a sunny patio complete with Adirondack chairs and a fire pit, and friendly experts to help get the perfect fit. The peaceful trail system includes terrain for all ability levels and great Lake Tahoe views.

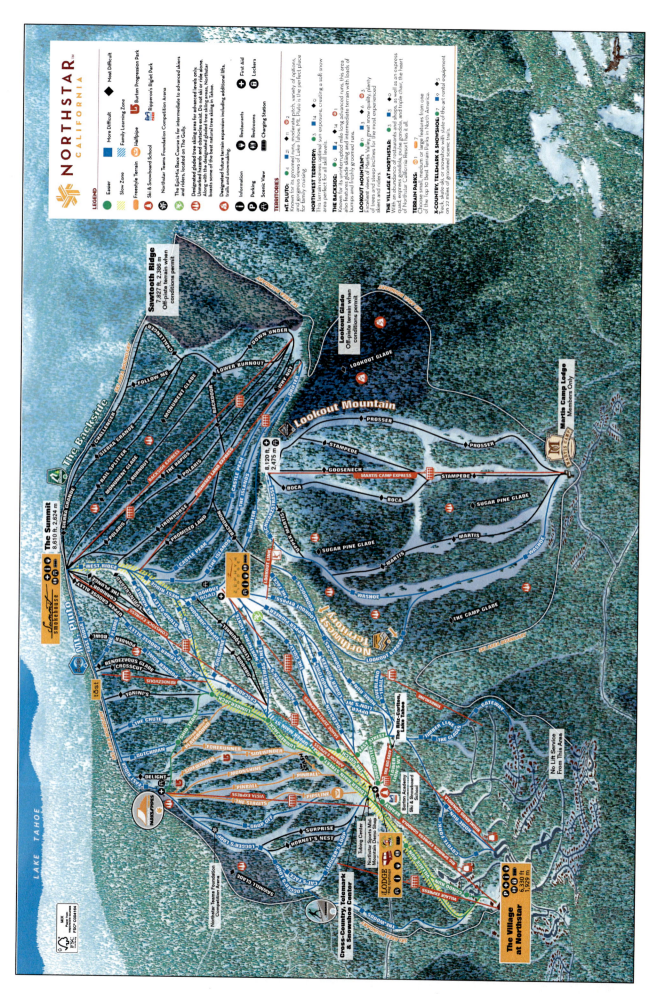

Kirkwood

Established: 1972	Acres: 2300	Vertical: 2000'	Annual Snowfall: 600"

Magical, raw, expansive and remote, Kirkwood is the stuff of legend. With the deepest, driest snow around and some of North America's most diverse and challenging terrain, Kirkwood offers big mountain riding with small town attitude. It's about adventure and challenge. At the end of the day, a uniquely rewarding experience that can only be had at a handful of places on Earth.

Kirkwood's unique location atop the Sierra Crest combined with elevations ranging 7,800 to 9,800 feet create a little something they like to call the K-Factor – a geographical predisposition to receive the lightest, the driest, and the most plentiful snow in the Tahoe region. With 2000 feet of vertical drop, and over 2300 acres of terrain from calm groomed beginner runs to hair raising cornices, cliffs and the most high angle grooming around, there's something for everyone at the 'Wood.

Kirkwood has a small village at the base and is home to several restaurants, a general store, ski rentals, gift shop, and many lodging options.

BACKCOUNTRY

Expedition:Kirkwood is for the avid adventurer looking to explore Kirkwood on a more intimate level. Kirkwood's unique terrain offers lift access to backcountry opportunities within the resort boundaries providing the perfect backdrop for a range of specialty clinics, private guides and backcountry awareness offerings. Beyond Kirkwood's boundaries, you'll find infamous terrain that has been featured in many ski/ snowboard flicks and is the proving ground for competitors in the North American Freeskiing Championships every spring.

Sierra-at-Tahoe

Established: 1946	Acres: 2000	Vertical: 2212'	Annual Snowfall: 480"

Sierra-at-Tahoe upholds the highest standards of fun and the unexpected, aimed at preserving the original soul of skiing and riding. They focus 100% of their attention on providing the best on-mountain experience Tahoe has to offer. From the amazing learn to ride programs, to award winning terrain parks, there is something for the whole family to enjoy without breaking the bank.

Sierra boasts 2,000 acres and 2,212 vertical feet of dynamic terrain with panoramic views of Lake Tahoe from the summit and one of the deepest snowpacks in the region, plus access to expert off-piste terrain in Huckleberry Canyon and incredible tree runs. It also Tahoe's closest big resort to Sacramento and the Bay Area. Sierra-at-Tahoe is located just 12 miles from South Lake Tahoe and offers Ski & Stay packages with local resorts and casinos. Known as the "locals spot," Sierra is a bastion of the authentic California ski experience, where unserious fun is taken seriously.

TERRAIN PARKS

Sierra's world class Park and Pipe offerings include a nationally recognized halfpipe and parks (6 in total!). With a strong focus on progression, Sierra strives to provide fun and progressive features for all ability levels.

PLACE TO LEARN

Learning to ski or snowboard is all about balance, control and movement. To help with this, Sierra has an expanded learning environment that features SMART TERRAIN®. Designated, sculpted terrain that fosters an elevated learning curve so guests can progress more efficiently and gain confidence in their new sport. With affordable options, sculpted learning terrain and certified instructors, it's no wonder why Sierra is the place to learn to ski or snowboard in Lake Tahoe.

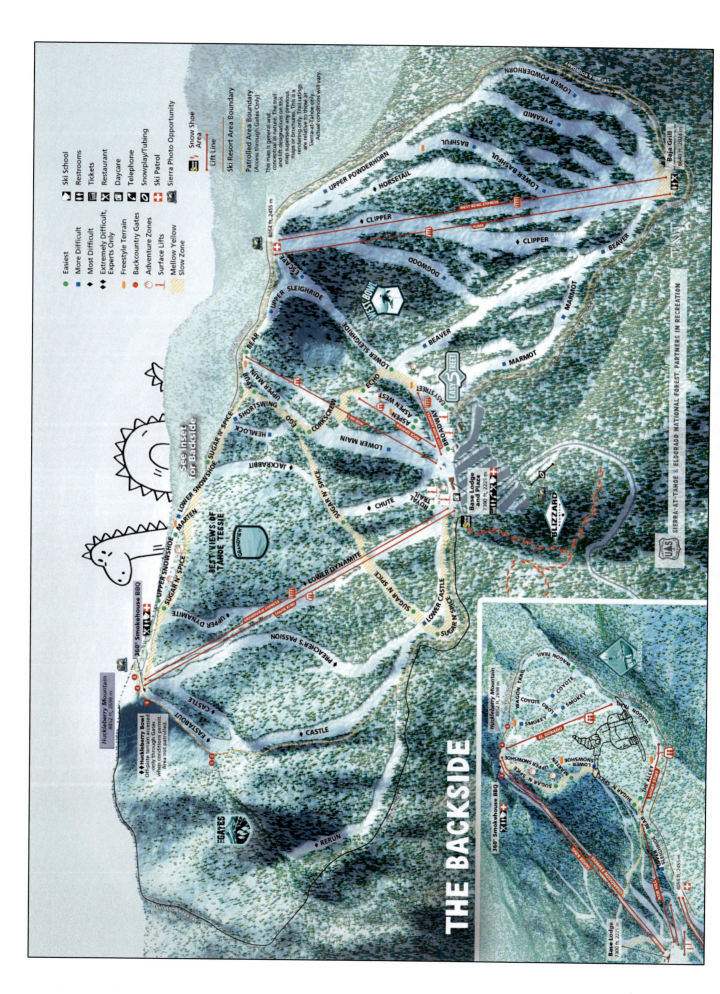

THE BACKSIDE

Bear Valley

Established: 1967	Acres: 1680	Vertical: 1900'	Annual Snowfall: 370"

Bear Valley is one of the best kept secrets of the Sierra Nevada mountains. It is located 126 miles east of Sacramento (2½ hour drive), which keeps the crowds to a minimum. The views are spectacular without the high cost of a big resort. With a small lodge and few condos, Bear Valley feels much the same as it opened in the 60s, as if time has stood still. Powder stashes can be found all day long since it doesn't get busy.

Called an "upside-down" mountain by the locals, the beginner and intermediate terrain is on the upper mountain while the expert terrain is on the lower half. The lodge and parking area is located conveniently at mid-mountain. Around the backside of the mountain is Bear Valley Village, but is not lift-accessible. After years of working with Alpine county, forest service and private land owners, the resort received approval in 2013 to install a village lift in the future.

The mid-mountain day lodge has three restaurants for keeping you fueled all day. Stop by Ebbett's Grill for some burger & fries or stop by the Sunrise Cafe for a cup of java or hot cocoa. Looking for an adult oriented place to hang out with friends? Stop by the Monte Wolfe Saloon with some friends and grab a quick drink and enjoy the view of vast Mokelumne Wilderness.

SNOWCAT TOURS

Sierra Wilderness Seminars in collaboration with Bear Valley Mountain offers guided snowcat tours for up to 8 people. Trek into terrain adjacent to the ski resort that is often "closed" or inconvenient to access. These areas often have some the of the best, and untracked, snow conditions at the resort. The convenience of having a professional guide lead you to the best snow, and a snowcat greet you at the bottom of a run is unmatched. Space is limited and advanced reservations are highly recommended.

NORDIC TRAILS

Bear Valley has one of the largest cross-country trail systems in the United States. 60 km of groomed trails provide endless opportunities to explore the area.

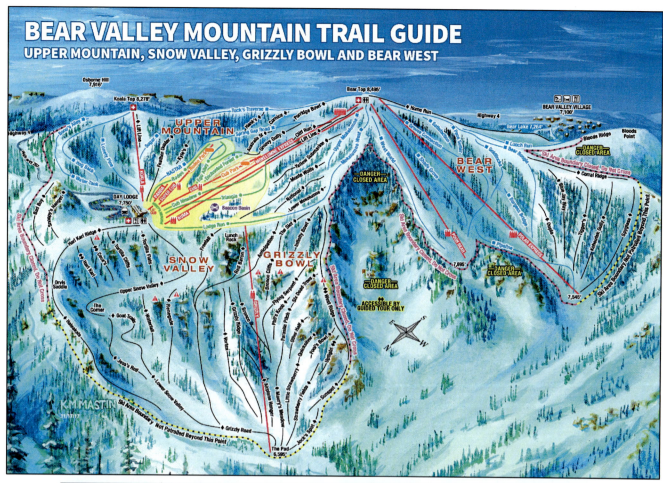

BEAR VALLEY MOUNTAIN TRAIL GUIDE
UPPER MOUNTAIN, SNOW VALLEY, GRIZZLY BOWL AND BEAR WEST

BEAR VALLEY MOUNTAIN TRAIL GUIDE
VILLAGE SIDE

Sugar Bowl

| Established: 1939 | Acres: 1650 | Vertical: 1500' | Annual Snowfall: 500" |

Perched atop Donner Summit, Sugar Bowl Resort has been family owned since the beginning in 1939. While visiting Sugar Bowl much of the historic charm is still maintained within the modern resort. Touches of Austrian character and Bavarian styling provide a glimpse into Hannes Schroll's and other founders' vision for this unique mountain.

Sugar Bowl has 1650 acres spread across four peaks so there is plenty to explore. The slopes off Judah are perfect for a family cruising together. Mt. Lincoln offers some of the most iconic steeps Sugar Bowl is known for including the infamous Silver Belt. Disney Peak provides the perfect mix of exciting groomed runs alongside open powder bowls. Lastly Crow's Peak provides access to some of the best trees and glades in the area.

VILLAGES

Sugar Bowl has two village areas: Both the Judah Side and Village Side offer all the amenities expected from a world-class resort, blissfully void of pretension and refreshingly lacking in attitude. The Judah Side offers convenient slopeside parking while the Village Side is accessed via Sugar Bowl's iconic gondola whisking guests away to America's only ski-in/ski-out snowbound village.

AMBASSADORS

The Ambassadors of Sugar Bowl have been selected not only for their amazing talents on-snow, but also for embodying the same values Sugar Bowl holds in the highest esteem. If you see them around the mountain take a chairlift ride or slap a high-five; this crew is as authentic as they come.

TERRAIN PARKS

Sugar Bowl has four terrain parks with jumps, hits, ramps, banks, fun boxes, jibs, rails, half pipes, quarter pipes, snowcross, bump terrain and other constructed or natural terrain features. Be prepared for a challenge at Sugar Bowl's freestyle terrain.

June Mountain

| Established: 1961 | Acres: 1500 | Vertical: 2590' | Annual Snowfall: 250" |

June Mountain offers 1,500 acres of uncrowded slopes, an easy-going atmosphere, breathtaking views of the surrounding lakes and peaks, and free lift tickets for kids 12 and younger which makes it a great place to take the family for a Sierra ski day.

The mountain consists of more than 80% of terrain that is beginner or intermediate, which makes it easier for families to ski together. If some are still learning, June Mountain has lessons for all ages.

All of this comes at an affordable price with lift tickets being discounted 20% for advance purchase, and kids 12 and under ski for free.

TERRAIN PARKS

The terrain parks were created with the family in mind. Three areas offer kids a chance to choose their adventure: Mambo Playground, Surprise's Fun Zone and Bucky's Adventure Zone.

BACKCOUNTRY TOURS

Sierra Mountain Guides provides tours of the backcountry terrain just a short hike from the summit of June Mountain. Tour price includes avalanche safety equipment, lift tickets, and lunch.

June Mountain is part of the Ikon Pass.

JUNE MOUNTAIN SUMMIT
10,090 ft. 3,075 m

RAINBOW SUMMIT
10,040 ft. 3,060 m

MATTERHORN
SUNSET
PRO BOWL
POWDER CHUTE
DAVOS DROP
DEER BOWL
SCHATZI
SCHATZI
BUNNER HILL
SUNRISE
CHAPARRAL
RAINBOW RIDGE
CUTBACK
SPIKE CAMP TRAIL
DANNY'S
ROSA MAE
LOTTIE JOHL
GUNSMOKE
BODIE
COMSTOCK
SAWTOOTH TRAVERSE
DESPERADO
DESPERADO RUN
MAMBO FL'VABOUND
CHALET
BABY FACE
SILVER
THE FACE
BULL CANYON
CANYON TRAIL
CANYON TRAIL
JUNE LAKE LOOP

STEW POT
SUNRISE CUTOFF
SUNRISE FREEZONE
BORN AGAIN
JUNE MEADOWS CHALET
CARSON
LOWER CARSON
CARSON CUTOFF
LOWER TICKET OFFICE

MATTERHORN CUTOFF
SKI PATROL FOR TICKET

NO LIFT ACCESS OR PATROL
ASSISTANCE BEYOND BOUNDARY
USE WILDERNESS AREA

NO LIFT ACCESS OR PATROL
ASSISTANCE BEYOND BOUNDARY
LINE. WILDERNESS AREA.

CALIFORNIA 39

China Peak

| Established: 1957 | Acres: 1400 | Vertical: 1678' | Annual Snowfall: 300" |

China Peak Mountain Resort is located in the Central Sierra, 60 miles east of Fresno, California, the closest mid-sized resort to a major city in the state. The resort ranks among California's top 10 in size and elevation, with a base of 7,000 feet and a peak of 8,709 covering 1,400 acres, the longest run extending 2.5 miles from top to bottom. For Californians living in the Central Valley or Central Coast, China Peak is their home resort, but it's also becoming a great alternative to more expensive destinations due to its affordability, excellent variety of terrain for all levels, family appeal and cozy Inn on site, one of only three hotel style slope side lodges in California skiing.

Lift lines are never an issue at China Peak, where one quad, four triples, two doubles and three moving carpets provide easy access to all of it's terrain. For beginners, China Peak boasts one of very few top to bottom low level runs in the state, Academy, 2.5 miles from the top of Chair 1 to the base area. The area is well known for an ample supply of mid-level cruisers, plus the steeps of China Bowl and The Face. With an average annual snowfall equivalent to most Tahoe area resorts of 25 feet per year, powder hounds will find hundreds of acres of fresh tracks long after the snow has fallen.

China Peak remains one of only a few privately owned resorts in the state, operated by a long time skiing family providing a welcoming feel to all guests, where the families' five professional level skiing sons can often be found ripping up the slopes. In addition to 47 rooms slope side at the Inn @ China Peak, the resort offers two base lodges and a hugely popular on mountain gathering spot, Buckhorn.

In the ever growing world of mountain resort corporatization, China Peak offers a throwback experience, where the resort's management staff averages over 20 years of service, and ownership actively engages with guests every day. It's a vibe many find welcome and more rare all the time.

Owning Winter Since 1958

CHINA PEAK

OWN WINTER.

Trail Map 2017/18

CHINESE PEAK
Elev. 8,709'

Homewood Mountain Resort

Established: 1961	Acres: 1260	Vertical: 1650'	Annual Snowfall: 450"

Photo courtesy of silent A photography

Opened in 1961, Homewood Mountain Resort remains one of Tahoe's classic family-friendly resorts with an epic peak to shore experience. Named the "gem of Lake Tahoe's West Shore" by SKI Magazine, the 1,260-acre mountain offers unobstructed views of the entire Lake and surrounding peaks and features 8 lifts and 64 runs with over 750 acres of guided snowcat accessible terrain. Homewood offers a truly unique four-season resort with flawless grooming, hidden powder stashes and an intimate West Shore setting located just steps from Lake Tahoe.

Photo courtesy of Kiwi Kamera

SNOWCAT ADVENTURES

Homewood Snowcat Adventures accesses over 750 acres of backcountry terrain on the flanks of Ellis Peak, above the resort's traditional ski area boundary.

Once transported to the peak, groups of up to 10 skiers and riders will enjoy guided access to a wide variety of terrain options – from perfectly-spaced tree runs to steeps, powder bowls, and intermediate-level glades – all leading guests back to the inbounds terrain at the resort.

DINING

Take in the full peak to shore experience and hop over to the West Shore Cafe and Inn for lakeside dining located just steps from the resort.

Dodge Ridge

Established: 1950	Acres: 862	Vertical: 1600'	Annual Snowfall: 350"

Located in the Stanislaus National Forest, just three miles from Pinecrest Lake off Hwy 108, Dodge Ridge is the closest ski area to the San Francisco Bay Area. At only three hours from San Francisco, Dodge Ridge an attractive option for weekend and day trip skiers who will not have to traverse any high mountain passes on their trek to the slopes.

Since its opening season in 1950, Dodge Ridge has remained a family owned resort with values that celebrate the skiers and riders who have started a life-long love of the sport. This family owned and family loved mountain provides terrain for all levels as expert skiers enjoy Granite Bowl and some of the best tree skiing available, along with miles and miles of groomed runs for beginner to intermediate skiers and all levels can take advantage of their cutting-edge lesson programs from beginner to expert.

Dodge Ridge has a single day lodge that has offers dining at Creekside Café, Boulder Bar, or The North Fork Bistro. If mid-mountain dining is what you are looking for, check out Local's Café at the bottom of Chair 7. Each restaurant offers a wide selection of food and beverages.

LESSONS

Dodge Ridge has always set itself apart in its lesson programming and is commonly referred to as the place where everyone learns to ski and ride. As one of the best values in the region, they offer instruction and terrain for every level of skier and rider with a focus on developing skills that allow anyone to progress and enjoy the sport for years to come.

TERRAIN PARKS

Three terrain parks provide a complete offering for the adventurous soul. Rocky's Road Park sets its self apart with the laid-back environment and is commonly a hiked, hang out area. Stagecoach Park is perfect for showcasing some new style and tricks while the Clementine Roller Park is ideal for skiers and riders who are new to freestyle terrain parks

LEGEND

- ● Easier
- ■ More Difficult
- ◆ Most Difficult
- ◆◆ Expert
- Terrain Parks

- Chairlift
- Surface Lift
- Conveyor Lift
- Rope Tow
- Ski Patrol

- Ski Area Boundary
- Slow Skiing Area

- Quad Chairlift
- Triple Chairlift
- Double Chairlift

DODGE RIDGE
We've Been Skiing • Riding Since 1950

1,600 VERTICAL FEET // 862 SKIABLE ACRES // 67 RUNS

GPS: 38° 11' 24.43" N
119° 57' 25.19" W

EL. 8,200'

EL. 7,045'

EL. 6,600'

Daily Conditions
- Daily weather, grooming, & snow reports
- ▢ Visit DodgeRidge.com
- ▢ Call the SnowPhone // (209) 536-5300
- ▢ Pick-Ups a Grooming Report Printed Daily
- ▢ Get Powder Report By Text: Text "powder" to (209) 259-4515 - must add (209) code message also automatically your provider

More On Safety
- ▢ Visit DodgeRidge.com
- ▢ Call the SnowPhone // (209) 536-5300
- ▢ Like Us on Facebook: DodgeRidge
- ▢ Check the Daily Safety Message on the Grooming Report Printed Daily

YOUR RESPONSIBILITY CODE

1. Always stay in control, and be able to stop or avoid other people or objects.
2. People ahead of you have the right of way. It is your responsibility to avoid them.
3. You must not stop where you obstruct a trail, or are not visible from above.
4. Whenever starting downhill or merging into a trail, look uphill and yield to others.
5. Always use devices to help prevent runaway equipment.
6. Observe all posted signs and warnings. Keep off closed trails and out of closed areas.
7. Prior to using any lift, you must have the knowledge and ability to load, ride and unload safely.

FACILITIES

- Ⓐ CREEKSIDE LODGE · WiFi
  - Creekside Cafe
  - Demo Center
  - Sport & Tech Shop
  - Restrooms
- Ⓑ RENTAL CENTER
  - FAMILY LODGE
  - Ticketing/Guest Services
  - Snowsports School
  - North Fork Bistro · WiFi
  - Restrooms
- Ⓒ CHAIR & TICKET BOOTH
- Ⓓ LOCALS CAFÉ
  - Restrooms
  - Ski Patrol
- Ⓔ LOCALS CAFÉ
  - Restrooms

Donner Ski Ranch

| Established: 1937 | Acres: 505 | Vertical: 750' | Annual Snowfall: 396" |

Among the oldest and most iconic ski areas in the Western U.S., Donner Ski Ranch is a family-friendly resort that features a wide variety of terrain, inviting skiers and riders of all abilities to enjoy the fully-featured mountain oasis.

Donner Ski Ranch is much larger than people realize. The view from the front is just the beginning. The mountain boasts more than 1,000 ft of vertical and an expansive back side, making it the second largest ski resort on Donner Summit. And, with one of the highest base elevations in the Sierras, Donner Ski Ranch gets some of the best powder. Combine this with their aggressive high-mountain and backside terrain, and Donner Ski Ranch is the perfect destination for advanced skiers and riders who want to escape the crowds and enjoy untouched lines.

For beginner and intermediate skiers, Donner Ski Ranch offers easy access to novice runs, group and private ski/snowboard lessons, equipment rentals, retail shop, and a tubing park that's great for kids of all ages.

Donner Ski Ranch isn't fancy. If you're looking for glitz and glamour, it's not for you. So, what does it offer? Fun, value, and an all-around good vibe. Sure, it has awesome terrain, great snow, and short lift lines, but what makes Donner Ski Ranch special is the people. They love skiing and love their hill. The reason people come back time and time again is simple -- it feels good there. They revel in teaching people to ski, watching kids grin ear to ear as they make their first turns, fresh powder stashes and face shots, untracked snow, bluebird days, and apré ski

at the Summit's greatest dive bar, right in the main lodge.

Donner offers more than 500 acres of varied terrain, 6 chairlifts, and 2 moving carpets, so there's something for everyone at Donner Ski Ranch. And, with daily ticket, season pass, and package pricing up to 75% less than other resorts, and close, free parking, Donner Ski Ranch is the #1 destination for family fun.

DAY LODGE

Donner Ski Ranch has been a family favorite for nearly 80 years, and for some, that love affair started with their humble main lodge. Rustic, simple and entirely void of pretense, their lodge features an on-site fully-equipped rental equipment shop, ticket office, cafe, bar, and huge wrap around deck, so no matter where you sit, you can relax and watch your family and friends as they charge the front side bunny slopes.

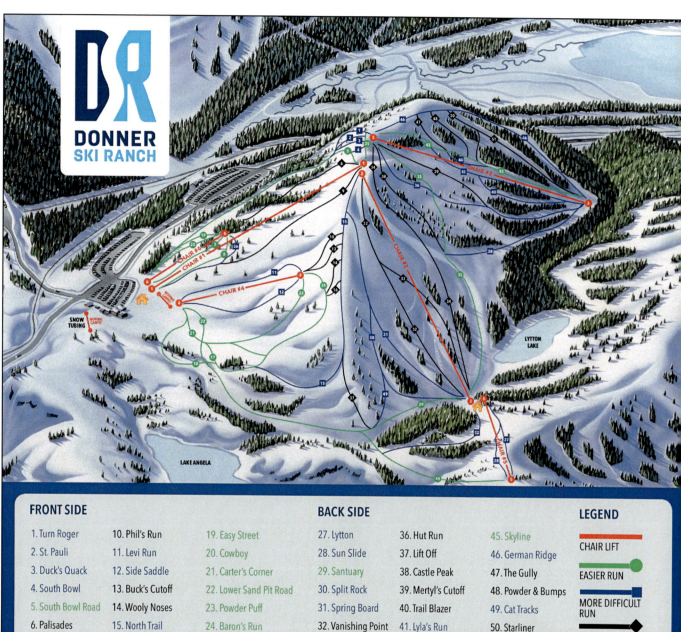

FRONT SIDE

1. Turn Roger
2. St. Pauli
3. Duck's Quack
4. South Bowl
5. South Bowl Road
6. Palisades
7. Easyrider
8. Corral
9. The Face
10. Phil's Run
11. Levi Run
12. Side Saddle
13. Buck's Cutoff
14. Wooly Noses
15. North Trail
16. Molly Hogan
17. Sand Pit Road
18. Not So Private Road
19. Easy Street
20. Cowboy
21. Carter's Corner
22. Lower Sand Pit Road
23. Powder Puff
24. Baron's Run
25. Snow Catch
26. Cross Over

BACK SIDE

27. Lytton
28. Sun Slide
29. Santuary
30. Split Rock
31. Spring Board
32. Vanishing Point
33. Half Pipe
34. Side Winder
35. Primrose Lane
36. Hut Run
37. Lift Off
38. Castle Peak
39. Mertyl's Cutoff
40. Trail Blazer
41. Lyla's Run
42. Lakeview
43. Crossunder
44. Race Course
45. Skyline
46. German Ridge
47. The Gully
48. Powder & Bumps
49. Cat Tracks
50. Starliner
51. Starr's Route
52. Boomerang

LEGEND

CHAIR LIFT

EASIER RUN

MORE DIFFICULT RUN

MOST DIFFICULT RUN

LODGE

Mt. Shasta Ski Park

Established: 1985	Acres: 425	Vertical: 1435'	Annual Snowfall: 275"

The Mt. Shasta Ski Park is located high on the flanks of mighty, 14,162' high, Mt. Shasta. Discover skiing and snowboarding at one of California's most unique resorts where you and your family can rest easy and enjoy an affordable winter adventure. The Mt. Shasta Ski Park is a full service resort which has something for everyone during both the day or night operations! Miles of trails cater to all skill levels thus providing fun for everyone in the entire family. The Park is a cruisers paradise and a powder hounds delight when Mother Nature pays a visit. Yet when nature is greedy, their state of the art snowmaking system replenishes it with the fresh white stuff.

Mt. Shasta is so sure that you'll have a great time that they even provide a guarantee! If for any reason you are not completely satisfied, return your ticket within the first hour of your purchase and receive a full refund on your lift ticket! In addition, their "Guaranteed to Learn" Introduction Package Programs promise you will be an experienced snow rider in no time or the next set of lessons are on them! The Learning Center teaching corral has a 100 foot Magic Carpet conveyor. Students simply step on to the conveyor that transports them effortlessly to the top of the learning slope.

TERRAIN PARKS

Trick riders and wannabes can access two terrain parks which feature all the hits, jibs, rails and a Super Pipe that guarantee to get the adrenaline rushing. For those new to winter activity, the park's learning center programs are considered some of the finest in the industry. Adults, kids and parents alike love what they teach 'em!

NIGHT SKIING

Join your friends for twilight skiing and snowboarding fun on Friday or Saturday night. Watch a beautiful sunset over the Eddies while getting in a few more runs. Two lifts provide access to nearly half of the trails from 3 to 8 pm.

TUBING

Mt. Shasta also offers a designated tubing area with beautifully groomed snow, a comfortable lodge with food/beverages, and free parking. Only available on Friday and Saturday.

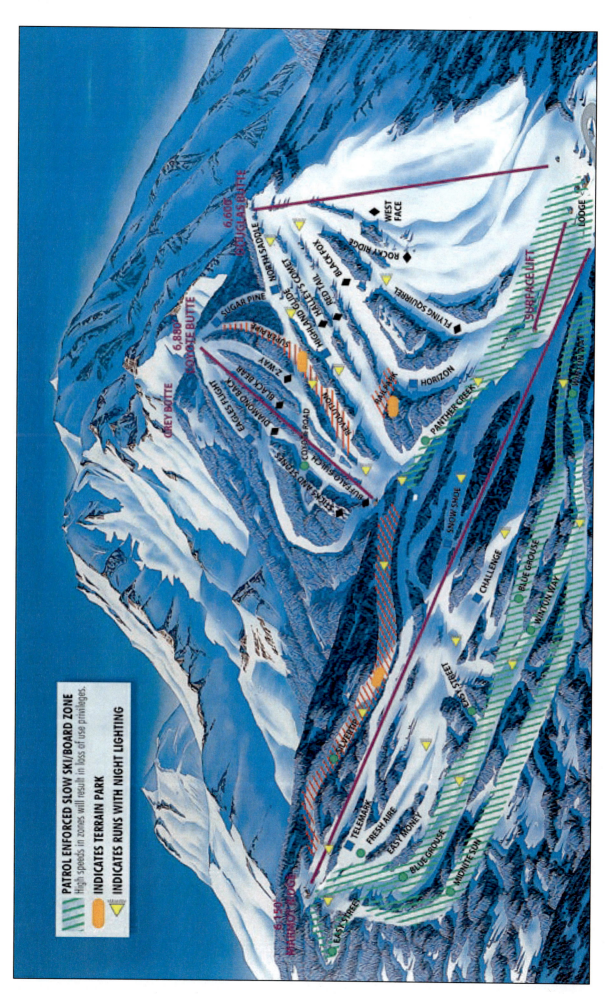

PATROL ENFORCED SLOW SKI/BOARD ZONE
High speeds in zones will result in loss of use privileges.

INDICATES TERRAIN PARK

INDICATES RUNS WITH NIGHT LIGHTING

DOUGLAS BUTTE
6,600'

COYOTE BUTTE
6,880'

GREY BUTTE

DIAMONDBACK RIDGE
6,150'

WEST FACE

ROCKY RIDGE

FLYING SQUIRREL

BLACK FOX

RED TAIL

HALLEY'S COMET

NORTH SADDLE

SUGAR PINE

SWITCHBACK

HIGHLAND GLIDE

Z-WAY

BLACK BEAR

REVOLUTION

HORIZON

HALF PIPE

EAGLES FLIGHT

DIAMOND BACK

COYOTE ROAD

BUFFALO GULCH

STICKS AND STONES

PANTHER CREEK

SNOW SHOE

CHALLENGE

BLUE GROUSE

WINTON WAY

SILVER TIP

EAST STREET

WINTON WAY

TELEMARK

FRESH AIRE

EASY MONEY

BLUE GROUSE

MIDNITE SUN

EASY STREET

EASY STREET

LODGE

SURFACE LIFT

Mt. Baldy

Established: 1952	Acres: 400	Vertical: 2100'	Annual Snowfall: 178"

Mt Baldy has been known for decades as hosting Southern California's best natural skiing and snowboarding terrain. At 10,064 feet, Mt Baldy is the highest summit in the San Gabriel Mountains. It is also one of the closest ski areas to Los Angeles (50 miles) and even closer to the Ontario Airport (25 miles). Mt. Baldy has all types of terrain from wide open glades, tree runs, bowls, moguls, groomers, and unique terrain park features placed sporadically around the mountain.

The top of chair #1 is where you will find a full service rental shop and Mt Baldy's one-of-a-kind Learning Center offering ongoing ski and snowboard instruction available from 9 am to 4 pm in Mt Baldy's Terrain Based Learning Center.

What many are finding out recently is that it is also a premiere summer time destination for hiking, tent cabin camping, zip lines, live music and quality dining at the Top of the Notch restaurant.

THE NOTCH

After a 15 minute ride on the Sugarpine Chair Lift, guests arrive to the Top of the Notch at 7,800ft. With a rich history beginning in the 1950s, the Top of the Notch provides a unique dining experience overlooking Southern California. Guests from San Bernardino, Los Angeles and San Diego Counties along with others enjoy nourishment at the Notch while experiencing all that the Angeles National Forest has to offer.

TUBING PARK

The tubing park is also located at the top of chair #1. It is approximately 100 yards long and can be 2 to 6 lanes wide. Participants take a short walk back to the top after each ride.

Lifts

Chair # 1 - 1300
Vertical Feet

◆ These double black
diamond trails provide a much

Trails and Runs

1. Snowball Point
2. Beginner's Gulch
3. Mullin's Mile
4. Bonanza Bowl
5. Fireroad
6. Toilet Bowl
7. Goldridge
8. Herb's Hollow
9. Andy's Alley
10. Robin's Run
11. Shortcut
12. Emile's
13. Skyline
14. The Tube
15. South Bowl
16. South Bowl Chutes
17. Turkey Shoot

Mt. Baldy is under special permit from the U.S. Forest

Mt. BALDY
Ski Lifts
Real Skiing/Real Close

KEY

▣ RESTROOMS
▣ RESTAURANT
▣ TICKETS

▣ SKI SCHOOL
✚ SKI PATROL
▣ BAR ▣ PARKING

● EASIER
■ MORE DIFFICULT
◆ MOST DIFFICULT
◆ EXPERTS ONLY

STOCKTON FLATS
SITE OF FUTURE EXPANSION

SNOW PHONE
Bud (909) 981-3344 Bud

TAKE I-10 TO MOUNTAIN
AVENUE EXIT IN UPLAND.
GO NORTH 16 MILES TO MT.
BALDY.

Boreal Mountain

| Established: 1965 | Acres: 380 | Vertical: 500' | Annual Snowfall: 400" |

Value, easy access and family-focused fun is what Boreal Ski Area is all about. Located northwest of Lake Tahoe right off of Interstate 80, Boreal is 45 miles from Reno, Nevada and 90 miles from Sacramento. Six lifts service 41 trails; along with Boreal's popular Playland snow tubing area.

Boreal is also home to Woodward Tahoe. Woodward Tahoe fosters lifestyle and action sports progression through daily programs and week-long camps. Experiences in snowboard, freeski, skateboard, BMX, slopestyle MTB, scooter, parkour, digital media and cheer are offered to recreationalists of all ages and abilities, as well as professional athletes. Programs are held in a safe and fun one-of-a-kind indoor facility and on state-of-the-art terrain parks. Boreal Mountain Resort is part of the POWDR Adventure Lifestyle Co. portfolio.

TERRAIN PARKS

Boreal has six terrain parks that vary in skill level: Neff Land, Shred Park, Half Pipe, Wave Pool, Mini-Shred Park, Mini Wave Pool, Start Park, and Micro-Park.

Boreal Mountain Resort has partnered with Neff Headwear to bring a new one-of-a-kind signature terrain park, Neff Land. Easily accessible from the high speed Accelerator chairlift, this pirate-themed Neff Land boasts over 30 ridable features including a life-sized ship mast, cannons, pirates and more.

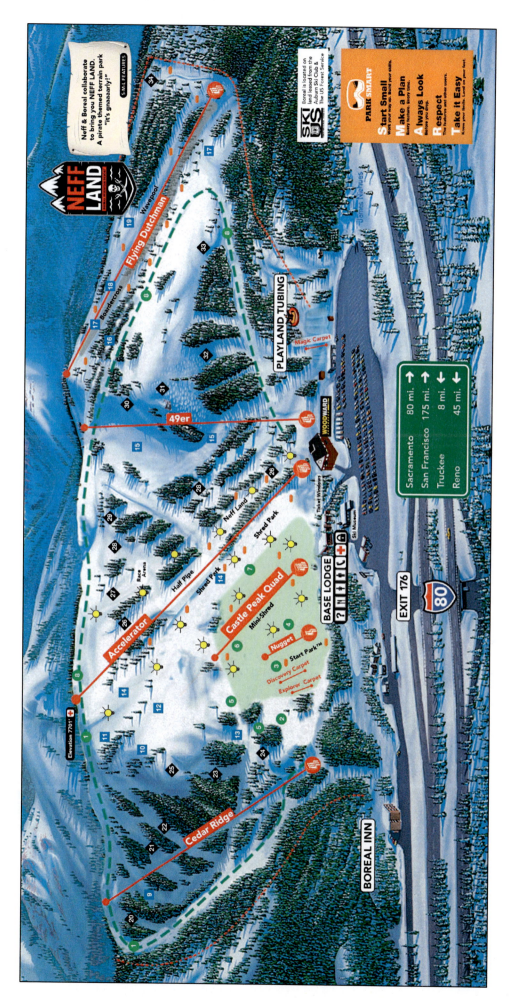

Neff & Boreal collaborate
to bring you NEFF LAND.
A pirate themed terrain park
"it's gnaaaarly!"

5-M.I. FEATURES

NEFF LAND

Boreal is located on
land leased from the
Auburn Ski Club &
The US Forest Service

SKI US

PARK SMART

Start Small
Work your way up. Build your skills.

Make a Plan
Every feature, every time.

Always Look
Before you drop.

Respect
The features and other users.

Take it Easy
Know your limits. Land on your feet.

Flying Dutchman

Wavepool

Boardercross

49er

PLAYLAND TUBING

Magic Carpet

WOODWARD

Ticket Windows

Neff Land

Shred Park

Half Pipe

Race Arena

Shred Park

Shred Park

Accelerator

Castle Peak Quad

Mini-Shred

Nugget

Start Park™

Discovery Carpet

Explorer Carpet

Elevation 7701'

Ski Museum

BASE LODGE

Sacramento	80 mi.	↑
San Francisco	175 mi.	↑
Truckee	8 mi.	↓
Reno	45 mi.	↓

EXIT 176

80

Cedar Ridge

BOREAL INN

James Niehues

Mountain High

Established: 1924	Acres: 290	Vertical: 1600'	Annual Snowfall: 132"

Mountain High Resort, located in Southern California's picturesque San Gabriel Mountains, has been one of the region's most popular winter destinations since 1924. Located just 90 minutes from Los Angeles and Orange County, it is by far the easiest resort to get to with no mountain driving.

With a top elevation of 8,200 feet, Mountain High gets plenty of snow. Plus, it whitens its slopes November through April with one of the largest snowmaking systems in North America. Enjoy three resorts, 16 lifts, 59 trails and night skiing every night until 10 p.m. during the peak season. For accommodations, Wrightwood, Calif. is the nearest town, located only three miles away at a height of 6,000 feet above sea level, where peace and quiet are major features.

EAST RESORT

The East Resort boasts the longest trails in the region serviced by a single high-speed quad lift. Its long, groomed, cruising trails make it perfect for carving. It is also home to the Olympic Bowl, the longest, steepest bump run in the region.

WEST RESORT

Nearly the entire West Resort is dedicated to terrain features, making it one of the largest terrain parks on the West Coast. Features like jumps, rails and fun boxes create a paradise for freestyle skiers and snowboarders up and down the mountain.

Mountain High West is home to the resort's Children's Sports Center and night skiing is available seven nights-a-week during peak season from 5 p.m. to 10 p.m. More than 85 percent of the resort is illuminated by lighting, including the terrain park.

NORTH RESORT

The North Resort consists of predominately beginner and intermediate terrain, which lends itself nicely to the mountain's family atmosphere. 70 acres of gently rolling terrain with historic log cabins are waiting for kids to explore. North Pole Tubing Park, a 20-acre, state-of-the-art tubing facility, is onsite for those who just want to enjoy the winter experience.

East Resort
El 8,200'

West Resort
El 8,000'

SOUTHERN CALIFORNIA'S CLOSEST WINTER RESORT

mountain HIGH

Grand View Bistro

Catalina Boardwalk
Discovery
Sunset
8

Goldrush
Sundance
Out Of Bounds
Wildcard
Pea Shot
Seps
Rangers
Cut 45
Stampede Magnum
Cut Off
Out Of Bounds
The Wedge
Pipeline
Borderline
Upper Chisolm
Calamity
Coffey's Chute
Exhibition
Vertigo
Lower Chisolm
McCoy Glades
Trestle
Crest Trail
Dragon
Conquest
O
Wild Fire
Inferno Ridge

Sundance
Canyon
Competition
Mountain High Express
Route 66
Olympic Bowl
Goldrush
Out Of Bounds
Wyatt
The Pocket
Groping
Catch Ya Later
Blue Ridge Express
Headwall
Freefall
Roadrunner
Silverspur
Smokeout
Cruiser
Woodworth Gulch
Creek Side
Coyote
6
Gunslinger
Hunts
Hot Shot
Back Fire
Burn Out
Conquest
Backdraft
The Reef
Out Of Bounds

Easy Rider
First Tracks
Runner
Snow Flake
Easy Street
Sunnyside
5

9
11
16
10
Angeles Crest Cafe
East Base
4
1 2
12
SA
3
13
Virtual Snow
Children's Academy
Bullwheel Bar & Grill

Big Pines Lodge
West Base

North Resort
El 7,800'

Out Of Bounds
Solitude
Waag's Woe
Howard's Run
Cascade
Diamondback
Sunrise Quad
Show Off
Round-A-Bout
Ski More Highway
North Lodge
Glades
Lower Round-A-Bout
14
15
Out Of Bounds
Out Of Bounds
Purgatory
7

Snow Summit

| Established: 1952 | Acres: 240 | Vertical: 1200' | Annual Snowfall: 100" |

Located in the heart of the San Bernardino Mountains, about two hours east of L.A., Snow Summit has been one of the most renowned winter sports locales in Southern California since it opened in 1952.

Snow Summit is known for having the most consistent snow conditions in Southern California thanks to an extensive snowmaking system, featuring more than 500 hydrants, 300 snow guns, and 40 fans capable of coverting 6,000 gallons of water to snow per minute. With that sort of capacity, and the most operating days per season in Southern California, it is no wonder Snow Summit was selected to host the inaugural Winter X Games in 1997.

Snow Summit has activities for non-skiing/snowboarding winter enthusiasts as well, including the Grizzly Ridge Tube Park (kids must be 42" to ride), a 30-foot rock climbing wall, and meadow area with fire pits and seating for musical performances, film premieres, and other aprés activities that are fun for the whole family.

LESSONS

Snow Summit is Southern California's learn to ride headquarters, with a variety of group and private lesson options for ages 3 and older, a 5,000 square-foot learning facility for kids and families, and a team of certified instructors who utilize progression-based techniques to a make learning to ski or snowboard a fun and natural experience for guests.

EARLY/LATE SESSIONS

Snow Summit also has options for early birds and night owls. The Fresh Tracks program, which lets guests beat the crowds and get on the slopes an hour earlier, is available on select dates, while night sessions are available on most Fridays and Saturdays during the season.

BIG BEAR MOUNTAIN RESORT

Founded in 2002, Big Bear Mountain Resort includes Snow Summit and Bear Mountain. Located just 3 miles apart, guests can use their lift tickets at either property on the same day, with courtesy shuttle service available throughout the season. Big Bear is also part of the Ikon Pass.

Bear Mountain

| Established: 1943 | Acres: 198 | Vertical: 1665' | Annual Snowfall: 100" |

Located in the San Bernardino Mountains, about two hours east of L.A., Bear Mountain has been pushing the progression of winter action sports for 75 years. One of the ski and snowboard industry's most innovative and influential destinations, Bear Mountain's terrain parks are heavily influenced by Southern California's iconic surf and skate scenes, with 200+ jibs and jumps, and the only halfpipes in Southern California. Perennially rated among the best terrain parks in the country, Bear Mountain regularly hosts some of the industry's biggest events, including photo and video shoots, competitions, and Big Bear Mountain Resort's annual winter kickoff event, Hot Dawgz & Hand Rails.

TERRAIN PARKS

Freestyle Park - This winter playground features four half pipes (8', 13', 18' & a Jib Pipe), over 100 features, and more jibs than any other terrain park in Southern California.

Red Bull Plaza –This urban inspired park sponsored by Red Bull has a little something for everyone, including features from Hot Dawgz & Hand Rails and multiple setups throughout the season to keep things fresh.

Skill Builder Park - The perfect place to get acclimated to terrain park features, the Skill Builder Park (SBP) is designed to help beginners build confidence before moving on to more advanced terrain and park features.

BIG BEAR MOUNTAIN RESORT

Founded in 2002, Big Bear Mountain Resort includes Bear Mountain and Snow Summit. Located just 3 miles apart, guests can use their lift tickets at either property on the same day, with courtesy shuttle service available throughout the season. Big Bear is also part of the Ikon Pass.

Snow Valley

| Established: 1937 | Acres: 240 | Vertical: 1041' | Annual Snowfall: 160" |

Snow Valley is the oldest continually operating ski resort in Southern California and the closest to the valley floor. Offering 240 acres served by 13 lifts, it has terrain for every level. Snow Valley is also home to Southern California's only high speed 6-passenger detachable lift. Snow Valley has a day lodge with several restaurants, or head up the hill to the base of Lift 3 at Deer Meadow Grille which offers a quick way to find refreshment without leaving the mountain. Kick back on the sun deck and watch the riders in the Hideout Jib Park while you take a break around the fire pit.

Looking for a different winter adventure? Try California's only lift-served Snow Play area, open daily from 10 am to 4 pm Fridays through Sundays and holiday periods, enjoy a scenic chairlift ride followed by a thrilling downhill sled ride.

BACKCOUNTRY

Slide Peak is the crown jewel of Snow Valley. When natural snow is abundant, Slide Peak comes to life, offering the best backcountry experience of any Southern California resort. In addition, there is much more backcountry terrain to be explored that you can't see from the base of the resort along Lifts 8 & 9.

TERRAIN PARKS

The EDGE™ is Snow Valley's premier terrain park with features for intermediate and advanced skiers and snowboarders. Additionally, the Hideout Jib Park features an assortment of rails and boxes and the Rim Progression Park offers smaller features, perfect for learning on. Offering nearly a mile of intermediate to advanced features that flow together from feature to feature, all accessed by its own chairlift, The EDGE™ is a locals favorite.

NIGHT SKIING

Enjoy an evening under the lights, skiing or snowboarding many of your favorite trails on the frontside of the mountain, including The EDGE, Mambo Alley, Eagle Flats & more! For those on a budget, night sessions also saves a bunch of money over regular priced all day lift tickets. Unique to Snow Valley is the Afternoon/Evening ticket available from 12 p.m. to 8 p.m. whenever night sessions are offered.

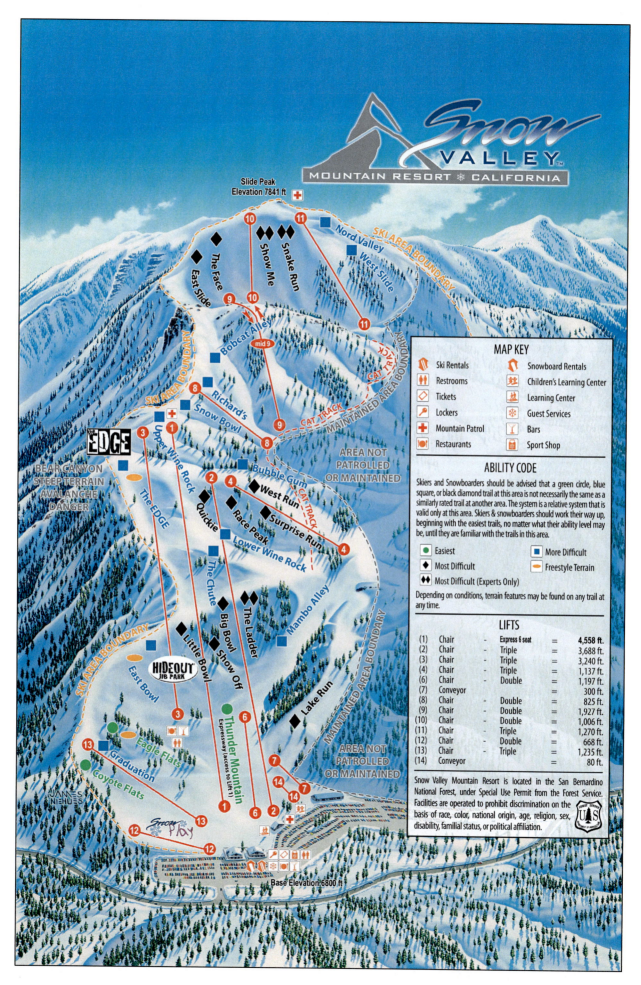

Snow VALLEY
MOUNTAIN RESORT ✳ CALIFORNIA

Slide Peak
Elevation 7841 ft

Nord Valley
West Slide

SKI AREA BOUNDARY

East Slide
The Face
Show Me
Snake Run

Bobcat Alley

mid 9

CAT TRACK

SKI AREA BOUNDARY

Richard's
Snow Bowl

The EDGE

Upper Wine Rock

Bubble Gum
CAT TRACK

MAINTAINED AREA BOUNDARY

AREA NOT
PATROLLED
OR MAINTAINED

BEAR CANYON
STEEP TERRAIN
AVALANCHE
DANGER

The EDGE

Quickie
Race Peak
West Run
Surprise Run

Lower Wine Rock

Mambo Alley

The Chute
The Ladder

SKI AREA BOUNDARY

Little Bowl
Big Bowl
Show Off

East Bowl
HIDEOUT JIB PARK

Lake Run

MAINTAINED AREA BOUNDARY

Thunder Mountain
Expressway (access to Lift 1)

AREA NOT
PATROLLED
OR MAINTAINED

JAMES
NIEHUES

Eagle Flats
Graduation
Coyote Flats

Snow Play

Base Elevation 6800 ft

MAP KEY

🎿	Ski Rentals	🏂	Snowboard Rentals
🚻	Restrooms		Children's Learning Center
◇	Tickets		Learning Center
🔑	Lockers	❄	Guest Services
✚	Mountain Patrol		Bars
🍴	Restaurants		Sport Shop

ABILITY CODE

Skiers and Snowboarders should be advised that a green circle, blue square, or black diamond trail at this area is not necessarily the same as a similarly rated trail at another area. The system is a relative system that is valid only at this area. Skiers & snowboarders should work their way up, beginning with the easiest trails, no matter what their ability level may be, until they are familiar with the trails in this area.

●	Easiest	■	More Difficult
◆	Most Difficult	🔶	Freestyle Terrain
◆◆	Most Difficult (Experts Only)		

Depending on conditions, terrain features may be found on any trail at any time.

LIFTS

(1)	Chair	-	Express 6 seat	=	4,558 ft.
(2)	Chair	-	Triple	=	3,688 ft.
(3)	Chair	-	Triple	=	3,240 ft.
(4)	Chair	-	Triple	=	1,137 ft.
(6)	Chair	-	Double	=	1,197 ft.
(7)	Conveyor			=	300 ft.
(8)	Chair	-	Double	=	825 ft.
(9)	Chair	-	Double	=	1,927 ft.
(10)	Chair	-	Double	=	1,006 ft.
(11)	Chair	-	Triple	=	1,270 ft.
(12)	Chair	-	Double	=	668 ft.
(13)	Chair	-	Triple	=	1,235 ft.
(14)	Conveyor			=	80 ft.

Snow Valley Mountain Resort is located in the San Bernardino National Forest, under Special Use Permit from the Forest Service. Facilities are operated to prohibit discrimination on the basis of race, color, national origin, age, religion, sex, disability, familial status, or political affiliation.

Soda Springs

Established: 1936	Acres: 200	Vertical: 550'	Annual Snowfall: 400"

Founded in 1935, Soda Springs is California's oldest continuously operating ski resort. Welcoming, relaxed, and perfect for families new to snow, Soda Springs is conveniently located directly off Interstate 80, less than 15 miles from Truckee. Soda Springs' 15 runs are serviced by five lifts. A progressive mountain layout starts with incredibly easy beginner slopes perfect for learning. The intermediate and advanced terrain will push your skill levels while exploring all the mountain has to offer.

OnePass

Since Soda Springs Resort is part of the POWDR Adventure Lifestyle Co. portfolio, you can buy a OnePass RFID card which is good at Soda Springs, Boreal Mountain, and Woodward Tahoe. And since it is tied to your credit card, you can use the OnePass for all your mountain purchases (food, rentals, lift tickets, etc.)

Snow Making

Many resorts make their own snow, but Soda Springs is the only resort in California that uses 100% recycled water in it's snowmaking. This is just one of the reasons Soda Springs earned the Golden Eagle Award for Environmental Excellence from the National Ski Areas Association & SKI magazine.

Planet Kids

Planet Kids is best described as a snow playground featuring tubing carousels, snow-tubing lanes, ski/snowboard specific learning areas, snow volcanoes to climb and more. Designed for children age 8 and under, this is a one-of-a-kind experience for making unforgettable family memories.

Mt. Waterman

Established: 1939	Acres: 150	Vertical: 1030'	Annual Snowfall: 72"

Mt. Waterman operates in the winter and summer months, offering ski, snowboarding in the winter and Mt. biking, disc golf and hiking in the summer. Mt. Waterman in the winter is a day ski & snowboard area. It has 3 chair lifts and 25 runs. 65% of the hill is advanced while offering beginner and intermediate runs at the top of the mountain. Lessons for skiing and snowboarding are available. It is an upside down hill in that the facilities are located at the top of Chair One.

Mt. Waterman offers scenic rides to the top of the mountain for all guests on foot to enjoy the mountain. Chair One can be taken back down the hill to the parking lot.

The Warming Hut offers amazing views, a fireplace to warm up and food and drink service. The Ticket Hut is located at the bottom of the mountain offering tickets, apparel and stickers for sale. Equipment rentals are not available on the hill.

Mt. Waterman in the summer offers Mt. bike trails, beginner intermediate and advanced, a professional 18 disc golf course, scenic chair lift rides and hiking. The warming hut is open for breakfast and lunch.

Chair one is in operation for round trip rides. There is music on the hill and fun events including disc golf tournaments, Mt. biking events, raffles, full moon walks.

Mt. Waterman is the closest ski area to the L.A basin and are now deemed a national monument. The Angeles Crest Highway out of La Canada has been repaved providing a nice and safe ride to the hill. There are no gas stations on the mountain so fill up before you come.

HISTORY

The first rope tow was established in 1939, followed by the first lift in 1941. The ski area was dormant between 2001 and 2008, after which Rick Metcalf bought it and re-opened it narrowly rescuing it from losing its USFS permit. Rick grew up learning how to ski at Mt. Waterman, so he knows just how much it means to the community to keep this ski area running for generations to come.

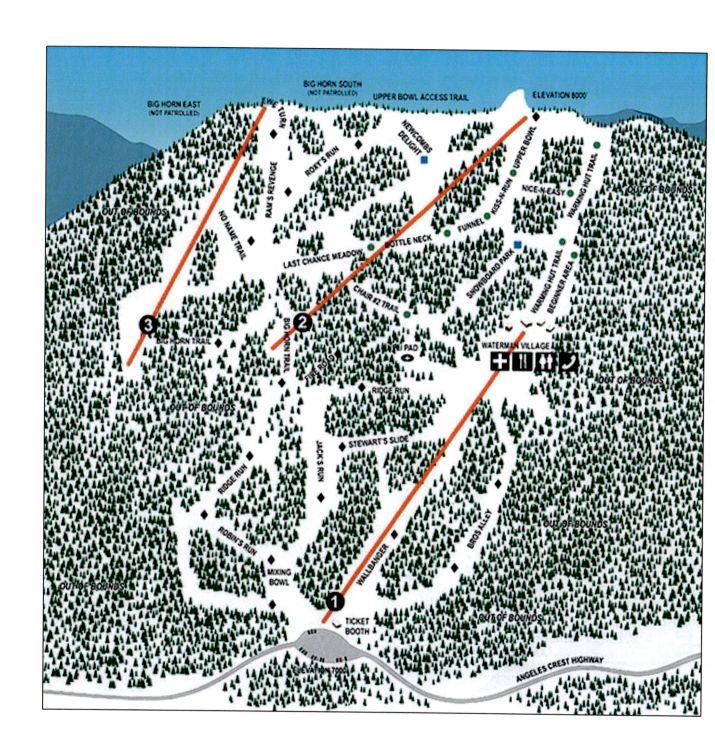

BIG HORN EAST
(NOT PATROLLED)

BIG HORN SOUTH
(NOT PATROLLED)

UPPER BOWL ACCESS TRAIL

ELEVATION 8000'

EWE TURN

NEWCOMBS DELIGHT

RAM'S REVENGE

ROXY'S RUN

OUT OF BOUNDS

NO NAME TRAIL

KISS-N-RUN

UPPER BOWL

NICE-N-EASY

FUNNEL

WARMING HUT TRAIL

OUT OF BOUNDS

BOTTLE NECK

LAST CHANCE MEADOW

CHAIR #2 TRAIL

SNOWBOARD PARK

WARMING HUT TRAIL

BEGINNER AREA

BIG HORN TRAIL

3

BIG HORN TRAIL

2

TUBE PAD

WATERMAN VILLAGE

OUT OF BOUNDS

OUT OF BOUNDS

TUBE HOLD

RIDGE RUN

STEWART'S SLIDE

OUT OF BOUNDS

RIDGE RUN

JACK'S RUN

ROBIN'S RUN

WALLBANGER

BROS ALLEY

OUT OF BOUNDS

MIXING BOWL

1

OUT OF BOUNDS

TICKET BOOTH

OUT OF BOUNDS

ELEVATION 7000'

ANGELES CREST HIGHWAY

Tahoe Donner

| Established: 1971 | Acres: 120 | Vertical: 600' | Annual Snowfall: 400" |

Tahoe Donner Downhill Ski Area is committed to being the best place for family fun and learning in the Tahoe region. With beautifully groomed runs and courteous staff, Tahoe Donner Downhill welcomes all ages to enjoy its wide-open bowls and uncrowded slopes. In addition, the size allows Tahoe Donner to deliver that personal touch that larger ski areas can't always provide. Family events, several of which are free, take place at various times throughout the season.

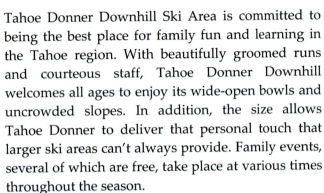

Located 18 miles from Lake Tahoe and just minutes off interstate 80 in Truckee, California, Tahoe Donner operates a wide variety of recreational facilities, including an award-winning championship golf course, a family-friendly downhill ski area, and a renowned cross country ski area with a newly constructed, state-of-the-art base lodge.

SNOWPLAY

Slip and slide at Tahoe Donner's Snowplay area. Experience exhilarating tubing runs or grab a sled and carve your own path, at a great value for the entire family.

CROSS COUNTRY SKIING

Tahoe Donner's cross country ski center offers guests over 100 kilometers of world-class groomed terrain to meet every need, from beginner to expert. Skiers can enjoy gliding through pines and aspen groves, climbing challenging peaks or cruising along gentle rolling hills or the flats of Euer Valley.

DOWNHILL SKI AREA:
THE BEST PLACE TO BEGIN

A ski or snowboard lesson is the best way for you to have the most fun on the snow. Tahoe Donner has great deals on lessons and programs designed for all levels. One of the only areas that starts teaching kids as young as 3 years old, Tahoe Donner is known for their learn-to-ski programs.

Adults can hone their skills with a group or private lesson with one of their pros. For any level skier or rider, Tahoe Donner is the best place to begin and continue learning!

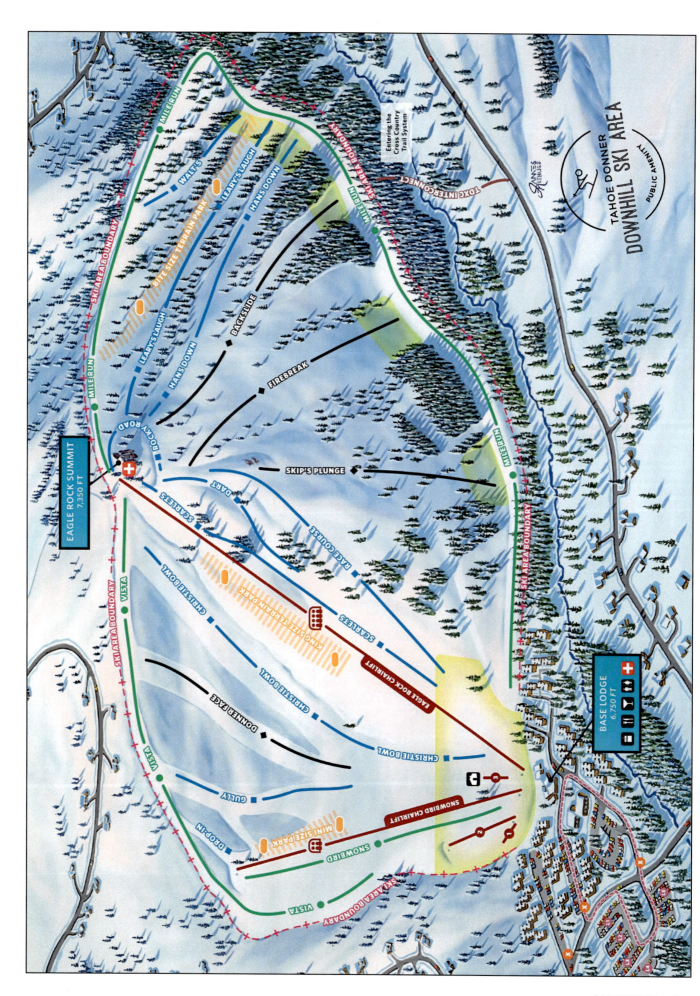

TAHOE DONNER SKI AREA
DOWNHILL SKI AREA
PUBLIC AMENITY

EAGLE ROCK SUMMIT
7,350 FT

BASE LODGE
6,750 FT

Entering the
Cross Country
Trail System

MILE RUN
WALT'S
LEARY'S LAUGH
HANS DOWN
BIKE SIZE TERRAIN PARK
LEARY'S LAUGH
HANS DOWN
BACKSLIDE
FIREBREAK
SKIP'S PLUNGE
ROCKY ROAD
DART
SCARLETS
RACE COURSE
SCARLETS
SKI AREA BOUNDARY
TDXC INTERCONNECT
MILE RUN
MILE RUN
SKI AREA BOUNDARY

EAGLE ROCK CHAIRLIFT
VISTA
CHRISTIE BOWL
CHRISTIE BOWL
CHRISTIE BOWL
DONNER FACE
GULLY
DROP-IN
VISTA
VISTA
SKI AREA BOUNDARY
TRIO SIZE TERRAIN PARK

SNOWBIRD CHAIRLIFT
MINI SIZE PARK
SNOWBIRD
VISTA
SKI AREA BOUNDARY

Yosemite Ski & Snowboard Area

YOSEMITE
SKI & SNOWBOARD AREA

Established: 1935	Acres: 88	Vertical: 800'	Annual Snowfall: 300"

Founded in 1935, Yosemite Ski & Snowboard Area is California's first ski resort and the perfect winter destination for families and beginner skiers. Yosemite Ski & Snowboard Area is the gateway to some of the most beautiful vistas in the High Sierra, offering five convenient lifts and 10 spacious, groomed runs. Yosemite Ski & Snowboard Area makes every mountain adventure fun and stress-free with their friendly, affordable ski and snowboard area that's perfect for skiers and riders of all levels. Here you'll find equipment rentals, top-notch instructors, a ski shop, cafeteria and lounge—and a fantastic sundeck, where you can watch your kids ski as you bask in the sunshine. (The ski school was established in 1928!)

Some of the special features of the ski area is the daily ranger-led snowshoe walks and the Nordic Center operates Glacier Point Ski Hut, which allows cross-country skiers the opportunity to enjoy a 10.5 mile trip each way with an overnight at the hut. Both guided and self-guided options are available.

OTHER WINTER ACTIVITIES

Yosemite also offers snowshoe trails, rentals, and guided hikes. For a few days when the moon is full each month, their naturalist guides offer a Full Moon Snowshoe Walk in the evenings. With the full moon above reflecting off the snow below, this is a magical time in Yosemite.

Yosemite Ski and Snowboard area also offers two two-hour sessions of tubing each day. The tubes are provided with the session fee. Perfect activity for the whole family. Please note personal sledding is not allowed at the ski area

YOSEMITE
SKI & SNOWBOARD AREA

Tubing

Cross-country trail to Old Glacier Point Road

GLACIER POINT RD.

● **Easiest**	■ **More Difficult**	◆ **Most Difficult**	▬ **Terrain Park**

1 Turtle
2 Beaver
3 Rabbit
4 Eagle
5 Red Fox
6 Wildcat
7 Chipmunk
8 Badger
9 Bruin
10 Grey Owl

A **Turtle** (Cable Tow)
B **Red Fox** (Double Chair)
C **Eagle** (Triple Chair)
D **Badger** (Double Chair)
E **Bruin** (Double Chair)

★ **Nordic Center**

★★**Day Lodge**
Food & Beverage
Lockers
Pups' Den
Ski School
Rentals
Ski Shop

✚ **Ski Patrol**
First Aid
Ranger Station

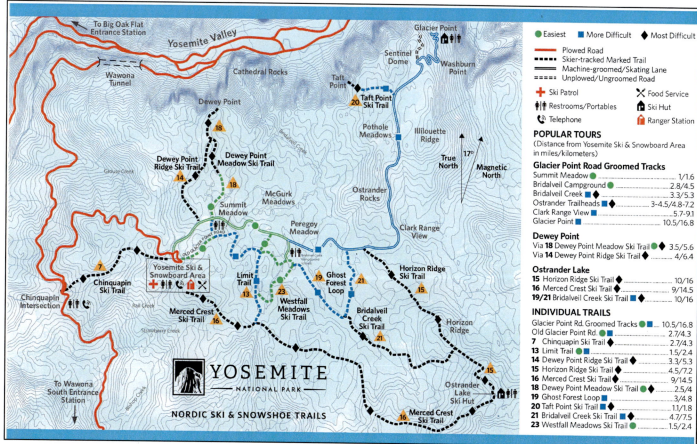

To Big Oak Flat Entrance Station

Yosemite Valley

Glacier Point

Sentinel Dome

Washburn Point

Wawona Tunnel

Cathedral Rocks

Taft Point

20 Taft Point Ski Trail

Dewey Point

Pothole Meadows

Illilouette Ridge

Grouse Creek

Bridalveil Creek

Dewey Point Ridge Ski Trail
14

Dewey Point Meadow Ski Trail

18

18

McGurk Meadows

Ostrander Rocks

True North

17° Magnetic North

Summit Meadow

Peregoy Meadow

Clark Range View

OLD GLACIER POINT ROAD

7

Chinquapin Ski Trail

Chinquapin Intersection

Rail Creek

Yosemite Ski & Snowboard Area

Limit Trail
13

23

Westfall Meadows Ski Trail

19 Ghost Forest Loop

21

Horizon Ridge Ski Trail

15

Strawberry Creek

Merced Crest Ski Trail
16

Bridalveil Creek Ski Trail

21

Horizon Ridge

To Wawona South Entrance Station

YOSEMITE
NATIONAL PARK

NORDIC SKI & SNOWSHOE TRAILS

Ostrander Lake Ski Hut

15

16 Merced Crest Ski Trail

● **Easiest**	■ **More Difficult**	◆ **Most Difficult**

━━━ Plowed Road
▪▪▪▪ Skier-tracked Marked Trail
═══ Machine-groomed/Skating Lane
▭▭▭ Unplowed/Ungroomed Road

✚ Ski Patrol
🚹🚺 Restrooms/Portables
📞 Telephone

✗ Food Service
🏠 Ski Hut
🏠 Ranger Station

POPULAR TOURS
(Distance from Yosemite Ski & Snowboard Area in miles/kilometers)

Glacier Point Road Groomed Tracks
Summit Meadow ● 1/1.6
Bridalveil Campground ● 2.8/4.5
Bridalveil Creek ■ ◆ 3.3/5.3
Ostrander Trailheads ■ ◆ 3-4.5/4.8-7.2
Clark Range View ■ ◆ 5.7-9.1
Glacier Point ■ 10.5/16.8

Dewey Point
Via 18 Dewey Point Meadow Ski Trail ● ◆ 3.5/5.6
Via 14 Dewey Point Ridge Ski Trail ◆ 4/6.4

Ostrander Lake
15 Horizon Ridge Ski Trail ◆ 10/16
16 Merced Crest Ski Trail ◆ 9/14.5
19/21 Bridalveil Creek Ski Trail ■ ◆ 10/16

INDIVIDUAL TRAILS
Glacier Point Rd. Groomed Tracks ● ■ .. 10.5/16.8
Old Glacier Point Rd. ● ■ 2.7/4.3
7 Chinquapin Ski Trail ◆ 2.7/4.3
13 Limit Trail ● ■ 1.5/2.4
14 Dewey Point Ridge Ski Trail ◆ 3.3/5.3
15 Horizon Ridge Ski Trail ◆ 4.5/7.2
16 Merced Crest Ski Trail ◆ 9/14.5
18 Dewey Point Meadow Ski Trail ● ◆ 2.5/4
19 Ghost Forest Loop ■ 3/4.8
20 Taft Point Ski Trail ◆ 1.1/1.8
21 Bridalveil Creek Ski Trail ■ ◆ 4.7/7.5
23 Westfall Meadows Ski Trail ● 1.5/2.4

Granlibakken

GRANLIBAKKEN
TAHOE
1922 **95** 2017

Established: 1922	Acres: 10	Vertical: 450'	Annual Snowfall: 184"

You can ski or ride right out your back door at Granlibakken Tahoe. Their intimate ski hill is perfect for beginner through intermediate skiers and snowboarders, with rental shop, ski school and warming hut on the premises. Rental shop and warming hut are open daily, all season. The ski hill and ski school are open Friday-Monday throughout the season; and daily during the winter season and during holiday periods.

Granlibakken also has a nice sledding hill where you can use your own

sled or rent one. And if you need more of a workout, Granlibakken offers plenty of Sierra terrain to explore. Enjoy the cross country ski trails around Granlibakken's 74-acre resort or head up to Paige Meadows to experience Tahoe's back country. Guests have easy access to popular cross-country trailheads which provide miles of ungroomed Lake Tahoe skiing and snowshoeing terrain

Granlibakken
Ski/Board Hill

Granlibakken
Sled Hill

Granlibakken
Ski, Snowboard and Snowplay area Since 1922

GRANLIBAKKEN
TAHOE

■ Paved road to the Truckee River
■ Nordic Trail around the property/Par Course
■ Nordic Trail to Rawhide and along the forest logging road to Page Meadows
■ Nordic Trail on road to Water Tower and top of the "Olympic Hill" Ski Jump
■ Ski lifts

725 Granlibakken Road, Tahoe City, CA 96145 • 800.543.3221 • Granlibakken.com

Colorado

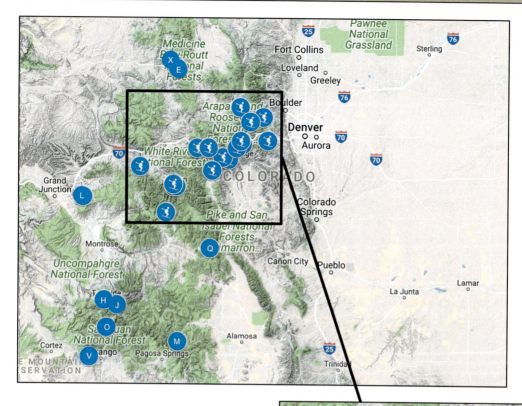

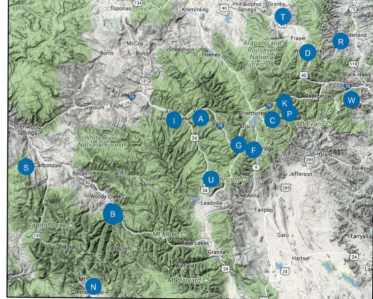

		Page
A.	Vail	72
B.	Aspen	76
C.	Keystone	84
D.	Winter Park	86
E.	Steamboat	88
F.	Breckenridge	90
G.	Copper Mountain	92
H.	Telluride	94
I.	Beaver Creek	96
J.	Silverton Mountain	98
K.	Loveland	100
L.	Powderhorn	102
M.	Wolf Creek	104
N.	Crested Butte	106
O.	Purgatory	108
P.	Arapahoe Basin	110
Q.	Monarch Mountain	112
R.	Eldora	114
S.	Sunlight Mountain Resort	116
T.	Granby Ranch	118
U.	Cooper	120
V.	Hesperus	122
W.	Echo Mountain	123
X.	Howelsen Hill	124

Vail

Established: 1962	Acres: 5289	Vertical: 3450'	Annual Snowfall: 353"

Coveted as one of the largest ski resorts in the world with more than 5,200 acres of developed ski and snowboard terrain, seven legendary Back Bowls spanning seven miles, and the most groomed terrain on the planet, Vail has been an extraordinary winter vacation destination for passionate skiers and snowboarders for more than 50 years.

Whether you love the feeling of gliding down a freshly laid carpet of groomed snow or revel in knee-deep powder, Vail has terrain to suit your style. Known for that light and fluffy Colorado powder, Vail also boasts the most groomed terrain on the planet. From the Front Side to the Back Bowls, there is intermediate-friendly terrain off of every lift, while experts can challenge themselves on iconic Vail runs and glades. Golden Peak and Bwana Terrain Parks offer small, medium, and large features for those looking for an added challenge.

Vail has unique Kid's Adventure Zones all over the mountain, featuring banked turns, tunnels, and small glades. These fun and safe areas are perfect to build confidence and challenge your child's skiing and riding abilities.

MOUNTAIN TOURS

Community Guest Service volunteers provide complimentary tours of Vail Mountain for any guest whose ability level is intermediate or above. There are general mountain tours and also tours of the Blue Sky Basin.

WINTER ACTIVITIES

Play in the afternoon and well into the night at Adventure Ridge with ski bikes, kids snowmobile track, a slippery slope of rip-roaring tubing lanes and more. Located at the top of the Eagle Bahn Gondola, Adventure Ridge is snow park the size of a football stadium, complete with family food favorites like Bistro Fourteen. The Eagle Bahn Gondola runs from breakfast till night. Drink hot chocolate and watch the sun set over the bowls. Adventure Ridge, a family experience Like Nothing on Earth.

VILLAGE

Nestled up to the base of the ski mountain, the village experience is at once timeless and vibrant. The highly regarded fine dining scene is matched by stellar shopping experiences. Looking for a fun place to unwind après ski? You'll have a hard time choosing which deck and drink special. Family and group friendly options abound with ice skating rinks, a high-end movie theater, ritzy bowling, sweets shops and event concert venues all within a few minutes' walk.

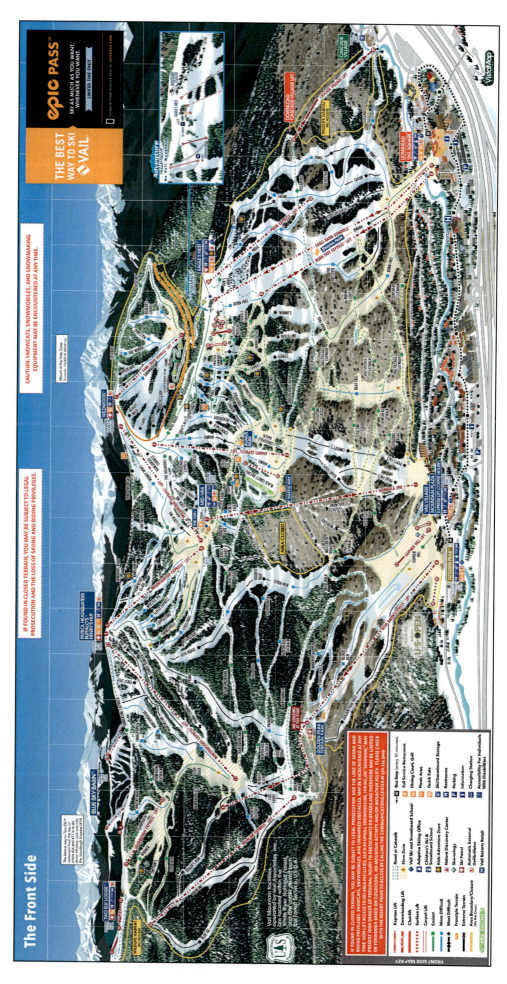

The Back Bowls™

Blue Sky Basin™

EARL'S BOWL™

PETE'S BOWL™

ELEVATION
11,480'
3,499m

BELLE'S CAMP™

WILDLIFE HABITAT NO ACCESS

WILDLIFE HABITAT NO ACCESS

WILDLIFE HABITAT NO ACCESS

WILDLIFE HABITAT NO ACCESS

WILDLIFE HABITAT NO ACCESS

ELEVATION
11,570'
3,527m

KELLY'S TOLL ROAD
to TEA CUP & SKYLINE EXPRESS

38

37 38

CHAMPAGNE GLADE

EARL'S EXPRESS™ LIFT

IN THE WUIDES

MONTANE GLADE

ENCORE

THE DIVIDE

SKYLINE EXPRESS™ LIFT

37

36

TEA CUP EXPRESS™ LIFT

MARMOT VALLEY

SLEEPYTIME ROAD

STEEP & DEEP

LOVER'S LEAP

SKREE FIELD

LITTLE OLLIE

HEAVY METAL

CLOUD 9
to TEA CUP & SKYLINE EXPRESS

39

DAWG HAUS

21

CLOUD 9

BIG ROCK PARK

to TEA CUP & SKYLINE EXPRESS

SILK ROAD

ORIENT EXPRESS™ LIFT

RESOLUTION

HORNSILVER

THE STAR

PETE'S EXPRESS™ LIFT

CHINA SPUR
to CHINA BOWL

POPPYFIELDS

GRAND REVIEW

39

BLUE SKY BASIN MAP KEY

Express Lift	
Chair Lift	
Area Boundary/Closure (Do Not Cross)	
More Difficult	
Most Difficult	
Road or Catwalk (May Include Flat Terrain)	

VistaMap

Aspen Snowmass

| Established: 1946 | Acres: 3332 | Vertical: 4406' | Annual Snowfall: 300" |

At Snowmass, you could spend your entire trip skiing and riding its terrain without covering the same ground twice. From the choice expert terrain of Burnt Mountain Glades, High Alpine and the Cirque, to the long blue groomers and impressive beginner facilities for newcomers, it is an easy choice. Then there's the events, activities and dining... See why Snowmass is more than just awesome terrain.

TERRAIN PARKS

Year after year, Snowmass' terrain parks are consistently placed toward the top of Transworld Snowboarding Magazine's rankings. Whether you are looking for a mountain to keep your family of shredders happy, or you're hoping to fine-tune your rail and half-pipe skills, Snowmass' three parks have you more than covered.

With approximately 100 features in total — including a 22-foot Zaugg-cut Superpipe — this mountain has earned its reputation as one of the best for terrain parks.

And best of all, you can ski all four Aspen resorts (Snowmass, Highlands, Buttermilk, and Aspen Mountain) under one pass, all within nine miles. Furthermore, all four areas are part of the Ikon Pass.

FIRST TRACKS

Join their staff for an early-morning, first run of the day on freshly groomed snow or powder. Offered on Wednesdays and Fridays beginning December 23, sign-up 24-hours in advance.

AMBASSADOR TOURS

Get to know Aspen Snowmass with community ambassadors. Tours serve as an orientation to the mountain on intermediate runs and take one to two hours. They are ideal for those who have never been to Snowmass Mountain or returning visitors who need a refresher. All skiers must be an intermediate level or better to join.

TUBING

Aspen Snowmass is thrilled to offer tubing facilities at Snowmass. The multiple lanes are lift served and carved into The Meadows at Elk Camp, with lighting facilities to illuminate the runs at night during Ullr Nights festivities and on special holidays.

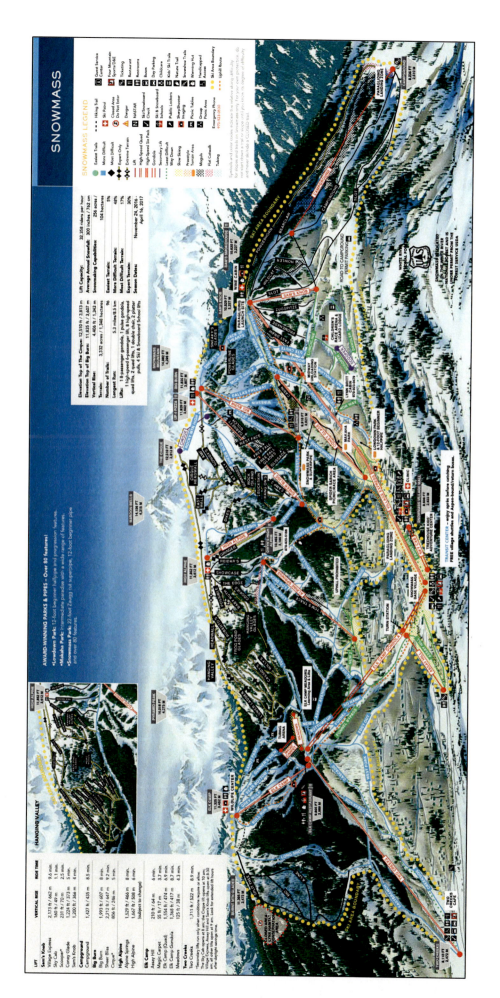

SNOWMASS

SNOWMASS LEGEND

Easiest Trails	• • • Hiking Trail	🏥 Guest Service Center
More Difficult	🚫 Closed Area	🚑 Ski Patrol
Most Difficult	🚫 Do Not Enter	Four Mountain Sports/D&E
Expert Terrain	⚠ Danger	Ticketing
Extreme Terrain	⚠ NASTAR	Restaurant
High-Speed Quad	Ski/Snowboard Check	Restrooms
High-Speed Six Pack	Ski & Snowboard Schools	Beds
Gondola	Childcare	Day Parking
Secondary Lift	Least Difficult Way Down	Public Lockers
Lift	Slow Skiing	SharpShooter Imaging
	Freestyle Terrain Area	Group Picnic Area
	Moguls	Snowshoe Trails
	Flat Cat/walk	Warming Hut
	Tubing	Nature Trail
		Handicapped Access
		Ski Area Boundary
		• • • Uphill Route

Symbols and colour codes indicate the relative difficulty for slopes and trails in Snowmass only. For your own protection, do not ski terrain that is beyond your ability, and if you know the degree of difficulty and never ski inside a CLOSED trail.

Specifications

Elevation Top of The Cirque:	12,510 ft / 3,813 m
Elevation Top of Big Burn:	11,835 ft / 3,607 m
Vertical Rise:	4,406 ft / 1,343 m
Terrain:	3,332 acres / 1,348 hectares
Snowmaking Capabilities:	256 acres / 104 hectares
Number of Trails:	96
Longest Run:	5.3 miles/8.5 km
Lifts:	1 8-passenger gondola, 1 pulse gondola, 1 high-speed 6-passenger lift, 8 high-speed quad lifts, 2 quad lifts, 1 double chair, 2 platter pulls, 4 Ski & Snowboard School lifts
Lift Capacity:	32,358 riders per hour
Average Annual Snowfall:	300 inches / 762 cm
Easiest Terrain:	5%
More Difficult Terrain:	48%
Most Difficult Terrain:	17%
Expert Terrain:	30%
Season Dates:	November 24, 2016 – April 16, 2017

AWARD-WINNING PARKS & PIPES – Over 80 features!

•Lowdown Park: 12-foot beginner halfpipe and progression features.

•Makaha Park: intermediate paradise with a wide range of features.

•Snowmass Park: 22-foot Zaugg cut superpipe, 12-foot beginner pipe and over 80 features.

HANGING VALLEY

Lift Specifications

LIFT	VERTICAL RISE	RIDE TIME
Sam's Knob		
Village Express	2,173 ft / 662 m	9.6 min.
Sky Cab	160 ft / 49 m	1.1 min.
Scooper*	231 ft / 70 m	2.5 min.
Coney Glade	1,224 ft / 373 m	5 min.
Sam's Knob	1,200 ft / 366 m	4 min.
Campground		
Campground	1,427 ft / 435 m	8.5 min.
Big Burn		
Big Burn	1,993 ft / 607 m	8 min.
Sheer Bliss	2,712 ft / 647 m	9.2 min.
Cirque*	806 ft / 246 m	5 min.
High Alpine		
Alpine Springs	1,529 ft / 466 m	8 min.
High Alpine	1,667 ft / 508 m	6 min.
(subject to change)		
Elk Camp		
Assay Hill	210 ft / 64 m	6 min.
Magic Carpet	55 ft / 17 m	3.7 min.
Elk Camp (Quad)	1,554 ft / 474 m	6.6 min.
Elk Camp Gondola	1,368 ft / 417 m	8.7 min.
Meadows	125 ft / 38 m	4.3 min.
Two Creeks		
Two Creeks	1,711 ft / 522 m	8.9 min.

Secondary lifts run only when conditions require or allow. The Sky Cab opens at 8 am; the Cirque Lift opens at 10 am; Village Express, Assay Hill and Sam's Knob lifts open at 8:30 am; all other lifts open at 9 am. Look for extended lift hours after daylight savings time.

Aspen Highlands

ASPEN SNOWMASS®

| Established: 1958 | Acres: 1040 | Vertical: 3365' | Annual Snowfall: 300" |

Of the four mountains, Aspen Highlands avoids the spotlight, which is perfectly fine with the locals and in-the-know skiers and riders who tackle its uncrowded slopes. Hike the ridge to Highland Bowl for the sweetest run of your life, or simply cruise along the mid-mountain groomers off the Cloud Nine chairlift. Views over the valley to the snow-covered Maroon Bells constantly will remind you: this is Colorado at its best.

Locals call the vibe at Aspen Highlands "duct tape to diamonds." The duct tape part is the do-it-yourself character of its terrain (e.g. want to ski to Highlands Bowl? You'll have to hike in). The diamonds part is easy to spot at Cloud Nine Alpine Bistro in the afternoon, when the Champagne bottles equal the number of skis left out front.

CLOUD NINE – SNOWCAT DINNERS

This cozy, European-style cabin with a backdrop of the iconic Maroon Bells is a highlight of any Aspen Snowmass vacation. Cloud Nine Alpine Bistro is a legendary for a reason: channeling authentic European Alpine culture in a warm, welcoming environment, it also happens to have the most boisterous après ski scene on any mountain in North America

Evening snowcat dinners are a chance to make some unforgettable winter memories. They start with a fun snowcat ride to the restaurant — leaving at 6 pm from the base of Aspen Highlands — and include an unparalleled culinary experience in a cozy cabin surrounded by a snowy paradise.

AMBASSADOR TOURS

Want to see all the good terrain? Ambassadors lead tours every day for approximately 1-2 hours, twice a day. Ambassadors are at your service. In addition to free orientation tours, they offer information on terrain and facilities, and goodies like apple cider and Clif Bars.

If you are history buff, be sure to catch the history tour in conjunction with the Aspen Historical Society on Mondays at 11am and 1pm — from the Guest Services Cabin near the Exhibition Lift.

Aspen is part of the Ikon Pass.

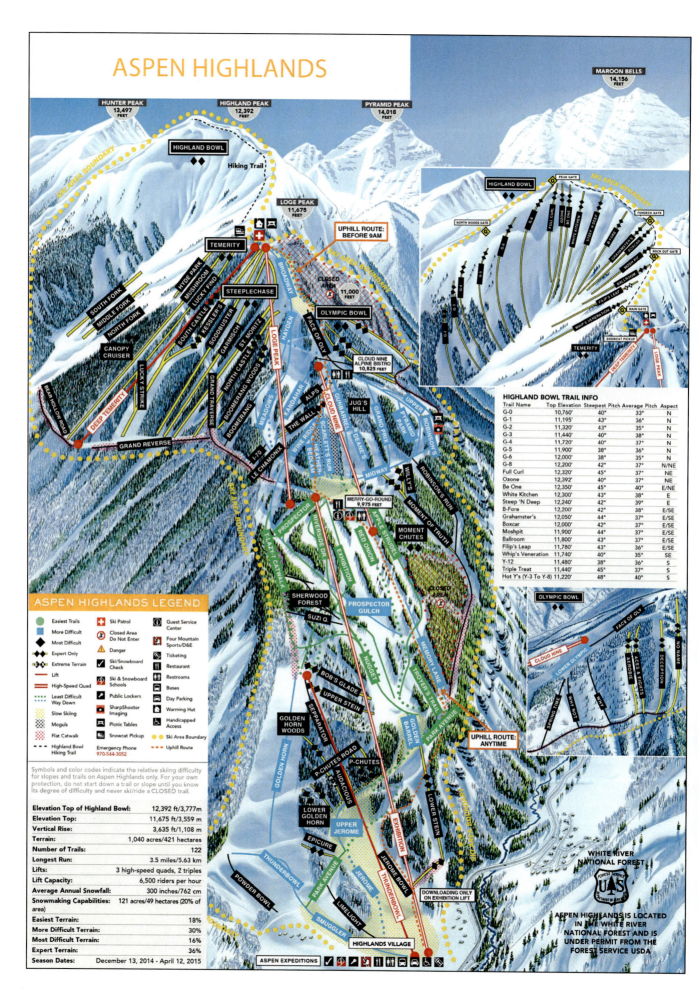

Aspen Mountain

| Established: 1946 | Acres: 675 | Vertical: 3267' | Annual Snowfall: 300" |

Rising from the heart of downtown Aspen, this is where it all began in the 1940s. In fact, at times it seems like the personality of the mountain and the town are one. Without a single beginner's run, Aspen Mountain presents a host of challenges, and some of the most awe-inspiring blue groomers in North America.

At Aspen Mountain you can ski down the same runs that hosted World Cup races, ride through gladed powder stashes, chase after the snowcat-towed Oasis Champagne Bar, or put together one quad-burning top-to-bottom after another. And all of this is just steps away from downtown Aspen. No wonder this mountain is a legend. It has it all – on-mountain dining, slope-side lodging, and some of the best terrain in Colorado.

And best of all, you can ski all four Aspen resorts (Snowmass, Highlands, Buttermilk, and Aspen Mountain) under one pass, all within nine miles. Furthermore, all four resorts are part of the Ikon Pass, too.

FIRST TRACKS

Join the staff for an early morning, first-run-of-the-day on freshly groomed snow or powder on Aspen Mountain. Offered daily beginning December 8, sign-up 24-hours in advance.

AMBASSADOR TOURS

Get to know Aspen Mountain like the locals do with community ambassadors. Ambassadors lead tours every day on Aspen Mountain. In addition to free orientation tours, they offer information on terrain and facilities, and goodies like apple cider and Clif

Bars. Tours serve as an orientation to the mountain on intermediate runs and take 1-2 hours.

POWDER TOURS

Aspen Mountain Powder Tours are available via luxury snowcats that take you to prime untracked glades and runs on the backside. A typical day averages 10,000 vertical feet of ungroomed wilderness skiing and boarding in an expanse of 1,100 acres that features open bowls, meadows and glades. Two guides and a driver lead each 12 person snowcat group, selecting terrain according to daily snow conditions and the group's experience.

Aspen is part of the Ikon Pass.

ASPEN MOUNTAIN

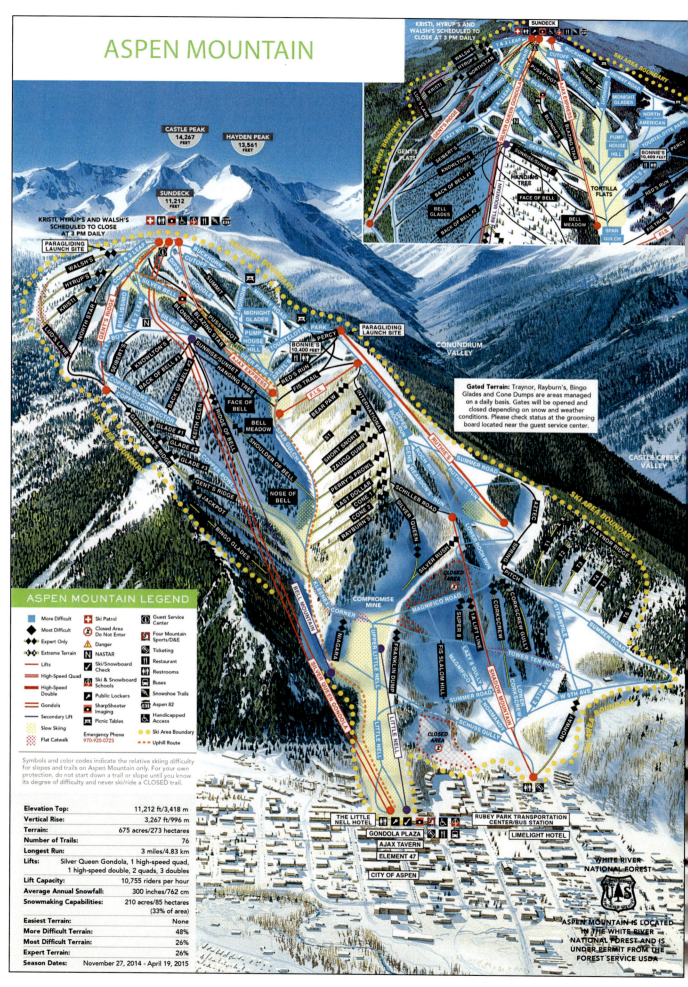

Gated Terrain: Traynor, Rayburn's, Bingo Glades and Cone Dumps are areas managed on a daily basis. Gates will be opened and closed depending on snow and weather conditions. Please check status at the grooming board located near the guest service center.

ASPEN MOUNTAIN LEGEND

■	More Difficult	✚	Ski Patrol	Guest Service Center
◆	Most Difficult	⊘	Closed Area Do Not Enter	Four Mountain Sports/D&E
◆◆	Expert Only	⚠	Danger	Ticketing
◆◆◆	Extreme Terrain	N	NASTAR	Restaurant
	Lifts		Ski/Snowboard Check	Restrooms
	High-Speed Quad		Ski & Snowboard Schools	Buses
	High-Speed Double		Public Lockers	Snowshoe Trails
	Gondola		SharpShooter Imaging	Aspen 82
	Secondary Lift		Picnic Tables	Handicapped Access
	Slow Skiing		Emergency Phone 970-920-0723	● Ski Area Boundary
	Flat Catwalk			● ● ● Uphill Route

Symbols and color codes indicate the relative skiing difficulty for slopes and trails on Aspen Mountain only. For your own protection, do not start down a trail or slope until you know its degree of difficulty and never ski/ride a CLOSED trail.

Elevation Top:	11,212 ft/3,418 m
Vertical Rise:	3,267 ft/996 m
Terrain:	675 acres/273 hectares
Number of Trails:	76
Longest Run:	3 miles/4.83 km
Lifts:	Silver Queen Gondola, 1 high-speed quad, 1 high-speed double, 2 quads, 3 doubles
Lift Capacity:	10,755 riders per hour
Average Annual Snowfall:	300 inches/762 cm
Snowmaking Capabilities:	210 acres/85 hectares (33% of area)
Easiest Terrain:	None
More Difficult Terrain:	48%
Most Difficult Terrain:	26%
Expert Terrain:	26%
Season Dates:	November 27, 2014 - April 19, 2015

ASPEN MOUNTAIN IS LOCATED IN THE WHITE RIVER NATIONAL FOREST AND IS UNDER PERMIT FROM THE FOREST SERVICE USDA

Aspen Buttermilk

Established: 1958	Acres: 470	Vertical: 2030'	Annual Snowfall: 300"

Buttermilk is one mountain with two personalities. Best known around the world for being home to the Winter X Games and the Red Bull Double Pipe event, the mountain has become an icon for freestyle riders and skiers, who hit up the Buttermilk Park to see what they're made of. But the mountain is also easy-going for beginners and families, boasting uncrowded beginner terrain and The Hideout, an innovative learning center for young skiers.

Spacious groomers, scenic views and a mellow, chilled-out vibe: there may not be a better mountain to learn to ski and ride than Buttermilk. But here's the secret: it's blue and black terrain is choice as well, often overshadowed by its neighboring mountains.

And best of all, you can ski all four Aspen resorts (Snowmass, Highlands, Buttermilk, and Aspen Mountain) under one pass, all within nine miles. Furthermore, all four Aspen resorts are part of the Ikon Pass.

TERRAIN PARKS

How good are the terrain parks at Buttermilk? In 2014, the resort was ranked No. 3 for Best Terrain Park by Transworld Snowboarding Magazine (just one place behind Snowmass). Depending on how you look at it, the entire heart of Buttermilk from the top to bottom is one terrain park after another, and that doesn't even include the S3 Park, where their Ski & Snowboard School can help you elevate your skills off the West Buttermilk Express Lift. Six parks for maximum fun.

AMBASSADOR TOURS

Get to know Buttermilk by tapping into the local insight of the community ambassadors. Tours serve as an orientation to the mountain on intermediate runs and take one to two hours. They are ideal for those who have never been to Snowmass

Mountain or returning visitors who need a refresher. All skiers must be an intermediate level or better to join.

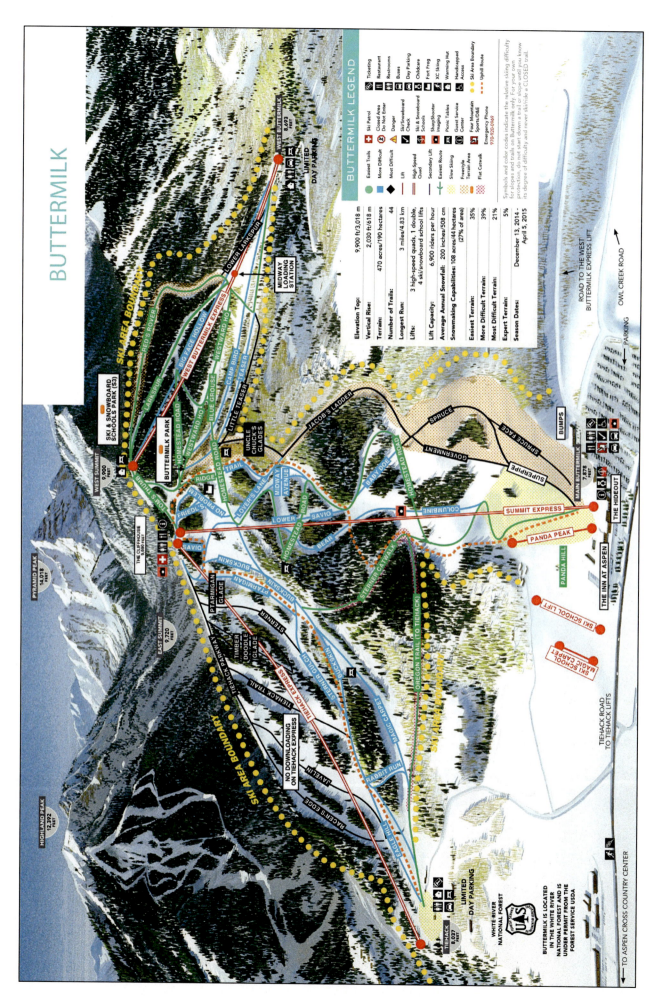

BUTTERMILK

BUTTERMILK LEGEND

✚	Ski Patrol	✷	Ski/Snowboard Check
⊘	Closed Area Do Not Enter	☒	Ski & Snowboard Schools
⚠	Danger		SharpShooter Imaging
	Lift		Guest Service Center
	High-Speed Quad		Four Mountain Sports/D&E
	Secondary Lift		Emergency Phone 970-920-0969
	Slow Skiing		

🎟	Ticketing	
🍴	Restaurant	
🚻	Restrooms	
🚌	Buses	
🅿	Day Parking	
	Childcare	
🐸	Fort Frog	
	XC Skiing	
	Warming Hut	
♿	Handicapped Access	

●	Easiest Trails
■	More Difficult
◆	Most Difficult

	Freestyle Terrain Area
	Flat Catwalk
● ● ●	Ski Area Boundary
	Easiest Route
● ● ●	Uphill Route

Symbols and color codes indicate the relative skiing difficulty for slopes and trails on Buttermilk only. For your own protection, do not start down a trail or slope until you know its degree of difficulty and never ski/ride a CLOSED trail.

Elevation Top:	9,900 ft/3,018 m
Vertical Rise:	2,030 ft/618 m
Terrain:	470 acres/190 hectares
Number of Trails:	44
Longest Run:	3 miles/4.83 km
Lifts:	3 high-speed quads, 1 double, 4 ski/snowboard school lifts
Lift Capacity:	6,900 riders per hour
Average Annual Snowfall:	200 inches/508 cm
Snowmaking Capabilities:	108 acres/44 hectares (27% of area)
Easiest Terrain:	35%
More Difficult Terrain:	39%
Most Difficult Terrain:	21%
Expert Terrain:	5%
Season Dates:	December 13, 2014 – April 5, 2015

WHITE RIVER NATIONAL FOREST

BUTTERMILK IS LOCATED IN THE WHITE RIVER NATIONAL FOREST AND IS UNDER PERMIT FROM THE FOREST SERVICE USDA

Keystone

| Established: 1970 | Acres: 3148 | Vertical: 3128' | Annual Snowfall: 230" |

Keystone Resort, located in Summit County, Colorado and just 75 miles from Denver, is the ultimate family resort destination! In winter, the ski resort boasts more than 3,000 acres of skiable terrain within the White River National Forest including three incredible peaks, five above-tree-line bowls, night skiing and an in-bounds cat skiing program. Home to the industry's-leading Kids Ski Free program, kids 12 and younger can ski and ride for free every day, all season long with just two or more nights of lodging booked through the resort, no blackout dates.

A true winter wonderland, in addition to skiing and snowboarding across more than 3,000 acres, at Keystone visitors can enjoy a variety of on- and off-mountain activities including scenic and dinner sleigh rides, Nordic skiing, snowshoeing, snow tubing at Adventure Point, Mountaintop Family Adventure Tours in a snowcat, and ice skating.

Keystone's Kidtopia continues to redefine the family resort experience with free activities and events on and off the snow every day of the week, for kids of all ages. Test your aim and compete with family members at the Giant Snowball Launch, learn about the wonders of winter at Super Snowy Science, march in the Village Parade and experience the world's largest Snow Fort on Dercum Mountain – the possibilities are endless for kids at Keystone!

NIGHT SKIING

Offering the longest ski day in all of Colorado, at Keystone families can enjoy the star-filled sky as they ski and snowboard on the resort's multiple lighted trails. Open until 8 p.m. during night operations and fireworks every Saturday make Keystone's night skiing is a unique experience.

CAT SKIING

Keystone is one of the only Colorado ski resorts that offers cat skiing. Warm, heated cats and endless acres of terrain, you'll have an unforgettable adventure.

Winter Park

WINTER PARK RESORT

| Established: 1940 | Acres: 3081 | Vertical: 3060' | Annual Snowfall: 353" |

With over a 75-year history, Winter Park Resort is Colorado's longest continually operated ski resort that features the Seven Territories across 3,081 acres of award-winning terrain. From groomers to black diamonds at the Winter Park Territory; world-class glade skiing in the Eagle Wind Territory; panoramic bowl skiing/riding in the Parsenn Bowl Territory; jumps and jibs in the Terrain Park Territory; off-the-beaten path powder stashes of the Vasquez Ridge Territory; steeps and deeps of the Cirque Territory; to the world-famous bumps at Mary Jane Territory, there is something for everyone at Winter Park Resort.

With 25 lifts, Winter Park has no problem moving people up the mountain at a pace of 40,000 per hour. Averaging over 320 inches of annual snowfall, 300 days of sunshine, and located just 67 miles northwest of Denver, Winter Park Resort is the closest major destination resort to Denver International Airport and a favorite among the Denver locals who call this place their "home mountain."

THE TO DO LIST

1. Step off the Gondola at 10,713 feet and walk into the warm, inviting ambiance of Sunspot for an unforgettable dinner
2. First tracks on fresh Cranmer corduroy
3. Hearing kids scream through the Village Way tunnel
4. Habanero Hot Chocolate at the Hill House after tubing
5. Watching GS racers on Hughes from the Zephyr chair
6. Free s'mores in the Village after a day on the slopes
7. Free ice skating lessons in the Village

RAIL ACCESS

Winter Park is the only Western resort that can be accessed by rail, courtesy of Amtrak. The Winter Park Express train takes you from Denver's Union Station directly to the platform at Winter Park.

Winter Park is part of the Ikon Pass.

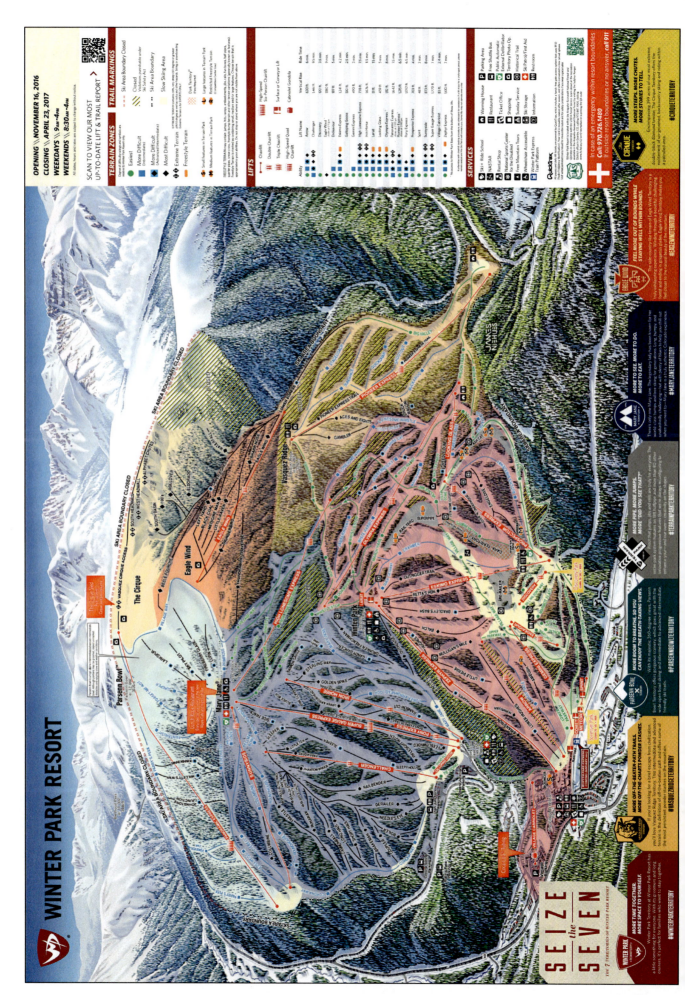

Steamboat

Steamboat.

Established: 1965	Acres: 2965	Vertical: 3668'	Annual Snowfall: 336"

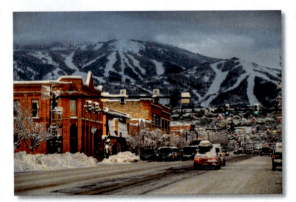

Steamboat is known around the world for snow so light and dry that it carries its very own trademark: Champagne Powder® snow. With 26 percent more trails and 10 percent more lifts than the average Colorado ski resort, guests spend less time in line and more time on the slopes enjoying that fine snow.

From expert chutes to kids-only slopes, Steamboat's wide variety of terrain offers the perfect run everyone. Even the nonskier has plenty of options — including horseback riding, sleigh rides, tubing, snowmobiling and snowshoeing — so the whole family can enjoy Colorado's beautiful Rocky Mountains with Steamboat's Yampa Valley as the backdrop.

Steamboat has been recognized as a "Premier Family Ski Resort" by Jetsetter and recently has ranked within the top 10 family ski resorts by Ski Magazine and Forbes.

And when the day is over, the family can experience world-class dining and mountain hospitality at more than 100 of Steamboat's restaurants and bars.

NIGHT SKIING

Steamboat is one of the few destination resorts that keeps the slopes open after dark. Night skiing and riding is open five nights a week with access to five trails and 1,100 vertical feet illuminated by the state-of-the-art Ultra-Tech™ lighting system.

GETTING THERE

With nonstop flights from 14 U.S. cities — more than any other ski destination — and convenient connections from airports worldwide, Steamboat's Champagne Powder® snow is more accessible than ever. And if you fly into Steamboat/Hayden Airport, you ski free the night of your arrival.

Photos courtesy of Larry Pierce/Steamboat Ski Resort

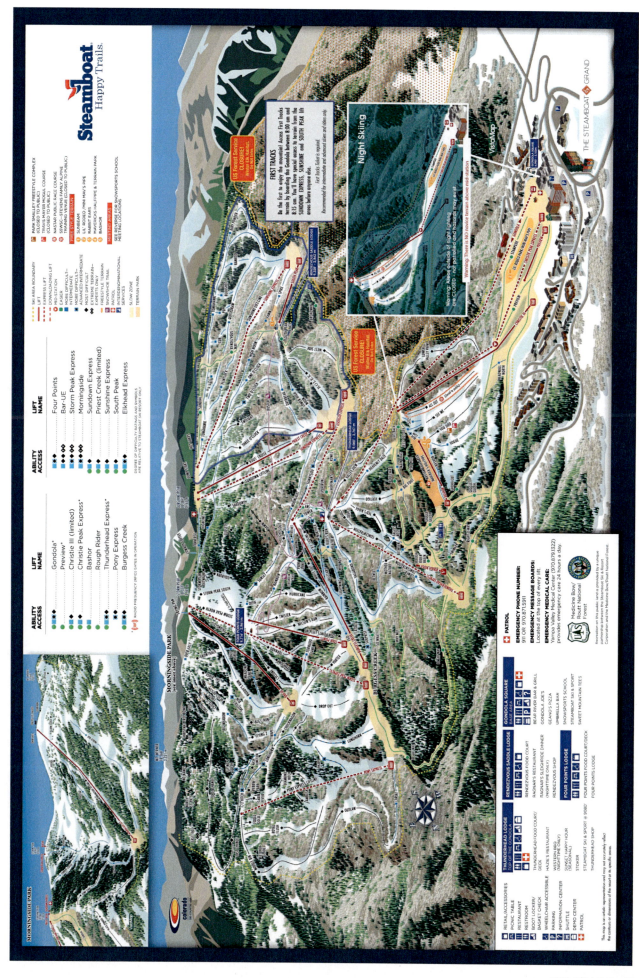

Breckenridge

Established: 1961	Acres: 2908	Vertical: 3397'	Annual Snowfall: 300"

Offering the perfect combination of mountain, town, and spirit, Breck is one of the greatest ski destinations in the world. The mountain spans 2,908 skiable acres and five unique, and astounding peaks. From Peak 10's steep groomers to Peak 9's world-class beginner terrain, to the variety on Peak 8, to the intermediate cruising runs on Peak 7 to the gorgeous above-treeline terrain on Peak 6 – there's something for everyone at any time of year. Plus Breck's elevation (the base is at 9,600 feet and Breck has the highest chairlift in North America) means the snow stays fresh longer.

The town is as real of a Colorado town as you can get. Founded in 1851, Breckenridge started as a mining town quickly in the 1960s. Now the town has 200 shops and restaurants that line the downtown and arts district. And with the town located at the base, there are plenty of slopeside lodging options.

Breck's spirit is really what makes this destination unique. With events like Ullr Fest in January and Spring Fever in April, there's always something happening in Breck. People come from around the country to relax, unwind, and just be themselves.

MOUNTAIN TOURS

Guest Service volunteers provide complimentary tours of Breckenridge Ski Resort for any guest whose ability level is intermediate or above. Tours are only available on intermediate runs. In addition, Breck has a guide service that offers guests the inside scoop on their best terrain, plus they teach basic backcountry skills and where to find the freshest powder.

Breckenridge is a Vail Resort, which means that an Epic Pass works here along with the EpicMix phone app for tracking your statistics.

BRECK

Breckenridge Ski Resort is made up of five distinct peaks, each with its own characteristics and features. Welcome!

Breckenridge Ski Resort is operated under a special-use permit with the White River National Forest.

PEAK 10

Experience the all-new 6-person Falcon SuperChair – it's your fast-track to Breck's most thrilling terrain. Peak 10 is comprised entirely of expert trails, where skiers will find groomed steeps, challenging moguls and technical tree chutes.

Peak 10
13,659ft / 4,157m

PEAK 9

Peak 9 is one of the best places to learn to ski. The family friendly learning zones and wide-open intermediate runs foster progression and offer endless fun. Test your skills at the Epilogue Face Course or head over to Peak 9's advanced northern face for a full day of adventure.

Peak 9
13,195ft / 4,022m

PEAK 8

The heart of Breck, Peak 8 offers something for everyone. Choose from legendary terrain parks, interactive trails for kids, and our widest selection of trails. Test your skills at the Epilogue Face Course or head over to Peak 9's advanced northern face and experts alike.

Peak 8
12,998ft / 3,962m

PEAK 7

An intermediate skier's paradise, Peak 7 features rolling terrain and gorgeous views. Looking for a cozy on-mountain retreat? The new Pioneer Crossing restaurant is conveniently located at the top of the Independence SuperChair and features upscale campfire food with a casual atmosphere.

Peak 7
12,651ft / 3,857m

PEAK 6

Peak 6 showcases above treeline terrain. Above treeline expert terrain with awe-inspiring views of the entire valley. Let Mother Nature be your guide through the wide open bowls of Peak 6, or feel the thrill of The Six Senses. Go beyond your expectations.

Peak 6
12,573ft / 3,832m

LEGEND

LIFT STATS

MOUNTAIN STATS

FAMILY ZONES

TERRAIN PARKS

Let Your Battery Reach Its Peak.

Free charging stations for your device, compliments of Verizon at the following places:

The Overlook
TenMile Station
DoubleTree by Hilton
The Maggie
Park Avenue Pub

Vista Haus
Ski Hill Grill
Pioneer Crossing
Sevens
Horizon Hut

verizon

Breckenridge.com

Copper Mountain

COPPER
MOUNTAIN

Established: 1972	Acres: 2490	Vertical: 2601'	Annual Snowfall: 302"

Located just 75 miles west of Denver, Colo. in the heart of the Rocky Mountains, Copper Mountain Resort is an ideal vacation destination with a laid-back, inclusive feeling for all. Three pedestrian-friendly village areas provide a vibrant atmosphere with lodging, retail outlets, restaurants, bars and family activities. During the winter months, Copper's naturally-divided terrain offers world-class skiing and riding for all ages and abilities.

Copper has three villages (East, West, and Center) which offer a variety of slope-side lodging and dining options.

MOUNTAIN TOURS

Copper's Ambassadors offer free mountain tours daily from mid-December through the beginning of April. This is a great way to learn how to get around and find the local's favorite places. Share the Resort Ambassadors' passion & knowledge for the mountain and the resort including history, wildlife, natural science and fun facts as you discover each of the diverse and distinctive areas Copper has to offer. Tours are available at 10 am and 1 pm.

Copper Mountain is part of the Ikon Pass.

FREE SNOWCAT

Jump on the snowcat for a free ride to experience parts of the mountain you only dreamed about last night. Copper's snowcat rides, to legendary Tucker Mountain, are the essence of skiing and riding liberty: catching a free ride, choosing your own line and never wiping the smile off your face. Tucker Mountain and Copper Bowl offer expert skiers and riders unprecedented access to over 273 acres and 12,000 vertical feet of Copper's amazing high alpine back bowls. Tucker Mountain Snowcat access is the closest thing to a backcountry experience that you'll ever find inside any resort.

TUBING HILL

All tubing hills are not created equal. You could go the classic straight lane route, or you can up your game with Copper. After a day on the slopes, kick off those ski boots and gather your entourage (AKA your family) and head to the hill.

ROCKY MOUNTAIN COASTER

The Rocky Mountain Coaster at Copper is the most recent year-round outdoor attraction in Center Village. With an overall length of 5,800 feet and a vertical drop of 430 feet, the raised alpine coaster track runs along the natural curvature of the mountain with zigs, zags, dips and 360 degree turns for guaranteed thrills all the way down to Copper's high alpine village.

Photos courtesy of Tripp Fay

Telluride

Established: 1972	Acres: 2000	Vertical: 4425'	Annual Snowfall: 309"

Forty-five minutes from the nearest stoplight at the end of a towering canyon sits Telluride, Colorado (elev. 8,750'), a National Historic Landmark surrounded by the highest concentration of 13,000' and 14,000' peaks in the United States. And nestled within the surrounding majesty is Telluride Ski Resort.

The resort lives up to its reputation as a skier's dream come true with legendary terrain, spectacular scenery and unspoiled character. With over 300" of snowfall and more than 300 days of sunshine, Telluride's elevation means the resort receives snow when other, lower-elevation resorts may not. Additionally, the area's ideal southern Colorado location means the temperatures in Telluride are generally a few degrees warmer than the resorts in northern Colorado, Wyoming and Montana.

Along with various ski in/ski out options for guests, Telluride Ski Resort offers terrain for every type of skier. The Plunge, Revelation Bowl and Gold Hill offer plenty of steeps for experts. See Forever and Prospect Bowl provide the ideal terrain for intermediates and the wide open, gentle slopes of Ute Park and The Meadows start beginners off right while enjoying the breathtaking scenery of the San Juans. For those seeking high-adventure thrills, Telluride's Helitrax earns the distinction as the ultimate heli-ski experience in the world, with over 200 square miles of stunning terrain.

MOUNTAIN TOUR

Kick off your first day with a complimentary mountain tour from one of Telluride's Mountain Ambassadors. Learn about the history of the mountain and get acquainted with its various areas of terrain. Mountain Tours depart daily at 10 a.m. from the top of the Coonskin Lift (Lift 7).

TRANSPORTATION

Above the historic mining town of Telluride is a modern mountain village connected by a free pedestrian gondola, the only one of its kind in North America. Between the two towns is San Sophia Station, where you can get off the gondola to visit the resort's flagship restaurant, Allred's. For many guests, one of perks of visiting Telluride is that you'll never have to get in a car once you're there.

Telluride is part of the Epic Pass.

Beaver Creek

Beaver Creek

| Established: 1980 | Acres: 1832 | Vertical: 3340' | Annual Snowfall: 323" |

Year after year, skiers of all levels flock to Beaver Creek and discover what they've always been looking for: legendary service, unmatched skiing and the intimacy and relaxation of one of the best mountain towns in the West. What makes Beaver Creek such a sought-after destination?

They spend all year paying attention to details so your vacation is unparalleled. Creating a world-class ski destination is a labor of love that transforms a beautiful mountain valley into a premium snow sport experience. That means you can expect the best experience from beginning to end, from the check-in at your preferred lodging to the staff on the mountain to the servers at dinner.

Ski School Ambassadors take guest service to a whole new level. Visiting Beaver Creek is the experience of a lifetime due to the emphasis their staff places on making every moment a memorable one.

More than a ski town. They know not every moment can be spent on the slopes (as much as you wish that were true). Browse upscale boutiques in Beaver Creek Village or lounge by a mesmerizing fire while enjoying a relaxing après ski cocktail.

They have six gourmet on-mountain dining options. Their mountain offers more than just fresh powder; they have several epicurean options slopeside so you can indulge whenever your appetite is piqued.

With over 1,800 acres of skiable terrain, their trails are World Cup worthy. Every year Beaver Creek hosts the Birds of Prey World Cup weekend. Once you've watched the pros tackle the trails, you can challenge yourself on the very same runs.

No nannies needed at Beaver Creek. They offer half or full day world class care for your young ones that aren't quite ready to strap on skis. They care for children aged two months to five years old.

The best homemade cookies, every day, free. Every day at three o'clock is Cookie Time in Beaver Creek. Their chefs serve over 500,000 freshly-baked cookies each year!

Silverton Mountain

Established: 2002	Acres: 1819	Vertical: 3087'	Annual Snowfall: 400"

Silverton Mountain is an experience unlike any other. Whether it is your first time here or your 100th, there is always something new to try and a new stash to find. If you've never been guided skiing, Silverton Mountain features world-class guides to show you the best terrain you've ever seen. Ready for more individual adventure with you and your crew? Show them around during the Unguided Skiing dates, and remember not to follow any sucker tracks! Their single-drop heli program is unique in the USA, and for $179 a drop, now is the time to try heli skiing/boarding in Colorado. Want to see more terrain than you can fathom? Check out Silverton's 6-run heli package that accesses over 29,000 acres of terrain.

Magazine Testimonials:

FREESKIER❄

"With one lift (dug by hand), no grooming and plenty of hike-to-insanity, Silverton remains an anomaly in American skiing. You wouldn't think the trial lawyers would let founder Aaron and Jen Brill get away with this one, but they do, and they have. Bring your avi gear, hire a guide (provided by Silverton), sign all the waivers and ski at your own risk, because Silverton is the real deal. Skiers with backcountry experience can go during periods when the mountain offers unguided skiing, otherwise Silverton is guide-skiing only. Check the website for details on when is the best time to go for you."
— Freeskier Magazine Travel Guide: Best Of The Best

Illustration by Mark Kowalchuk

skiing
magazine

"BEST RESORT YOU'VE NEVER SKIED: Silverton Mountain, Colorado Owners Jen and Aaron Brill deliver the best no-frills, no-beginners, no-bullshit steep skiing on the continent, and they do it with nothing more than a recycled double chair. But Silverton is more than San Juan couloirs and knee-deep powder. It's post-ski beers with literally every skier who rode the lift that day, a yurt-style 'lodge,' and a rental shop with reverse-camber fatties."

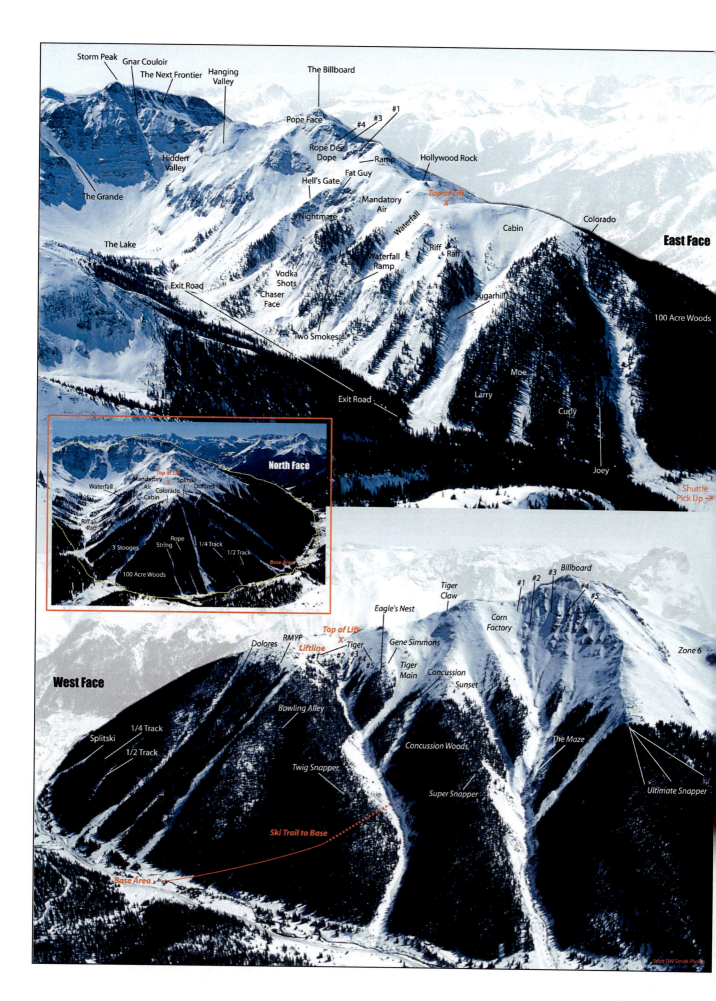

Storm Peak
Gnar Couloir
The Next Frontier
Hanging Valley
The Billboard
Pope Face
#1
#4 #3
Hidden Valley
Rope Dee Dope
Ramp
Hollywood Rock
The Grande
Hell's Gate
Fat Guy
Top of Lift
X
The Lake
Nightmare
Mandatory Air
Waterfall
Cabin
Colorado
East Face
Riff Raff
Exit Road
Vodka Shots
Chaser Face
Waterfall Ramp
Sugarhill
100 Acre Woods
Two Smokes
Moe
Exit Road
Larry
Curly
Joey
Shuttle Pick Up →

North Face
Top of Lift X
Mandatory Air
Splitski
Waterfall
Colorado
Dolores
Cabin
Riff Raff
3 Stooges
Rope String
1/4 Track
1/2 Track
Base Area
100 Acre Woods

Tiger Claw
#1 #2
#3
Billboard
#4
#5
Eagle's Nest
Corn Factory
Dolores
RMYF
Top of Lift X
Liftline
Tiger
Gene Simmons
Zone 6
#1
#2 #3 #4 #5
Tiger Main
Concussion
West Face
Sunset
Splitski
1/4 Track
Bowling Alley
Concussion Woods
The Maze
1/2 Track
Twig Snapper
Super Snapper
Ultimate Snapper
Ski Trail to Base
Base Area

Scott DW Smith Photo

Loveland

Loveland has been Denver's local mountain since 1937, making Loveland the second oldest ski area in Colorado. Throughout the years, Loveland Ski Area has focused on providing an exceptional Colorado ski & snowboard experience at an affordable price with products like the Loveland Pass Card, 4-hour flex ticket, and 4-Pak deals.

Loveland Ski Area is typically one of the first ski areas in the nation to open and offers a season that runs from mid-October through early-May. The Race-To-Open starts in late September when snowmaking operations begin and culminate with Opening Day.

Loveland Ski Area offers skiers and riders 1,800 acres of varied terrain and two separate base areas: Loveland Valley and Loveland Basin.

Loveland Valley caters to beginners with gentle, un-crowded slopes perfect for those new to the sport. With their own chair lifts, surface lifts and wide open terrain, beginners don't have to worry about intimidating runs crossing their path or sharing trails with intermediate and advanced skiers and snowboarders. Loveland Valley is home to the Loveland Ski & Ride School that offers affordable lessons for beginners of all ages.

Loveland Basin offers terrain for every level of skier and snowboarder: steeps, trees, cruisers, open bowls and everything in-between. The Ridge, served by Chair 9 which takes skiers and snowboarders to 12,700', offers intermediate and expert level skiers and riders terrain just the way they like it – open, steep and deep! With 4800 acres to choose from right off the lift and an additional 100 acres of hike-to terrain for the true adventurer, the Ridge offers an experience like no other.

Free Snowcat Skiing

Enjoy free snowcat skiing along the Continental Divide and explore some of Loveland's most exhilarating terrain with a free ride on the Ridge Cat. Take in the amazing 360 degree views as you are whisked along the North side of The Ridge in the comfort of an 18 passenger snowcat. The Ridge Cat provides access to Field of Dreams, Velvet Hammer, Tickler, 13,010 and Marmot when conditions permit.

Powderhorn

Established: 1966	Acres: 1600	Vertical: 1650'	Annual Snowfall: 250"

Powderhorn Mountain Resort is tucked alongside the northern edge of Western Colorado's beautiful Grand Mesa. The mountain offers breathtaking views and over 1,600 acres of mountain terrain. The Flat Top Flyer high speed detachable quad lift offers year round activities such as lift-served downhill mountain biking in the summer, and downhill skiing, snowboarding, and a dedicated tubing hill in the winter.

Powderhorn averages over 250 inches of light, dry Colorado powder each winter and boasts some of the best tree-skiing in the Rocky Mountains. Summers feature miles of mountain bike trails and scenic lift rides with unparalleled views of the valley. Powderhorn is a hidden gem resort in the Colorado Rockies, known for friendly staff, minimal lift lines, and proximity to Grand Junction.

Powderhorn offers all levels of terrain, a full-service Ski & Ride and Bike Center, rental equipment, base area dining, shopping, and lodging. Powderhorn is a perfect destination for families, groups, couples, and friends seeking a unique and authentic adventure.

So welcome to Powderhorn: Where the pace is slower and the smiles are broader.

LODGING

There are plenty of options in the area if you need a fun & comfortable place to stay. On the mountain, they offer a hotel and condominiums for every size family. They also offer many lodging partners in Grand Junction, Palisade and Mesa, including some great wine country packages.

Powderhorn is only 40 miles east of Grand Junction (which has a regional airport) and 230 miles west of Denver.

Powderhorn
MOUNTAIN RESORT

TRAIL LEGEND

- ● EASIEST
- ■ MORE DIFFICULT
- ◆ MOST DIFFICULT
- ◆◆ EXPERTS ONLY
- ▮ FREESTYLE TERRAIN
- ▮ LIFT

- ✚ FIRST AID/SKI PATROL
- SKI SCHOOL
- CROSS COUNTRY
- SNOWSHOE AREA
- PICNIC AREA
- RENTALS

- RESTROOMS
- WHEELCHAIR ACCESSIBLE
- FOOD
- SUNDAY SERVICE

- DOUBLE CHAIR
- HIGH SPEED QUAD CHAIR
- SLOW SKIING AREA
- TERRAIN BASED LEARNING AREA
- LODGING
- TICKETS

HOURS OF OPERATION

Lift Ticket Window	8:30am - 3:00pm
Ski Area Lifts	9:00am - 4:00pm
West End Lift	9:00am - 3:30pm
Tubing Hill	9:00am - 4:30pm
Ski School Desk	8:30am - 2:00pm

Pre-registration is recommended for all lessons

Rental Shop	8:30am - 5:00pm
Children's Learning Center	8:30am - 3:30pm
Sunset Bar & Grille	8:00am - 6:00pm
Alpine Trader	8:30am - 4:30pm

Powderhorn Mountain Resort is located in the Grand Mesa, Uncompahgre and Gunnison National Forest and operates under a special use permit from the Forest Service USDA.

MOUNTAIN STATS

- Base Elevation: 8,200 ft.
- Summit Elevation: 9,850 ft.
- Vertical Drop: 1,650 ft.
- Skiable Acres: 1,200
- Average Snowfall: 250 inches
- Lifts: 5
  - 1 High Speed Quad, 2 Doubles,
  - 2 Surface

  ● 20% Beginner
  ■ 50% Intermediate
  ◆ 30% Advanced/Expert

RECCO Powderhorn Mountain Resort is equipped with the RECCO Rescue System.

ACCESS TO BACKCOUNTRY

ACCESS TO BACKCOUNTRY

Trail names
RED EYE, BEAR CLAW, WEST END, SWEET MISERY, DIXON, SECOND THOUGHTS, HOOKER, RED EYE, UPPER THUNDERBIRD GLADE, LOWER THUNDERBIRD GLADE, MAD DOG GLADE, HOOLIGAN, SNOWCLOUD, LOWER SNOWCLOUD, BRONCO, BOARDWALK, THUNDER MOUNTAIN GLADE, MUDSLIDE, COW CAMP, TENDERFOOT, SVEN'S BEND, WHISTLE PIG, DUDE, LOWER SNOWCLOUD, EASY RIDER, BOTTOM'S UP, E-Z, TUBING HILL, MAGIC CARPET, SUNSET GRILLE, LOOK OUT, LOWER PEACEPARK, FLAT TOP FLYER, BASE LODGE, SLOPESIDE INN, GOLDENWOODS CONDOS, VALLEY VIEW CONDOS, ADMINISTRATION, PARKING, MAVERICK, BILL'S RUN, LOWER EQUALIZER, UPPER PEACEPARK, PEACEMAKER, GREENHORN, STAGECOACH, EQUALIZER, YOO HOO, HAROLD'S WAY, QUICK DRAW, SHOWDOWN, WONDERBUMP, CANNONBALL, POWDERKEG, RACER'S GLADE, RACER'S EDGE

Wolf Creek

WOLF CREEK
THE MOST SNOW IN COLORADO®

Established: 1939	Acres: 1600	Vertical: 1604'	Annual Snowfall: 430"

Wolf Creek has always been known for its uniqueness in the ski industry since it's opening in 1939, sporting the reputation of "The Most Snow in Colorado". Wolf Creek is acclaimed for its deep-powder skiing, friendly atmosphere, delicious homemade food, affordable pricing and low-density skiing experience. Wolf Creek's average annual snowfall is 430 inches, allowing for early November openings and late Spring closings.

Wolf Creek Ski Area is located on US Highway 160. The unique location eliminates the frustration of traveling on a heavily congested corridor for guests to ski. Being located in Southern Colorado off the I-70 corridor also gives guests the perk of smaller crowds and feeling like you have the mountain all to yourself. Exploring all varieties of terrain is simple with a refined lift system inclusive of ten lifts, ranging from high-speed detachable quads and triple chairlifts to rolling conveyors. Wolf Creek has gradual sloping, wide green runs for beginners to excellent expert terrain. Tree skiing is endless and advanced skiers and boarders have chutes, glades, bowls, ridges and steeps to choose from that will give an out of bounds backcountry experience. Finding intermediate groomers to cruise down isn't hard to find with trails groomed nightly.

LESSONS

Skiers and snowboarders looking for lessons have an excellent selection through Wolf Creek's Ski School, which offers both private and group lessons for all ages and ability levels. Wolf Pups, the children's ski school, is renowned and very popular for little ones ages five through eight. Children have a designated Wolf Pup Building inclusive of a rental shop and magic carpet, solely for their use. Healthy and delicious lunches and snacks are prepared by the Wolf Pup's own chef. First Day Beginner Skiers now have their own learning and welcome area.

With Wolf Creek Ski Area being family owned and operated for over forty years, family friendly events are scheduled during the entire ski season. The low-density skiing experience at Wolf Creek Ski Area makes Wolf Creek a destination hot spot for powder hounds, families and new skiers alike.

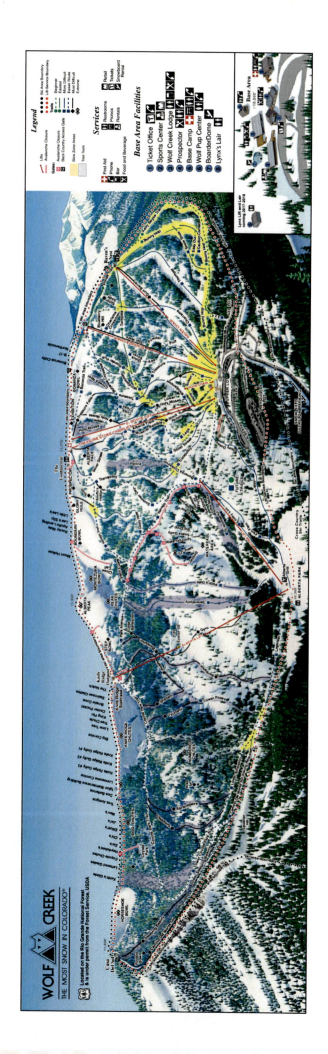

Crested Butte

Established: 1961	Acres: 1547	Vertical: 3062'	Annual Snowfall: 300"

Located off the beaten path of I-70, Crested Butte is known for more time on the slopes and less time in lift lines. The 1,547 acres of skiable terrain offers something for all ages and abilities. With over half of the mountain geared to intermediate and beginner skiers and a centrally located base area; it is a great place for families and groups with all ability levels.

For the more adventurous skiers and snowboarders, Crested Butte is a dream with some of the best lift-served extreme terrain in the nation. Home to first winter X games, the longest extreme skiing competition in the world, quirky costume events, and their friendly vibe, Crested Butte is a place you want to add to your skiing and snowboarding bucket list.

TERRAIN PARKS

Crested Butte offers five terrain parks spread around the resort. The Progression and Cascade Terrain Parks are part of a complete freestyle pod off the Painter Boy and Gold Link lifts. This translates to a literal playground for the park enthusiast, highlighted by the ability to progress from one park – and one feature size – to the next.

The Cascade Terrain Park also is ideal for larger park features, offering a consistent fall line for the jib park. Cascade is blessed with good afternoon light, allowing for better visibility, and its proximity to the mountain operations headquarters means that the snowcat operators have easier access and more time for perfectly shaping and manicuring features.

DINING

Crested Butte is a full service resort ski area, complete with 10+ dining options. Stop at Butte 66 and enjoy the best deck in the base area and special in-house barbeque, salads, milkshakes, burgers and more. Need a filling breakfast, try the all you can eat buffet or end your day playing pool and enjoying a new alpine menu at the WoodStone Grille, located in the Grand Lodge. On the slopes, pick up a Bavarian themed bite to eat and incredible views at the Umbrella Bar at Ten Peaks – Crested Butte's newest on-mountain dining option. Overall, this is just a small sample of the delicious and eclectic restaurant options.

LODGING

Crested Butte features a wide variety of slopeside and conveniently located condominiums. From ski-in, ski-out luxury to value oriented options, there is something for everyone!

Crested Butte is part of the Epic Pass.

Purgatory

| Established: 1965 | Acres: 1525 | Vertical: 2029' | Annual Snowfall: 260" |

Purgatory Resort is located in the rugged San Juan Mountains in southwestern Colorado, and 25 miles north of historic downtown Durango. Carved by glaciers thousands of years ago, Purgatory is a unique blend of steep tree skiing trails and wide-open cruisers with stunning views. Averaging 260 inches of snow annually, Purgatory is known for consistent, dry powder from frequent storms, followed by sunny, bluebird days, which creates perfect conditions for pure alpine nirvana. Renowned as a family-friendly resort and named "Best Ski Value" by TripAdvisor, there are many ways to enjoy the incredible winter wonderland at Purgatory, including dog sledding, scenic snowcat tours, snowshoeing, sleigh rides, snowmobile adventures, tubing, and Nordic skiing on 20 km of groomed trails.

Purgatory Lodge has all the amenities you'll want during a ski vacation, including great restaurants, shops, pool/spa, fitness center, private lounge, game room, and concierge. Purgatory Resort features a variety of cuisine with 9 restaurants and bars in the base Village area and on-mountain. Enjoy hearty breakfast dishes, lunch and dinner menus of gourmet burgers, fresh salads, grilled sandwiches, pizza, steaks, fish, and more.

SNOWCAT

Purgatory Snowcat Adventures offers a full day of powder-filled skiing or snowboarding in the San Juan backcountry. Guides help identify perfect lines and navigate the expansive backcountry terrain totaling 35,000 acres and is Colorado's largest cat skiing operation.

Purgatory Snowcat Adventures also offers scenic 30-minute tours with breathtaking views of the San Juan Mountains. Enjoy a unique evening on mountain via Snowcat Coach, complete with a 5-course gourmet dinner paired with wine or beer.

Arapahoe Basin

Established: 1946	Acres: 1331	Vertical: 2530'	Annual Snowfall: 350"

Founded in 1946, Arapahoe Basin maintains its status in Colorado as "The Legend," with 70 years of vibrant history. Known for its long seasons, laidback vibe and pristine variety of terrain. It's about the people. It's about the feeling you get when you arrive. It's about the skiing. *It is really about the skiing.*

At A-Basin, they pride themselves on having long seasons. As soon as summer is winding down, A-Basin begins preparations as one of the annual contenders in Colorado's "Race to Open." Snowmaking typically begins in late September; the ski area generally opens in mid-October and closes in early June. There have been seasons where A-Basin has remained open until the 4th of July, and back in 1995, the ski area remained open until August 10.

It's not only a long season, but a quality season at A-Basin. *SKI* magazine has recently (2016) ranked A-Basin in the top 10 for Best Challenge, Best Character, and Best Value – proving that skiing at an authentic Colorado mountain doesn't have to break the bank.

TERRAIN OF ALL LEVELS

Of course, they are known for their steeps but they have terrain for all levels. You can take an affordable lesson with their Snowsports school on A-Basin's two mellow learning areas, or take sweeping turns down intermediate groomers (something they are expanding).

KIDS FREE 2 SKI PROGRAM

A-Basin believes that all kids deserve to try skiing or snowboarding, and that parents shouldn't have to break the bank to take their child to the mountain. This program gives kids ages 6-12 two free days at the mountain with no blackout dates and no purchase necessary, just sign up before the deadline. (See website – signup is in December) And they get 50% off a half-day lesson.

A-Basin is part of the Epic Pass.

THE BEAVERS

Montezuma Bowl

THE STEEP GULLIES
NO CHAIRLIFT
30 MINUTE HIKE REQUIRED
Go ONLY

Monarch Mountain

MONARCH
MOUNTAIN

Established: 1939	Acres: 800	Vertical: 1162'	Annual Snowfall: 350"

Perched at the top of the continental divide on scenic HWY 50, independently owned Monarch Mountain is a hidden gem that has something for everyone. Monarch boasts 1,162 vertical ft. of diverse, skiable terrain that can accommodate skiers and snowboarders of all levels, from beginner to expert. If you're a powder hound in search of the softest, deepest powder in Colorado, look no further. Monarch receives more than 350 inches of natural snow every year. What Monarch boasts in annual snowfall, it lacks in crowds, so you can find ample powder stashes even days after a storm. With 670 lift-served skiable acres and an extra 130 acres of hike-to-ski access in Mirkwood Basin, Monarch has 800 skiable acres inbounds.

Monarch Mountain's free parking, affordable lift tickets, ease of access and helpful staff make it the perfect destination for those looking for a genuine Colorado mountain experience. Monarch is located two hours west of Colorado Springs and just 20 miles west of Salida; a small mountain town known for its creative arts community, charming downtown, and plethora of year-round outdoor recreational opportunities.

CAT SKIING

If backcountry is more your speed, the guided Snow Cat operation will wear out any expert skier with an additional 1,000 acres of steep, technical terrain.

LESSONS

Monarch is the perfect classroom. Whether it's your first time on skis or if you just want to polish your skills, the Monarch Ski and Ride School offers an array of robust programs that will help you reach your goals. A convenient single base area makes it easy to keep groups together while giving individuals the confidence and freedom to explore on their own.

MONARCH
MOUNTAIN

Hours of Operation

Lifts	9:00 a.m. – 4:00 p.m.
Lodge	8:00 a.m. – 5:30 p.m.
Rental Shop	8:00 a.m. – 4:30 p.m.

Terrain

Base Elevation	10,790 feet
Summit Elevation	11,952 feet
Vertical Drop	1,162 feet

GATE ACCESS TO
MIRKWOOD ◆◆

Total Skiable Acres	800 acres
Lift Access Acres	670 acres
Hiking Access Terrain	130 acres

CAT SKIING
TERRAIN

ELATION RIDGE

ORCS

MIRKWOOD BOWL

MIRKWOOD GLADES

STAIRCASE

EAST TREES

RETURN TO BASE AREA

LODGEVIEW

OUROBOROS

GENO'S MEADOW

NEVER SUMMER

UPPER HALL'S SWEET

LOWER HALL'S SWEET

B & G PASS

BREEZEWAY

PICANTE

SNOWBURN

DRIFT STRAITS

HIGH ANXIETY

SHAGNASTY

MR. B'S

OUTBACK

SHEER ROCKO

MIRAGE

PANORAMA

TILT

SNOWFLAKE

CATERPILLAR

TUMBELINA

OUTHOUSE

FREEWAY

CURVELINE

SHORT-N-SWEET

CHRISTMASTREE

QUICKDRAW

NO NAME

DOQ1

GARFIELD

EXAMINER

PIONEER

AJAX

K'MANCHE

CLEANZER

CURECANTI

SHORT CIRCUIT

TOPPER

GUNBARREL

GUNNISON

SALIDA

ROUTE 50

TRAM TO UPPER LOT

CONDO

SKI AREA
BOUNDARY

SKI AREA
BOUNDARY
NOT PATROLLED

SKI AREA
BOUNDARY
NOT PATROLLED

SKI AREA
BOUNDARY
NOT PATROLLED

PEAK LOCATOR

Legend

Ski Area Boundary	Easiest Way Down
Double Lift	Easiest
Quad Lift	More Difficult
Surface Lift	Most Difficult
	Extreme Terrain
Uphill Travel Route	Ski & Ride School Area
Egress Trail	Patrol Duty Station
Terrain Park	Patrol HQ
Slow Skiing Zone	Beacon Training Park
	Interpretive Information

MIRKWOOD ◆◆

Mirkwood Basin offers 130 acres of double-black diamond extreme skiing. Formerly only accessible by Monarch Cat Skiing, it boasts some of the best terrain in Colorado. To access Mirkwood, take the Breezeway lift, cross under the big wooden gate with the Mirkwood sign, then hike about 10 – 20 minutes to the summit. There is no grooming and conditions may be variable. Skiing with a partner is highly recommended. Mirkwood closes at 2:30.

Monarch Mountain is located in the San Isabel National Forest and operates under a Special Use Permit from the US Forest Service. Monarch Mountain is an Equal Opportunity Service Provider.

Eldora

eldora

Established: 1962   Acres: 680   Vertical: 1600'   Annual Snowfall: 300"

Eldora is skiing, snowboarding, cross-country and snowshoe friendly! Eldora opened for skiing in 1962. Eldora receives 300 inches of snow per year, but when the snow is lacking, Eldora uses Colorado's best snowmaking system to provide 100% coverage of groomed terrain, more than any other resort in Colorado!

There is terrain for everyone from the most difficult trail being Corona Bowl – a double black diamond, to steeps, glades, blue groomers, a terrain park, and even a beginner section dedicated to families. Eldora has 680 acres of skiable terrain. The longest run is 3 miles long!

Eldora has two day lodges at the base as well as a warming hut at the top of Corona Bowl (10,800 ft!) called "The Lookout." The Lookout serves up panoramic views from the Continental Divide to the Great Plains, as well as tasty soups and sandwiches.

Eldora is part of the Ikon Pass.

Eldora is only 21 miles from Boulder and 47 miles from Denver. It is easy to get to from Boulder because of the RTD Ski-n-Ride bus service. Eldora is the only resort with scheduled bus service.

NORDIC TRAILS

Eldora's Nordic Center is complemented by an extensive network of trails – starting just a few steps past the ski lifts and meandering through serene forests, across expansive alpine meadows and past dramatic mountain backdrops. The trails, 40 kilometers in all, are designated for classic cross-country skiing, skate skiing or snowshoeing. The Nordic Center has rentals, lessons and clinics.

TRAIL MAP LEGEND

● Easiest	▭ Race Training & Events	┊ Road	✚ First Aid
■ More Difficult	**WOODWARD** Terrain Parks	┊ Alpine Touring Trail-Uphill Only	⊪ Restaurant
◇ Difficult	▭ Slow Zone	━ Lift Line	USFS Access
◆◆ Most Difficult		╌╌ Area Boundary	

This institution is an equal opportunity provider and is operated under special use permit with the Roosevelt National Forest. Eldora employees are committed to sustaining the region's environmental, cultural, and economic health. We encourage visitors to support this effort through recycling, conserving electricity and water, and using the Boulder County Regional Transit District (RTD).

Our trail maps are made of 100% recyclable paper.

Sunlight Mountain Resort

sunlight Mountain Resort

Established: 1966	Acres: 680	Vertical: 2010'	Annual Snowfall: 250"

With nearly 700 skiable acres and a 2,000 vertical foot drop, Sunlight offers big skiing at an affordable price. About 75% of Sunlight's terrain is rated as beginner or intermediate, making it the perfect place for beginners. Here you don't just learn to ski or snowboard, you learn to shine. Sunlight offers some of the most affordable ski lessons in the nation.

But that is Sunlight's gentle side. Sunlight is also home to the steepest lift-served run in the state. Named "The Heathen," this is one of several double-black diamond runs tucked away under the pines and in the shadows of the East Ridge. The Heathen falls out from under your boots at a breathtaking 52°.

In other areas on the mountain, rich Aspen groves makes the tree skiing at Sunlight some of the best in the state. And if you like long, rolling cruisers, then you'll love the 2.5 mile Ute trail.

All 67 trails lead right back to the lodge where you can stow your brown bag lunch or pick up something hot at the grill. No hassles. No hype. It's exactly what you've been missing.

The historic 19-room Sunlight Lodge Bed & Breakfast offers vintage lodging right on the mountain. The lounge features après ski specials all season long, and snowmobile tours leave right from the property.

Sunlight is located just 12 miles south of Glenwood Springs, where you can après ski in the world's largest hot springs pool and still find a room for under $100 a night. And when you book Sunlight's Ski Swim Stay package, kids 12 and under ski free. You'll also find plenty of affordable restaurants, many within an easy walk of Glenwood's historic downtown.

SNOWMOBILE TOURS

Whether you're new to snowmobiling, a family with children, or someone looking for a full-throttle adventure, Sunlight Mountain has a snowmobile tour for you! Consistently ranked as one of the best snowmobile tours in the state, they offer a variety of tour options.

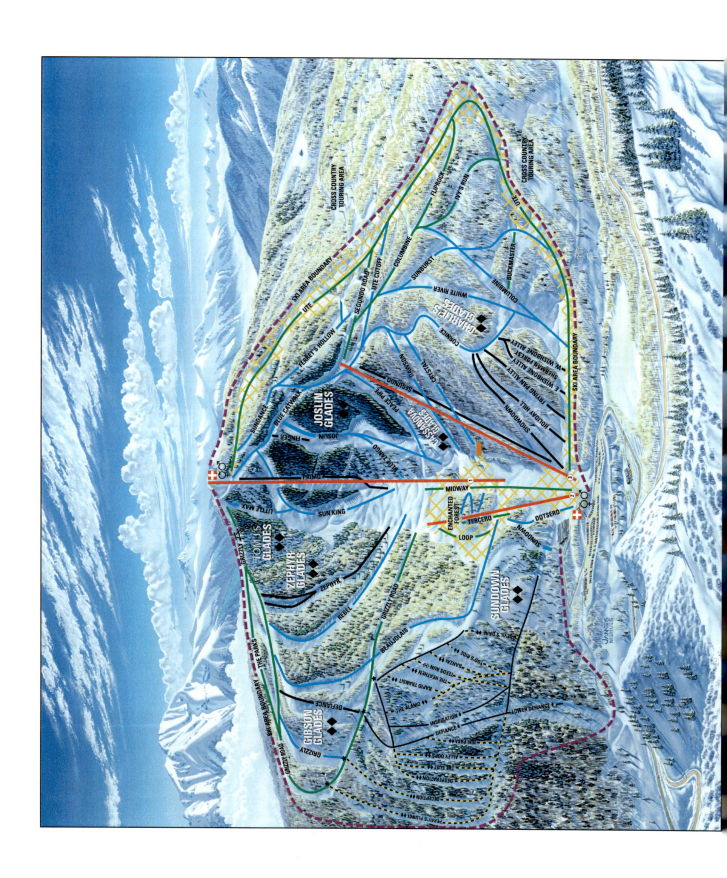

Granby Ranch

Established: 1983	Acres: 406	Vertical: 1000'	Annual Snowfall: 220"

Granby Ranch is the perfect place for families to ski and ride! They are located just 90 miles west of Denver and only 20 miles west of Winter Park. Granby Ranch is a family-owned ski resort, designed for skiers and riders of all ages and abilities. There's no need to hunt for parking, or battle for space to turn on the slopes. Granby Ranch offers easy lift access, gladed skiing, and a terrain park with progressive features. Add to that wide-open terrain that includes beginner, intermediate, and advanced runs.

And here's what Colorado locals know—Granby Ranch is a favorite for experienced skiers who want their kids to learn in a safe, friendly environment. There is close parking near the base, easy-access lifts, and ski terrain that was created specifically to be family friendly. All trails begin at one point and end at the base, so parents and children can ski at their own level without getting lost.

There is slope-side lodging at the base in the form of condos, townhomes, cabins, and luxury homes. After your Colorado cross-country skiing or snowshoeing trip, head back to Base Lodge and Granby Ranch Grill to warm your toes by the fire with après ski specials, late-night menu, s'mores by the fire pit, or an inspired dinner that includes steak, seafood, and pasta selections. The base lodge also has a cafeteria and the 8350 Bar & Grill.

If you want to extend your skiing into the evening, try renting the whole mountain for a fun group event. Check the website for more details.

CROSS COUNTRY SKIING

Granby Ranch brings you miles of cross-country skiing and snowshoeing trails. You'll find two Nordic trail networks located on the East Mountain (lift-access available during skiing hours) and at the golf course.

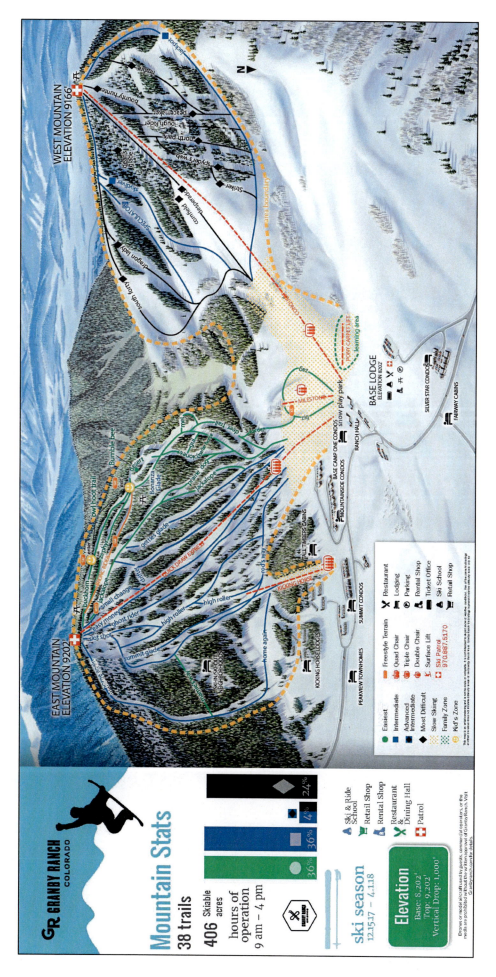

Cooper

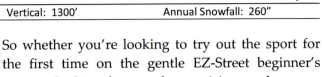

Established: 1945	Acres: 400	Vertical: 1300'	Annual Snowfall: 260"

Pure, authentic, down-to-earth skiing. That's what they are all about at Cooper. The mountain offers you 39 trails served by four lifts, spanning 400 lift-served acres. And if you're in the mood for an even bigger adventure, snowcat skiing tours on Chicago Ridge deliver you long, epic runs on 2,600 acres of wide-open powder bowls and glades.

What makes the skiing at Cooper better than anywhere else? The snow! Mother Nature graces them with an average of about 260" of natural fluffy stuff each season, and their high base elevation (10,500') means that the snow stays dry and light. And they can supplement Mother Nature's efforts as well, with a unique grooming philosophy. Unlike their neighbors, Cooper doesn't believe in over-grooming trails, which results in hardpack conditions. Instead, they rotate their grooming terrain, which means you always get the softest snow surface possible, while still providing you with plenty of groomed variety every day.

So whether you're looking to try out the sport for the first time on the gentle EZ-Street beginner's area, or looking for seamless cruising corduroy, or in the mood to bash some big bumps or weave through the glades, Cooper's got you covered.

SNOWCAT TOURS

Chicago Ridge Snowcat Tours is operated by Ski Cooper on 2,600 acres of open powder bowls, glades and timber in the San Isabel and White River National Forests. This is an area roughly the size of Vail's Back Bowls, with similar length, pitch and vertical. Guests soak in spectacular scenery as they climb along the Continental Divide with dozens of Colorado's highest peaks in view – a beauty scene unlike anywhere else. They'll take you as high as 12,600 feet. The slopes vary from 3,000 to 10,000 feet in length with vertical drops up to 2,000 feet per run.

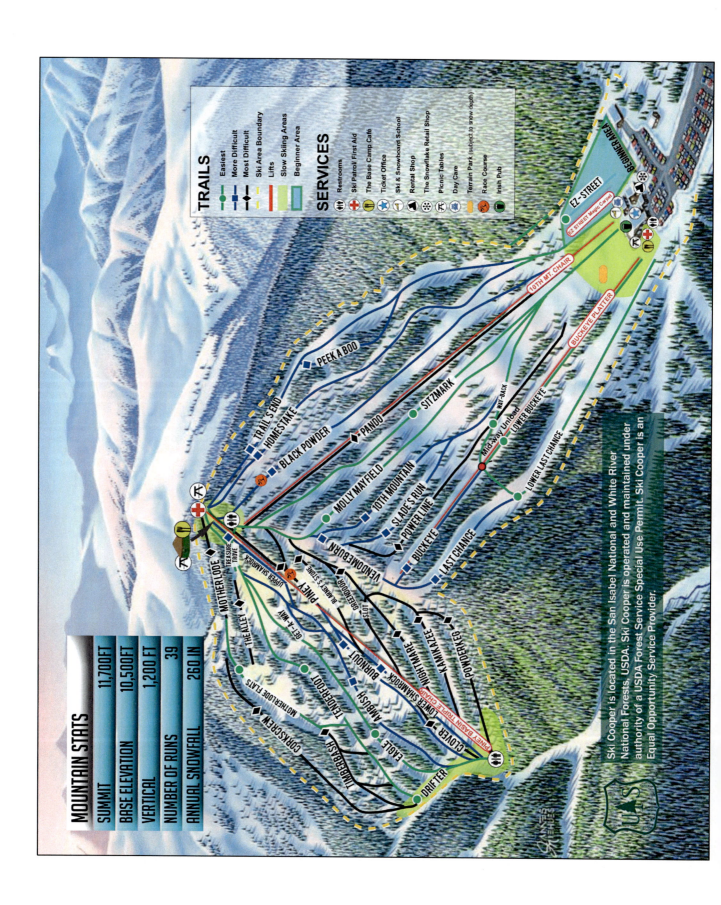

MOUNTAIN STATS

SUMMIT	11,700FT
BASE ELEVATION	10,500FT
VERTICAL	1,200 FT
NUMBER OF RUNS	39
ANNUAL SNOWFALL	260 IN

TRAILS

- Easiest
- More Difficult
- Most Difficult
- Ski Area Boundary
- Lifts
- Slow Skiing Areas
- Beginner Area

SERVICES

- Restrooms
- Ski Patrol/ First Aid
- The Base Camp Café
- Ticket Office
- Ski & Snowboard School
- Rental Shop
- The Snowflake Retail Shop
- Picnic Tables
- Day Care
- Terrain Park (subject to snow depth)
- Race Course
- Irish Pub

Ski Cooper is located in the San Isabel National and White River National Forests, USDA. Ski Cooper is operated and maintained under authority of a USDA Forest Service Special Use Permit. Ski Cooper is an Equal Opportunity Service Provider.

BEGINNER AREA

EZ-STREET

EZ STREET Magic Carpet

10TH MT. CHAIR

BUCKEYE PLATTER

WAY BACK

Mid-Way Unload

LOWER BUCKEYE

Lower Last Chance

PEEK A BOO

TRAIL'S END

HOMESTAKE

BLACK POWDER

PANDO

SITZMARK

MOLLY MAYFIELD

10TH MOUNTAIN

SLADE'S RUN

POWER LINE

BUCKEYE

LAST CHANCE

VENDOME BURN

UPPER SHAMROCK

PINEY

BLARNEY'S STONE

GREENHORN

SLOTS

NIGHTMARE

KAMIKAZEE

POWDERKEG

LOWER SHAMROCK

PINEY BASIN TRIPLE CHAIR

CLOVER

MOTHERLODE

TREASURE TROVE

THE ALLEY

GET-A-WAY

BURNOUT

AMBUSH

EAGLE

CLOVER

DRIFTER

MOTHERLODE FLATS

TENDERFOOT

CORKSCREW

TIMBERBASH

Hesperus

| Established: 1962 | Acres: 80 | Vertical: 700' | Annual Snowfall: 150" |

A double chairlift takes skiers and riders up to the 8,888' summit for over 700 feet of vertical fall-line skiing. A rope tow offers access to beginner terrain and the tubing hill. Best known for night skiing and riding, Hesperus also offers tubing by the hour, ski and snowboard rentals, ski and ride school, and a snack bar and day lodge.

New for 2018, Hesperus installed additional lights for night skiing, opened a new yurt for added indoor space, and expanded its rental shop. Hesperus is open for night skiing on weekdays (Monday through Friday), 4 pm to 9 pm. On weekends and holidays, the ski area is open from 9 am to 4 pm.

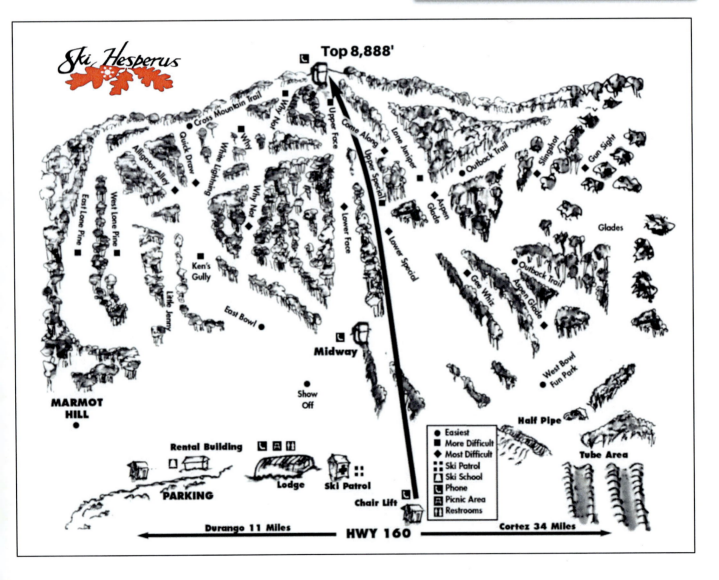

Echo Mountain

Established: 1960	Acres: 60	Vertical: 600'	Annual Snowfall: 275"

Echo Mountain was originally opened from 1960-1975 as Squaw Pass Ski Area and was a Denver family favorite as it was much closer to the front range than areas further into the mountains. After closing in 1975, it changed ownership a couple of times and laid dormant until 2005 when it was resurrected as Echo Mountain Park with a sole focus on terrain parks. A few years into the concept, a Ski School was opened and Echo began targeting a broader customer base. Echo Mountain was a private ski race training facility from 2012-2015. Then in 2016 it re-opened to the public with a renewed vision for the area to broaden it's appeal and offer a close, affordable option for snow sports and outdoors enthusiasts in Colorado's rapidly growing front range.

Now Echo Mountain has a new beginner area with a full-service ski school. But the mountain isn't just for beginners… the long blue groomers are great for speed (after all, the area was a race training facility). If you'd rather take on the challenge of glade skiing, Echo Mountain has that, too. And don't forget to check out the night skiing! The best part is that Echo Mountain is only a 50 minute drive from downtown Denver, with a beautiful Colorado mountain vista around every turn.

Howelson Hill

City of
Steamboat Springs

| Established: 1915 | Acres: 50 | Vertical: 440' | Annual Snowfall: 150" |

Howelsen Hill Ski Area is owned and operated by the City of Steamboat Springs and holds a unique place in the history of skiing. It has sent more skiers to international competition than any other area in North America.

Howelsen Hill boasts a remarkable heritage. It is Colorado's oldest continuously operated ski area, since 1915, and has the largest and most complete natural ski jumping complex in North America. Howelsen has been the training ground for more than 89 Olympians making over 150 Winter Olympic appearances.

Howelsen Hill has night skiing on Wednesdays and Thursday until 8pm.

Other activities at Howelsen include snowshoeing, cross country skiing (20km), and Fat Tire Biking.

.

Howelsen Hill Ski Area

Welcome to historic Howelsen Hill Ski Area
Colorado's oldest continuously operated ski area - since 1915

Easier		Freestyle Terrain		Terrain Park		Closed Area Do Not Enter		Parking		Ski Patrol/First Aid		Food Services
More Difficult		Lift		Closed Area		Caution/Danger		Ticket Office		Restrooms		Handicap Access
Most Difficult		Ski Area Boundary									

STATISTICS

Elevation:	6,696 base, 7,136 peak	
Trails:	16	
Lifts:	4	
(Includes: Double chair, Poma surface, Small Magic Carpet, & the Boardwalk)		
Cross-Country Trails:	21km	
Snowmaking:	50%	

CONTACT INFORMATION

Howelsen Hill Ski Area:	(970) 879-8499
Nordic Hotline:	(970) 871-7084
Parks, Open Space & Recreational Services:	(970) 879-4300
Tubing at Howelsen Hill:	(970) 819-8010
Steamboat Springs Winter Sports Club:	(970) 879-0695

MORE INFO
steamboatsprings.net
steamboatxcski.org
steamboatsprings.net
tubingsteamboat.com
SSWSC.org

TERRAIN PARK USER'S GUIDE

MAKE A PLAN Every time you use freestyle terrain, make a plan for each feature you want to use. Your speed, approach and take off will directly affect your maneuver and landing.
LOOK BEFORE YOU LEAP Scope around the jumps first, not over them. Know your landings are clear and clear yourself out of the landing area.
EASY STYLE IT Start small and work your way up. (Inverted aerials not recommended.)
RESPECT GETS RESPECT From the lift line through the park.

WARNING
Under Colorado law, a skier assumes the risk of any injury to person or property resulting from any of the inherent dangers and risks of skiing and may not recover from any ski area operator for any injury resulting from any of the inherent dangers and risks of skiing including: changing weather conditions; existing and changing snow conditions; bare spots; rocks; stumps; trees; collision with natural objects, man-made objects or other skiers; variations in the terrain; and the failure of skiers to ski within their own abilities.

YOUR RESPONSIBILITY CODE:
1. Always stay in control, and be able to stop or avoid other people or objects.
2. People ahead of you have the right of way. It is your responsibility to avoid them.
3. You must not stop where you obstruct a trail, or are not visible from above.
4. Whenever starting downhill or merging into a trail, look uphill and yield to others.
5. Always use devices to help prevent runaway equipment.
6. Observe all posted signs and warnings. Keep off closed trails and out of closed areas.
7. Prior to using any lift, you must have the knowledge and ability to load, ride and unload safely.

Idaho

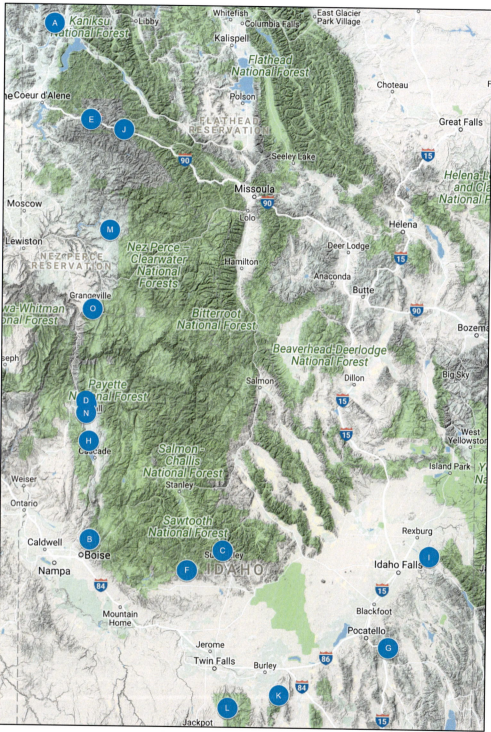

		Page
A.	Schweitzer Mountain	126
B.	Bogus Basin	128
C.	Sun Valley	130
D.	Brundage Mountain	132
E.	Silver Mountain	134
F.	Soldier Mountain	136
G.	Pebble Creek	138
H.	Tamarack	140

		Page
I.	Kelly Canyon	142
J.	Lookout Pass	144
K.	Pomerelle	146
L.	Magic Mountain	148
M.	Bald Mountain	149
N.	Little Ski Hill	150
O.	Snowhaven	151

Schweitzer Mountain

schweitzer
MOUNTAIN RESORT IDAHO

| Established: 1963 | Acres: 2900 | Vertical: 2400' | Annual Snowfall: 300" |

Schweitzer Mountain Resort is a year-round, family friendly destination located in the Idaho Panhandle, 85 miles from Spokane, WA and 66 miles south of the Canadian border into British Columbia. As the largest ski area in Washington and Idaho, the resort boasts 2900 acres of varied terrain for skiing and snowboarding as well as 32 kilometers of Nordic trails for cross-country, snowshoeing and snowbiking during the winter season. Other activities for non-skiers like an on-site spa, dining, and shopping are all located in the intimate village.

Stand at the top and stare at three mountain ranges, Canada and three states. Enjoy a variety of terrain from smooth corduroy groomers to wide open bowls and gladed runs. Then return to the top at hair-flying speed thanks in part to Stella. Stella, as you will soon discover, is Idaho's only six-person, high-speed lift.

FOR FAMILIES

Schweitzer is well designed for family ski vacations with a convenient village close by, and an activity center that sponsors movies, campfires, treasure hunts, crafts, to name just a few of the activities.

SKY HOUSE

Whether you're a skier, snowboarder, or just visiting the summit on foot – visit the new two-story lodge and enjoy fabulous 360 degree views from either their full-service bar & restaurant, The Nest, or from the Red Hawk café.

the front side — SCHWEITZER BOWL

Check out the new lodge at the summit opening this winter!
Featuring a restaurant, full bar, cafeteria, restrooms and
of course – amazing views!

Legend:
- ● EASIER SKIING
- ■ INTERMEDIATE
- ◆ MORE DIFFICULT
- ◆◆ MOST DIFFICULT (Use extreme caution. Check with patrol for current conditions.)
- TERRAIN PARK
- EASIER WAY DOWN
- ✚ SKI PATROL
- SKI AREA BOUNDARY
- NIGHT SKIING
- SLOW SKIING ZONES
- ⍩ RESTAURANTS (restrooms available)
- TREES/GLADED TERRAIN

Explore schweitzer — let life unfold – #schweitzerlife

SIZE 2,900 acres of fun
TERRAIN 10% beginner, 40% intermediate, 35% advanced, 15% expert
LONGEST RUN Little Blue Ridge Run
VERTICAL DROP 2,400 feet
TOP ELEVATION 6,400 feet
AVERAGE ANNUAL SNOWFALL 300"
TOTAL UPHILL CAPACITY 12,502 per hour

schweitzer MOUNTAIN RESORT IDAHO

the back side — OUTBACK BOWL

Lift Summary

NAME	TIME
BASIN EXPRESS	4 min.
LAKEVIEW TRIPLE	4.5 min.
GREAT ESCAPE	5 min.
STELLA	5.5 min.
MUSICAL CHAIRS	6 min.
SUNNYSIDE	8 min.
SNOW GHOST	13 min.
IDYLE OUR	4 min.
MUSICAL CARPET	4 min.

Daily Hours Of Operation
9am - 3:30pm

Bogus Basin

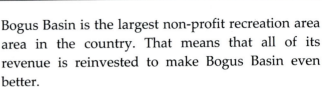

Established: 1942	Acres: 2600	Vertical: 1800'	Annual Snowfall: 250"

Explore miles of lift-serviced alpine skiing and snowboarding and a 36 km Nordic trail system. With 91 named runs, 3 high speed quads, 10 lifts, 2600 acres of terrain, and 360 degree mountain access, you can spend days, exploring all that Bogus Basin has to offer.

Bogus Basin has a rental shop, ski school with lessons for all levels/ages, and three day lodges that provide a variety of dining options. For lodging, try one of the mountain- top condos. The view is amazing and it is ski in/out.

All of this is easily accessible since Bogus Basin is only 18 miles from Boise.

Bogus Basin is the largest non-profit recreation area area in the country. That means that all of its revenue is reinvested to make Bogus Basin even better.

NIGHT SKIING

Bogus Basin is the perfect place to let off some steam and get out after work. The night culture at Bogus Basin is all about fun and adventure. Nights are a great time to see Bogus Basin in its full glory. Bogus Basin is positioned against a backdrop of the spilled jewels. The valley lights allow one to appreciate what a unique treasure Bogus Basin really is. (open until 10pm daily)

TUBING HILL

An 800 ft. downhill slide with the convenience of a conveyor lift back to the top so you can ride again and again. This is the perfect winter activity for groups looking for an exciting and accessible winter activity.

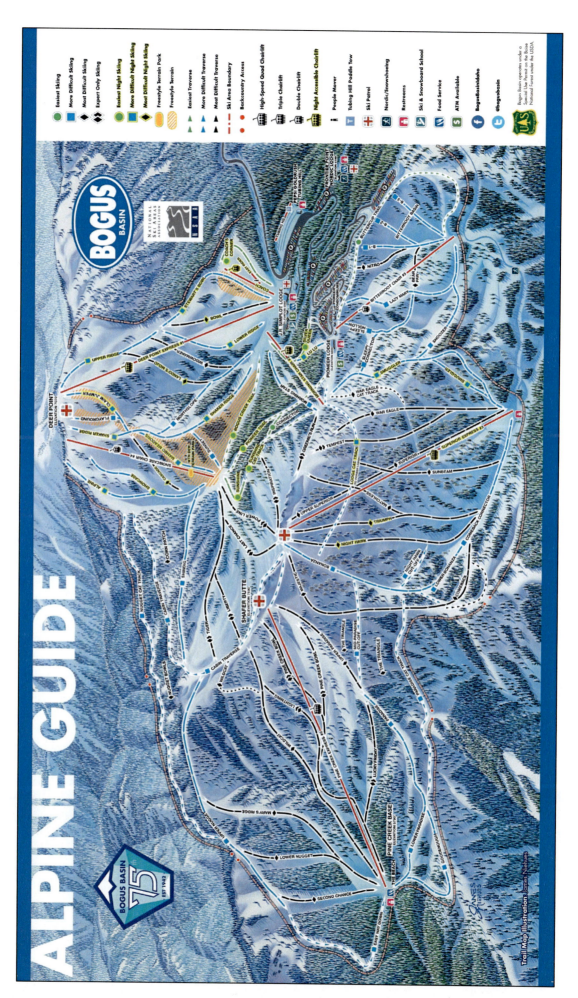

Sun Valley

Established: 1936	Acres: 2054	Vertical: 3400'	Annual Snowfall: 220"

Sun Valley is America's first destination ski resort, built in 1936 by the Union Pacific Railroad. With more than 3,400 vertical feet and over 2,000 acres of varied terrain, Sun Valley offers skiers and boarders something special on not just one mountain, but two. Bald Mountain's consistent pitch, lack of lift lines and variety of terrain have earned it a reputation as one of the world's finest ski mountains. Thirteen chairlifts and 65 varied runs await skiers and boarders on both sides of Baldy. There is over 55 acres of glade ski and boarding terrain.

Meanwhile, Dollar Mountain is the perfect place to get introduced to downhill sports and features two high-speed quads, terrain parks with features such as rails, bumps, jumps, and a family cross course.

Sun Valley has four day lodges. There are two bases at the foot of Baldy: River Run and Warm Springs.

Sitting high at 8,800 feet along Seattle Ridge is the Seattle Ridge Day Lodge. This lodge opens up onto jaw-dropping views of the surrounding Wood River Valley. Lastly is Carol's Day Lodge at Dollar Mountain, complete with European décor and a kid-friendly menu.

LODGING & DINING

The finest in lodging and dining may be found in the Sun Valley Village, just minutes away from the base areas of Bald and Dollar Mountains. The Sun Valley Lodge was completely renovated and reopened in June 2015, with a 20,000 sq. ft. Spa and fitness center, and all the modern amenities sophisticated travelers have come to expect.

OTHER SNOW ACTIVITIES

Sun Valley offers numerous snow activities including ice skating on one of the few outdoor ice rinks in the country (or on the indoor rink), cross-country skiing on 40+ km of groomed trails, and classic horse-drawn sleigh rides through the hills. If indoor sports are more your thing, the Sun Valley Lodge even has its own bowling alley.

Brundage Mountain

| Established: 1961 | Acres: 1920 | Vertical: 1921' | Annual Snowfall: 320" |

A visit to Brundage Mountain Resort is a getaway full of pleasant surprises. Generously wide groomed runs and a lack of crowds add to the relaxed feeling you'll find exploring this 1,900 acre gem. Plentiful Rocky Mountain powder makes it a delight to sample the ski area's many powder fields and untracked glades. Five well-placed chairlifts handily spread out the skiers and riders, so visitors are more likely to find solace on an open trail than they are to find themselves standing in a lift line. A high-speed quad makes for a quick ride to the summit, where you'll enjoy a 360 degree view that includes silhouettes of Idaho's Seven Devils Wilderness, Oregon's Eagle Cap Wilderness, and sweeping vistas of the Payette Lakes. The views highlight the fact that, in spite of the predictable heavy snowfall, Brundage Mountain enjoys a great many days of clear skies and bright sunshine.

SNOWCAT PROGRAM

Unique among mid-sized resorts is Brundage Mountain's jumbo-sized backcountry SnowCat program. Brundage Snowcat Adventures operates on an expansive 18,000 acres of Payette National Forest backcountry. Terrain includes four different peaks featuring open bowls, steep chutes and powder-packed glades. Brundage Mountain also offers guided backcountry snowmobile tours for those looking to explore the beautiful surroundings or reach idyllic destinations like Burgdorf Hot Springs.

An overnight stay in nearby McCall, just 8 miles from the Brundage base area, provides an experience of its own. This charming mountain town hugs the shores of Payette Lake and offers a wide array of dining and lodging choices.

Dubbed "The Last Great Place" in 2017 by Skiing Magazine, Brundage Mountain combines a top-notch skiing experience with a low-key vibe that's getting harder to find in today's world of corporate consolidation.

Brundage Mountain remains family-owned by the descendants of one of the resort's original founders. This little-known resort offers all the modern amenities, including delicious locally-sourced food, but retains the charm of a ski area operated by, and devoted to, people who simply love to ski.

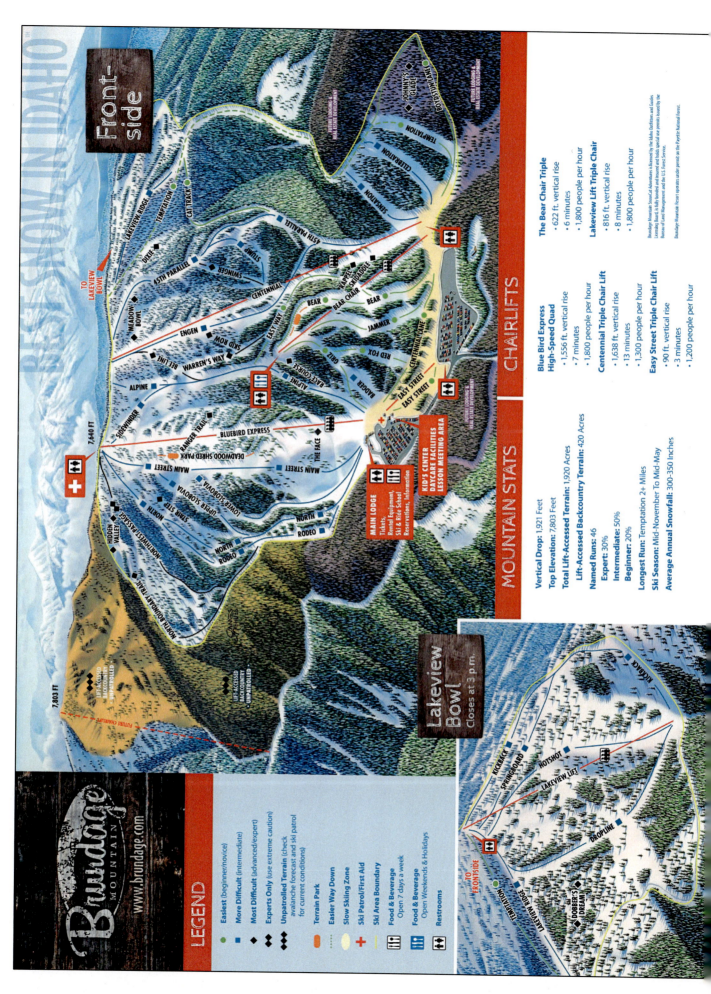

Brundage Mountain

www.brundage.com

LEGEND

- Easiest (beginner/novice)
- More Difficult (intermediate)
- Most Difficult (advanced/expert)
- Experts Only (use extreme caution)
- Unpatrolled Terrain (check avalanche forecast and ski patrol for current conditions)
- Terrain Park
- Easier Way Down
- Slow Skiing Zone
- Ski Patrol/First Aid
- Ski Area Boundary
- Food & Beverage Open 7 days a week
- Food & Beverage Open Weekends & Holidays
- Restrooms

BEST SNOW IN IDAHO
Front-side
7,803 FT
7,640 FT
LIFT-ACCESSED BACKCOUNTRY UNPATROLLED
FUTURE CHAIRLIFT
TO LAKEVIEW BOWL
HIDDEN VALLEY
NORTH BOUNDARY TRAIL
NORTHWEST PASSAGE
NORTH
STAIR STEP
UPPER SLOBOVIA
LOWER SLOBOVIA
NORTH
RODEO
MAIN STREET
DEADWOOD SHRED PARK
RANGER TRAIL
BLUEBIRD EXPRESS
SIDEWINDER
ALPINE
BEE LINE
WARREN'S WAY
SKID ROW
ENGEN
MEADOW BOWL
45TH PARALLEL
DIXIE
LAKEVIEW RIDGE
TEMPTATION
CAT TRACK
SWINGER
STUMP
CENTENNIAL
EASY WAY
THE FACE
ALPINE
RACE COURSE
GRIZ
BADGER
RED FOX
JAMMER
BEAR
BEAR CHAIR
RAPPEL
SKIDADDLE
SENSATION
CELEBRATION
TEMPTATION
JOHNNY'S GLADE
BOYDSTUN LANE
CENTENNIAL LANE
EASY STREET
MAIN LODGE
Tickets, Rental Equipment, Ski & Ride School Reservations, Information
KID'S CENTER
DAYCARE FACILITIES
LESSON MEETING AREA
FUTURE LODGING & REAL ESTATE DEVELOPMENT

Lakeview Bowl
Closes at 3 p.m.
TO FRONTSIDE
TEMPTATION
LAKEVIEW RIDGE
DOBBER'S DREAM
DROPLINE
LAKEVIEW LIFT
HOTSHOT
SPRINGBOARD
KICKBACK
KICKBACK

MOUNTAIN STATS

Vertical Drop: 1,921 Feet
Top Elevation: 7,803 Feet
Total Lift-Accessed Terrain: 1,920 Acres
Lift-Accessed Backcountry Terrain: 420 Acres
Named Runs: 46
Expert: 30%
Intermediate: 50%
Beginner: 20%
Longest Run: Temptation 2+ Miles
Ski Season: Mid-November To Mid-May
Average Annual Snowfall: 300-350 Inches

CHAIRLIFTS

Blue Bird Express High-Speed Quad
- 1,556 ft. vertical rise
- 7 minutes
- 1,800 people per hour

Centennial Triple Chair Lift
- 1,638 ft. vertical rise
- 13 minutes
- 1,300 people per hour

Easy Street Triple Chair Lift
- 90 ft. vertical rise
- 3 minutes
- 1,200 people per hour

The Bear Chair Triple
- 622 ft. vertical rise
- 6 minutes
- 1,800 people per hour

Lakeview Lift Triple Chair
- 816 ft. vertical rise
- 8 minutes
- 1,800 people per hour

Brundage Mountain SnowCat Adventures is licensed by the Idaho Outfitters and Guides Licensing Board, is fully bonded and insured and holds special use permits issued by the Bureau of Land Management and the U.S. Forest Service.

Brundage Mountain Resort operates under permit on the Payette National Forest.

Silver Mountain

| Established: 1968 | Acres: 1600 | Vertical: 2200' | Annual Snowfall: 340" |

Silver Mountain has 77 trails spread across two mountains – Kellogg Peak and Wardner Peak. With over 1600 acres, there is plenty of mountain for everyone resulting in short lift lines, and very diverse terrain. There are extensive gladed areas and hidden gems that make it possible to find fresh powder stashes days after the last storm, and the longest surface lift in the area makes for an extremely friendly beginner experience. With 340" of snow annually, this is Idaho skiing at its finest.

There's plenty to see and do at Silver Mountain Resort in the summer. Silver's gondola is the longest in North America and offers views of the surrounding mountains, and easy access to the hiking on Kellogg Peak and the fire lookout. With over 30 single track trails, Silver's Mountain Bike Park has been voted the best bike park in the Northwest for three years running.

INDOOR WATER PARK

The amazing thing about Silver Mountain is that it's home to the largest indoor water park in Idaho, and there is something for everyone in the family to do. It has a FlowRider wave for surfing and boogie boarding; lazy river, spray park, rope bridges, and water slides. The waterpark is kept at a consistent 84 degrees, so it can be enjoyed any time of the year.

TUBING

There's no hiking back to the top thanks to a 700' moving carpet that effortlessly whisks you and your snow tube back to the top for another run. Four lanes of snow tubing fun you won't want to miss! Silver's snow tube park is open most weekends and holidays throughout the season.

Silver Mountain Resort prohibits the operation or use of unmanned aerial systems, or drones, without prior written authorization from the Resort.

YOUR RESPONSIBILITY CODE
1. Always stay in control.
2. People ahead of you have the right of way.
3. Stop in a safe place for you and others.
4. Whenever starting downhill or merging, look uphill and yield.
5. Use devices to help prevent runaway equipment.
6. Observe signs and warnings, and keep off closed trails.
7. Know how to use the lifts safely.

LEGEND
- Easiest
- More Difficult
- Most Difficult
- Expert
- Terrain Park
- First Aid
- Moving Carpet
- Food & Beverage
- Slow Skiing Area
- Area Boundary
- New Ski Run

Kellogg Peak 6,300 ft.

Wardner Peak 6,200 ft.

GONDOLA

Soldier Mountain

| Established: 1947 | Acres: 1180 | Vertical: 1425' | Annual Snowfall: 100" |

A family-friendly mountain seated on the southern fringe of the Sawtooth National Forest, Soldier Mountain offers back country Snow Cat skiing/boarding, overnight yurt stays and a great time on the slopes!

There is something for everyone at Soldier, and even after a fresh snowfall, you often get runs all to yourself!

CAT SKIING

Soldier Mountain is home to the only cat skiing operation in South-Central Idaho. While Soldier Mountain is a small, family-friendly ski area, it also boasts some of the best back country skiing in the state. Cat skiing at Soldier is just a little bit different than the typical back country experience. Soldier Mountain wants to give you a memorable day in the snow where you get to choose the lines you ski or board, as opposed to staying in tight formation following your guide.

Soldier is a very unique mountain, with 3,000' of vertical that tops out at almost 10,000'. With 2,000 acres of skiable backcountry terrain, Soldier Mountain has it all: big open lines, rolling glades, steep trees and extreme chutes.

LESSONS

Whether you're a beginner or a double black diamond skier, there is always something new to learn. Through innovative age appropriate teaching techniques, Soldier Mountain instructors help build the skills and the confidence you or your child needs to have fun while exploring more challenging terrain. The PSIA certified school has an amazing group of instructors to get you skiing and riding in no time. There is a consistent education program which builds on skills you learn each lesson so you can pick up where you left off each time you come to the mountain.

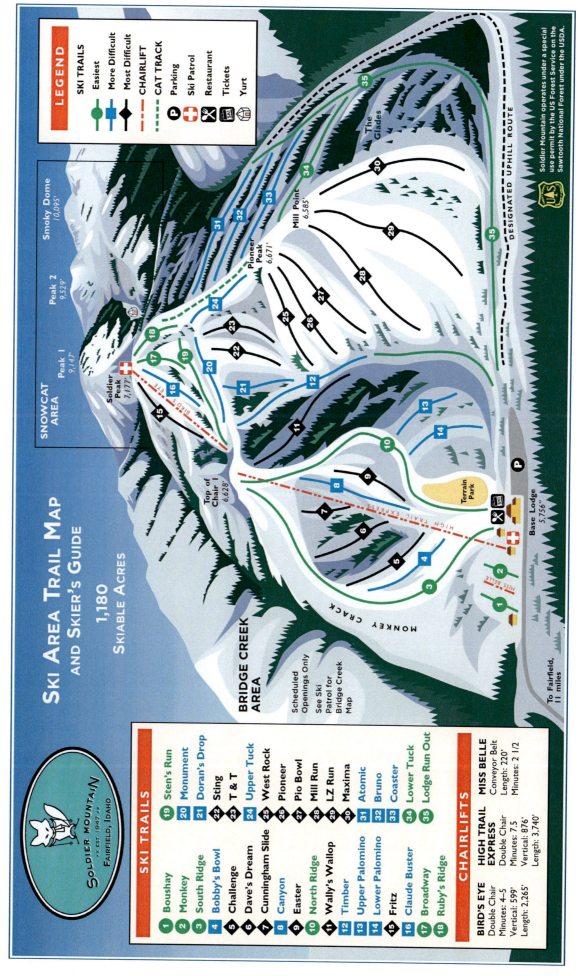

SKI AREA TRAIL MAP
AND SKIER'S GUIDE

1,180 SKIABLE ACRES

SOLDIER MOUNTAIN
EST. 1947
FAIRFIELD, IDAHO

LEGEND

SKI TRAILS
- Easiest
- More Difficult
- Most Difficult
- CHAIRLIFT
- CAT TRACK
- Parking
- Ski Patrol
- Restaurant
- Tickets
- Yurt

Soldier Mountain operates under a special use permit by the US Forest Service on the Sawtooth National Forest under the USDA.

Map labels
- Smoky Dome 10,095'
- Peak 2 9,529'
- Peak 1 9,147'
- The Glades
- Mill Point 6,585'
- Pioneer Peak 6,671'
- Soldier Peak 7,177'
- SNOWCAT AREA
- Top of Chair 1 6,628'
- BRIDGE CREEK AREA
- Scheduled Openings Only
- See Ski Patrol for Bridge Creek Map
- MONKEY CRACK
- Terrain Park
- Base Lodge 5,756'
- HIGH TRAIL EXPRESS
- MISS BELLE
- BIRD'S EYE
- DESIGNATED UPHILL ROUTE
- To Fairfield, 11 miles

SKI TRAILS

1 Boushay	19 Sten's Run
2 Monkey	20 Monument
3 South Ridge	21 Doran's Drop
4 Bobby's Bowl	22 Sting
5 Challenge	23 T & T
6 Dave's Dream	24 Upper Tuck
7 Cunningham Slide	25 West Rock
8 Canyon	26 Pioneer
9 Easter	27 Pio Bowl
10 North Ridge	28 Mill Run
11 Wally's Wallop	29 LZ Run
12 Timber	30 Maxima
13 Upper Palomino	31 Atomic
14 Lower Palomino	32 Bruno
15 Fritz	33 Coaster
16 Claude Buster	34 Lower Tuck
17 Broadway	35 Lodge Run Out
18 Ruby's Ridge	

CHAIRLIFTS

BIRD'S EYE
Double Chair
Minutes: 4–5
Vertical: 599'
Length: 2,265'

HIGH TRAIL EXPRESS
Double Chair
Minutes: 7.5
Vertical: 876'
Length: 3,740'

MISS BELLE
Conveyor Belt
Length: 220'
Minutes: 2 1/2

Pebble Creek

Established: 1949	Acres: 1100	Vertical: 2200'	Annual Snowfall: 250"

A family favorite for decades, Pebble Creek is a small, yet challenging ski area located near Pocatello in southeastern Idaho. An excellent beginner area at the base and steep challenges above can satisfy the beginner or thrill-seeking needs of the whole family. Two terrain parks provide something for every level of freestyler. All of this is accessed with just three lifts, that cover over a 1,100 acres (650 lift-served) on 54 trails with an amazing vertical drop of 2,200 feet. It's a big small mountain.

Pebble Creek is a local hill will local charm. The base lodge has a ski school, ski rentals, a cafeteria, and a bar for enjoying après drinks.

Many local skiers call Pebble Creek the hidden gem of Idaho ski areas. If you want to avoid crowds and enjoy great tree skiing and hiking, visit Pebble Creek.

NIGHT SKIING

A great way to extend your day, night skiing on Friday and Saturdays begins at 4 pm and finishes at 9:30 pm. Enjoy a whole different type of skiing under the stars for only $20/ticket.

HOT SPRINGS

After a day on the slopes, a great place to soak and for lodging is Lava Hot Springs. Ideally located just 25 minutes south of Pebble Creek, you can enjoy 102 to 112 degree odor free geothermal hot pools.

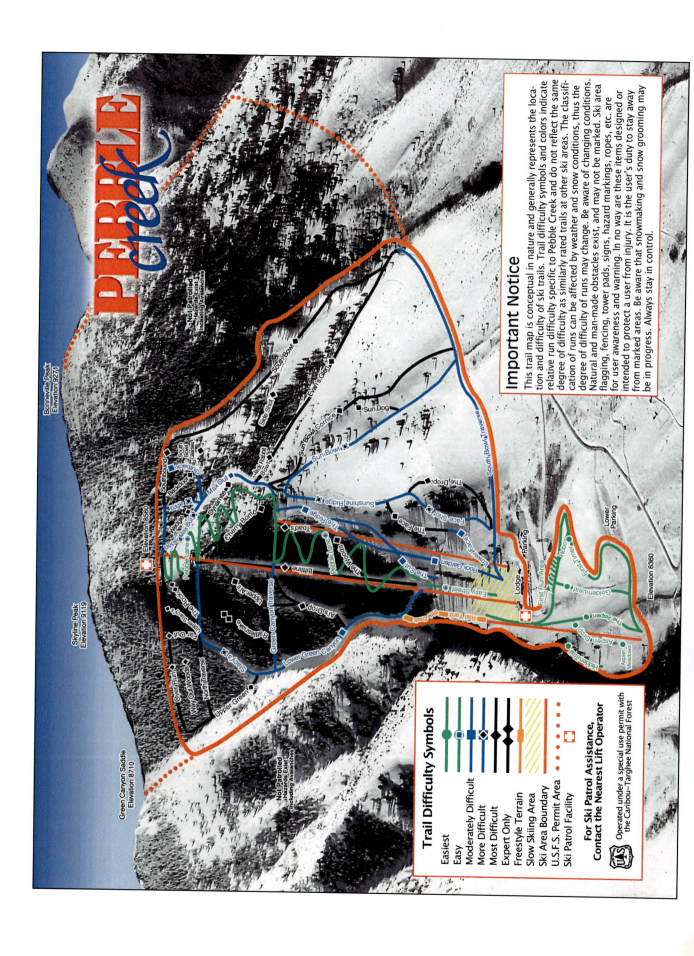

PEBBLE creek

Bonneville Peak
Elevation 9271

Skyline Peak
Elevation 9119

Green Canyon Saddle
Elevation 8710

Not Patrolled
Hazards Exist
Including Avalanches

Not Patrolled
Hazards Exist
Including Avalanches

Elevation 8560

Elevation 6360

South Bowl

Evan's Cleft

Sale Shot

Sun Dog

Sun Bowl Cornice

Sun Bowl

Sun Bowl Traverse

The Drop

South Bowl Traverse

Sunshine Ridge

The Face

Race Shot

Lower Face

Rock Garden

The Gut

Easy Street

Side Track

Rail Yard

Lodge

Lower Parking

Parking

First Run Area

First Tunnel

Robo

Golden Leaf

The Aspen

Aspen Drop

Hickerbill Trail

Aspen Meadows

South Bowl

Backdoor

Overdrive

Southbowl

Edge

Max Out

Dynamite

Cherry Bomb

Upper Max Out

Pebble Pane

Wedge

The Ridge

Pebble Lane

The Woods

Toad's

Liftline

Upper Arks

A's Drop

Green Canyon Traverse

Rattlesnake

Lower Green Canyon

The Rocks

Upper Stairs

Short's

Far Out

Over Run

Way Out Woods

Upper Green

North Traverse

Trail Difficulty Symbols

● Easiest
⊙ Easy
■ Moderately Difficult
◆ More Difficult
◆ Most Difficult
◆ Expert Only
▬ Freestyle Terrain
▨ Slow Skiing Area
▬ Ski Area Boundary
⋯ U.S.F.S. Permit Area
□ Ski Patrol Facility

For Ski Patrol Assistance,
Contact the Nearest Lift Operator

Operated under a special use permit with
the Caribou-Targhee National Forest

Important Notice

This trail map is conceptual in nature and generally represents the location and difficulty of ski trails. Trail difficulty symbols and colors indicate relative run difficulty specific to Pebble Creek and do not reflect the same degree of difficulty as similarly rated trails at other ski areas. The classification of runs can be affected by weather and snow conditions, thus the degree of difficulty of runs may change. Be aware of changing conditions. Natural and man-made obstacles exist, and may not be marked. Ski area flagging, fencing, tower pads, signs, hazard markings, ropes, etc. are for user awareness and warning. In no way are these items designed or intended to protect a user from injury. It is the user's duty to stay away from marked areas. Be aware that snowmaking and snow grooming may be in progress. Always stay in control.

Tamarack

Established: 2004	Acres: 1000	Vertical: 2800'	Annual Snowfall: 300"

In the heart of Idaho's magnificent west central mountains and overlooking Lake Cascade, Tamarack Resort is the first newly permitted four-season resort in North America in more than two decades. The resort features an extraordinary blend of mountain, meadow and lakeside amenities. The perfect springboard to adventure.

With six lifts that provide access to 1000 acres of terrain from 42 different runs, there is something for everyone – glades, steeps, cornices, and cruisers. And since it's East-facing, there is minimum wind and maximum snow retention.

Tamarack also offers other winter activities including snow mobile rentals, snow shoeing trails, and Nordic trails.

EXPRESS CARD

The Express Card is perfect for those who plan to ski up to 4 days this winter, and don't want the commitment of a season pass. The Express Card comes preloaded with a lift ticket for your first day. Then, you can return to the resort up to 3 more times and save $10 per visit. You can proceed directly to the chairlift. When your Express Card is scanned, your credit card will be charged. There is no need to return to the ticket window thanks to this wireless technology.

ON-MOUNTAIN DINING & LODGING

Having only been open since 2005, Tamarack has grown to offer all the usual amenities of a large resort including on-mountain dining and mountain-side lodging. There is even on-site daycare for guests of the Tamarack Resort.

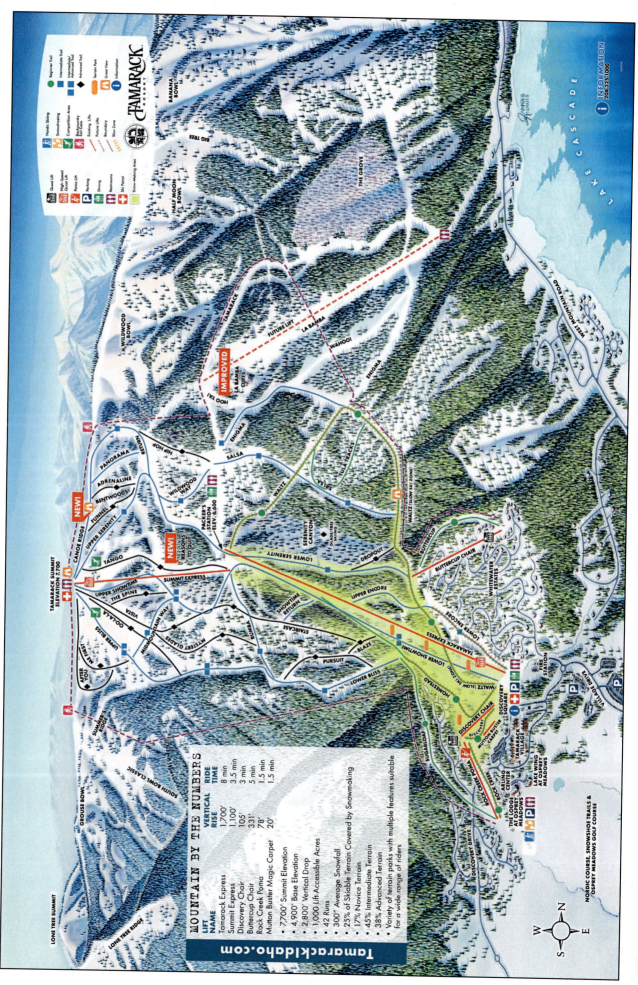

MOUNTAIN BY THE NUMBERS

LIFT NAME	VERTICAL RISE	RIDE TIME
Tamarack Express	1,700'	8 min
Summit Express	1,100'	3.5 min
Discovery Chair	105'	3 min
Buttercup Chair	33'	5 min
Rock Creek Poma	78'	1.5 min
Mutton Buster Magic Carpet	20'	1.5 min

- 7,700' Summit Elevation
- 4,900' Base Elevation
- 2,800' Vertical Drop
- 42 Runs
- 1,000 Lift-Accessible Acres
- 300" Average Snowfall
- 25% of Skiable Terrain Covered by Snowmaking
- 17% Novice Terrain
- 45% Intermediate Terrain
- 38% Advanced Terrain
- Variety of terrain parks with multiple features suitable for a wide range of riders

TamarackIdaho.com

NORDIC COURSE, SNOWSHOE TRAILS & OSPREY MEADOWS GOLF COURSE

Kelly Canyon

Kelly Canyon Ski Resort is a 30 minute drive northeast of Idaho Falls. Founded in 1957, the resort has been described by accomplished skiers as the perfect place to learn to ski and board with terrain suited for all levels of skiers and snowboarders.

Kelly Canyon Ski Resort has a family friendly atmosphere for winter enthusiasts of all ages offering lift tickets, yummy food, lessons, and rental gear at affordable prices.

LONGEST TERRAIN PARK IN THE REGION is located at Kelly Canyon where riders can choose between the Feature Park, the Rail Park, and the Jump Park. Unique features include the Teeter -Totter, the Blue Hole, and the Wrecking Ball. The Jump Park includes a quarter pipe, multiple jumps and rollers, and two 25' earth kickers known as Whammy and Double Whammy for those looking for big air. Each Park has great spectator visibility for riders to showcase their moves.

NIGHT SKIING is a hallmark at Kelly Canyon Ski Resort. The majority of the ski runs at Kelly Canyon (not just the beginner hill) are lit for skiing and boarding until 9:30 p.m. Night skiing is a unique and wonderful experience offering a pleasing complement to skiing and boarding during the day. Night skiing and boarding at Kelly Canyon are available Monday through Saturday.

FAT BIKING on designated slopes at Kelly Canyon Ski Resort is great fun accessed by starting at the lodge or using the lift to haul your bike to the top of the mountain. The Resort welcomes fat biking, snowshoeing, and nordic cross country enthusiasts to its expanding trail system known as the SHRED TRAILS! The Shred Trails are many miles of groomed uphill-downhill terrain accessing beautiful forest seclusion and spectacular vistas.

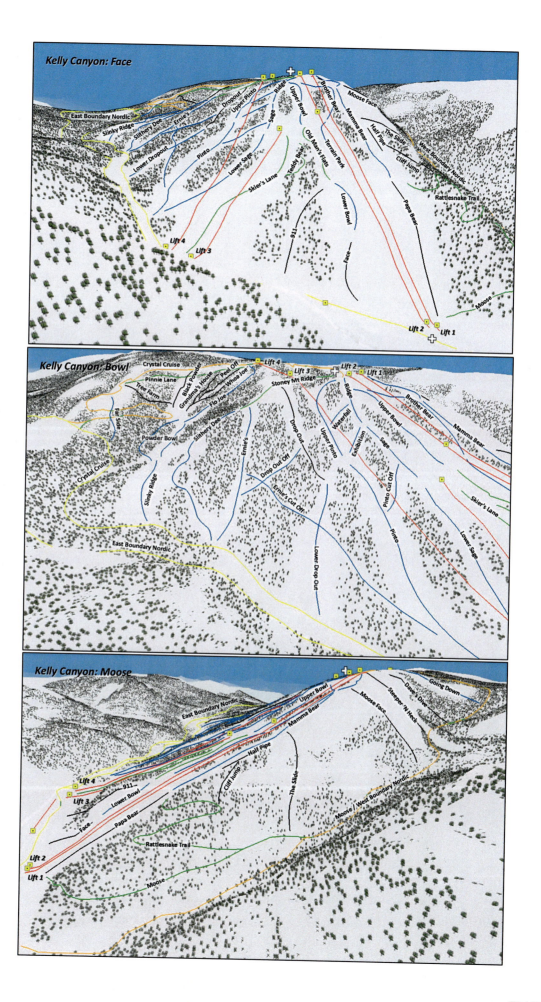

Kelly Canyon: Face

East Boundary Nordic
Slinky Ridge
Slither Dee
Ernie's
Dropout
Upper Pinto
Sage
Ridge
Upper Bowl
Brother Bear
Mamma Bear
Moose Face
The Slide
Half Pipe
Cliff Jump
West Boundary Nordic
Lower Dropout
Pinto
Lower Sage
Old Man's Flats
Terrain Park
Teddy Bear
Skier's Lane
Lower Bowl
Rattlesnake Trail
911
Papa Bear
Face
Lift 4
Lift 3
Moose
Lift 2
Lift 1

Kelly Canyon: Bowl

Crystal Cruise
Pinnie Lane
Tree Farm
Black Powder
Grandma's House
Peel Off
Whoa Joe
Lift 4
Stoney Mt Ridge
Lift 3
Lift 2
Lift 1
Far Side
Flo Joe
Ridge
Waterfall
Upper Bowl
Brother Bear
Slithery Dee
Ernie's
Drop Out
Upper Pinto
Exhibition
Sage
Mamma Bear
Powder Bowl
Crystal Cruise
Slinky Ridge
Drop Out Off
Ernie's Cut Off
Pinto Cut Off
Skier's Lane
East Boundary Nordic
Lower Drop Out
Pinto
Lower Sage

Kelly Canyon: Moose

East Boundary Nordic
Upper Bowl
Moose Face
Stepper 'N Heck
Dave's Dive
Going Down
Mamma Bear
Half Pipe
Lift 4
911
Cliff Jump
The Slide
Lift 3
Lower Bowl
Moose / West Boundary Nordic
Lift 2
Papa Bear
Face
Lift 1
Rattlesnake Trail
Moose

Lookout Pass

| Established: 1936 | Acres: 540 | Vertical: 1150' | Annual Snowfall: 400" |

Lookout's passion is to turn a good day of skiing and riding into a great day! They never set out to be the biggest. They strive to be the best in all they do and provide a ski and ride experience as it was meant to be - pure, exhilarating, .exceptional, and at an affordable price!

Turns out, the Lookout Pass family of friends wanted the same things too. A genuine, family friendly atmosphere with world class grooming and untouched powder on those magical powder days.

The number that sets them above the rest is 400" of annual snowfall, the lightest and driest in the region! They're the only Inland Northwest Ski Area that's actually in the Northern Rocky Mountains, at the crest of the Bitterroot Range.

And because many of their slopes face north and northeast, all that great snow stays light and fun.

FAMILIES LOVE LOOKOUT
Lookout Pass was voted the most family-friendly mountain resort in the Pacific Northwest by visitors to OnTheSnow.com for good reason...

The adult weekend lift ticket is almost half of what you pay at some other places. Juniors, teens and college students save even more, and kids six and under ski free. The variety of terrain means there's something for all ability levels yet the mountain layout is family friendly making it easy to keep track of your entire clan and see how much fun they are having. Lookout Pass is also wind protected and usually fog free making for an abundance of enjoyable days on the mountain.

HISTORIC LODGE
Lookout's original historic base lodge is the second-oldest ski lodge in the northwest. The cedar interior exudes the delightful warmth reminiscent of vintage lodges of the 1940's. The recent lodge expansions; including the 2011 main floor mountain seating and deck addition, preserve Lookout's rustic ambience and provide their guests with nice amenities like the International Food Court, Loft Pub & Grub, and a retail gift shop.

TERRAIN PARKS
Their terrain parks are geared for you! With 3 different parks, (Boarderline, Rolling Thunder, and Huckleberry Jam), and up to 35 features with something for everyone. They are sure that you will enjoy yourself with what they provide.

EXPANSION NEWS!
Work has already begun on adding 438 acres and two new chairlifts to the summit of Eagle Peak in the next year or so. Stay tuned!

LUCKY FRIDAY GLADES

INTERSTATE

MONTANA FACE

IDAHO FACE

NIAGRA

MOOSE LIPS

BLACK BEAR

BONANZA

GOLDEN EAGLE

GOLD

SILVER

COPPER SPUR

HUCKLEBERRY JAM

HUCKLEBERRY RIDGE

LAST CHANCE GLADES

SKI AREA BOUNDARY

QUICKSILVER

CHAIR 1

COPPER

GRUB STAKE

5650'

SUCCESS - CHAIR 4

SUCCESS

Slow Skiing Area

CROSS COUNTRY TRAIL

SKI AREA BOUNDARY

LODGE

Interstate 90

Parking

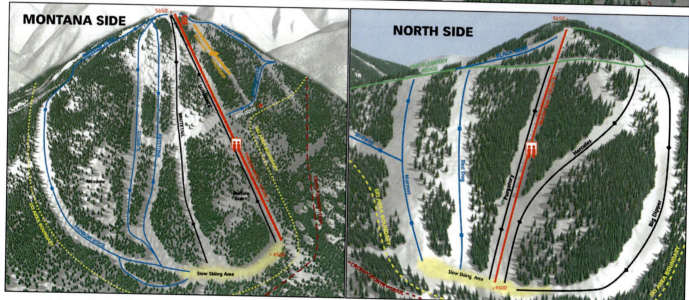

MONTANA SIDE

5650'

HOGBACK

SUNDANCE

SUNDANCE

CLOUT9

KEYSTONE

WHITETAIL

TO LODGE

SKI AREA BOUNDARY

CROSS COUNTRY TRAIL

Meadow

Buffalo Gulch

RAINBOW RIDGE

SKI AREA BOUNDARY

Slow Skiing Area

4500'

NORTH SIDE

5650'

HUCKLEBERRY RIDGE

BLACK BEAR

Midway

Marmot

Red Dog

Purgatory

Hercules

Big Dipper

SKI AREA BOUNDARY

CROSS COUNTRY TRAIL

SKI AREA BOUNDARY

Slow Skiing Area

4500'

BEGINNER	● 20% EASIER
INTERMEDIATE	■ 50% MORE DIFFICULT
ADVANCED/EXPERT	◆ 20% MOST DIFFICULT
EXPERT	◆◆ 10% EXTREME
FREESTYLE TERRAIN	

Pomerelle

Established: 1963	Acres: 500	Vertical: 1000'	Annual Snowfall: 500"

Pomerelle Mountain Resort is located just 25 miles off I-84 (Declo/Albion exit #216) in southern Idaho. Then, it is an easy drive via Idaho 77. It is one of the best little, local ski resorts in the West. Ask anyone who frequents the area. They would prefer to keep it a secret! The small, day/night resort is a relaxed, fun-filled, personalized retreat nestled in the Sawtooth National Forest.

With an annual snowfall of 500-inches, it is usually one of the first Idaho ski resorts to open each year and guests enjoy very short lift lines during the season. Pomerelle offers 24 groomed ski runs, plus ample gladed tree skiing and riding. The area sits at an elevation of 8,000-feet and caters to family-oriented ski/snowboarding enjoyment.

If Pomerelle is anything, it is a learning mountain. The Snow Sports School specializes in teaching tots-to-seniors of all abilities and is a PSIA member school. Kids age six and younger ski free with a paying adult guest.

The Pomerelle Day Lodge comprises the Cafeteria, Rental Shop for both alpine/snowboard equipment, Accessory Shop and Ski Patrol. The several terrain parks feature some of the best free-riding training facilities in Idaho. Competitive events are scheduled throughout the winter season.

Forest Service nordic (non-groomed/non-patrolled) trails are located adjacent to the resort; these are available for complimentary usage. Check with resort office for info.

NIGHT SKIING

Pomerelle also offers night skiing Tuesday through Saturday from 4 to 9 pm. Night skiing is a great time to see the mountain under the moonlight and with even shorter lift lines.

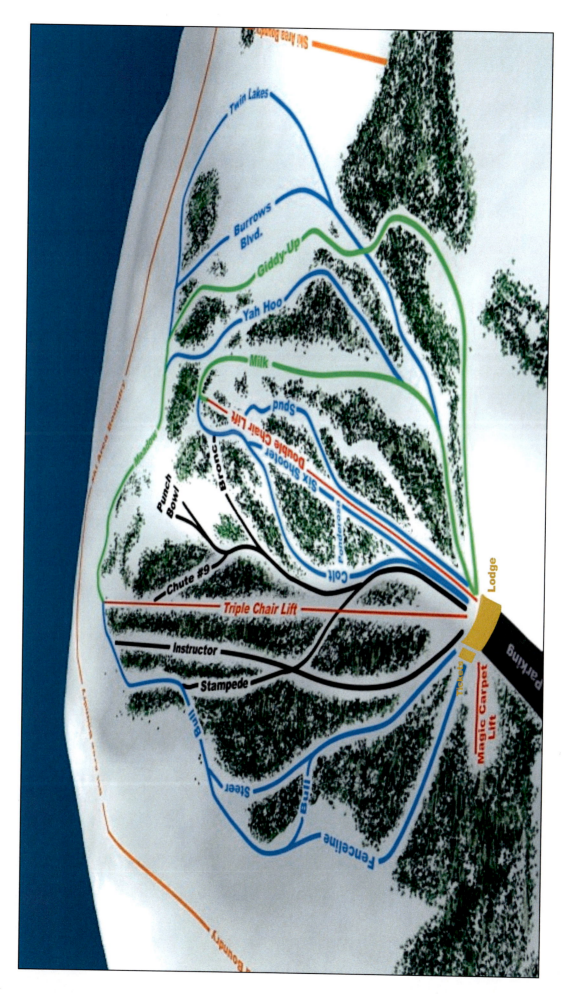

Magic Mountain

| Established: 1938 | Acres: 120 | Vertical: 740' | Annual Snowfall: 230" |

Magic Mountain Resort is a great family mountain and a sweet little day trip for skiers and snowboarders alike. There's terrain for all skill levels, including a terrain park, natural rocks and cliffs, and a great beginner's package if you're just starting out. And for the price, this little slice of southern Idaho paradise can't be beat.

For the non-skiers, there is a tubing hill with four lanes of tubing. Don't worry about walking up the hill – sit in the tube and let the tow rope bring you back to the top.

And be sure to visit the lodge for lunch or if you need your skis tuned. The rental shop will take care of you.

Magic Mountain is the little mountain that skis like a big mountain!

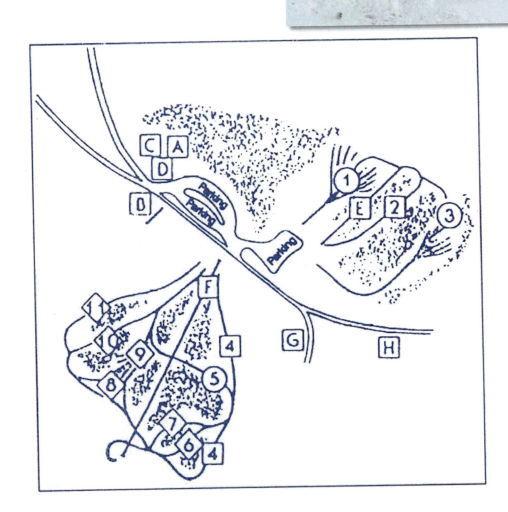

Bald Mountain

Established: 1959	Acres: 140	Vertical: 684'	Annual Snowfall: 100"

Bald Mountain Ski Area is located amongst the vast Clearwater Mountains along the Gold Rush Historic Byway in North Central Idaho. Established in 1959, Bald Mountain Ski Area is operated by the Clearwater Ski Club with the purpose of providing affordable family winter fun. "If you learn to ski at Bald Mountain, you can ski anywhere", has been a tag line since the beginning

The ski hill sits on 140 acres that the Club leases from Potlatch Corporation, with 19 named runs and several places where you can find your own line. With the exception of a few paid lift operators they are an all-volunteer operated place and consider themselves a winter time neighborhood. It has a day lodge with a café and a separate rental shop.

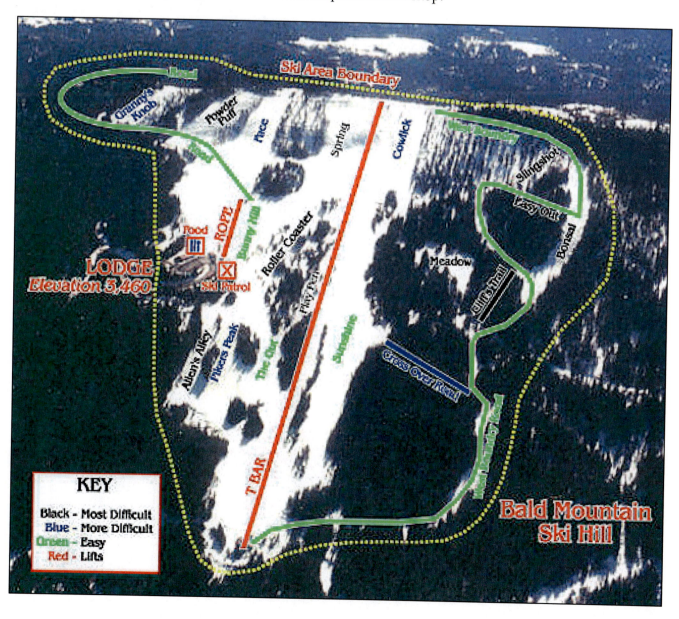

Little Ski Hill

Established: 1937   Acres: 50   Vertical: 405'   Annual Snowfall: 180"

For over 80 years, the Little Ski Hill has been the place for youth to learn how to ski, board and have a great time in the snow. Its 405 feet of vertical drop are accessed by a T-bar lift and a terrain park. Little Ski Hill also has 30 kilometers of groomed cross-country ski trails located at the Little Bear Basin Nordic facility. Every week something is going on whether it is a freeride series or a town league ski race. It's a great way to spend the day (or night) the next time you're in McCall.

Night skiing is available until 8 pm on Tuesdays through Thursday, and extended night operations on Friday and Saturday until 9 pm.

The Little Ski Hill is run by the non-profit Payette Lakes Ski Club.

LITTLE SKI HILL

Race Run

The Face

Main Run

Outback/Terrain Park

To Bear Basin Nordic Center

MCCALL, IDAHO
ELEVATION 5200
ESTABLISHED 1937

Snowhaven

| Established: 1948 | Acres: 40 | Vertical: 400' | Annual Snowfall: 60" |

Snowhaven Ski & Tubing Area is a small ski course and tubing hill owned and operated by the City of Grangeville. They pride themselves on great customer service and awesome snow, for a reasonable price. One T-bar and one rope-tow are used to access the top of the hill.

The tubing hill has one of the longest tubing runs in the state. A ride down the run features an approximate 150-foot vertical drop. Once the ride is completed a 600-foot-long lift carries you back to the top of the two 1100-foot-long runs for another tubing adventure.

Nearby are 16 km of Nordic trails and a 100 miles of snowmobile trails maintained by the Sno-Drifters Club of Grangeville.

Only open on weekends (and holidays), 10 am to 4 pm.

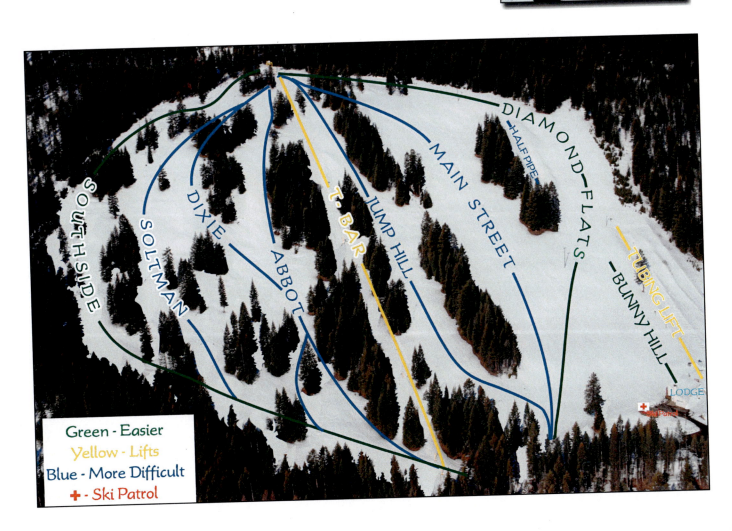

Green - Easier
Yellow - Lifts
Blue - More Difficult
+ - Ski Patrol

FUN FACTS

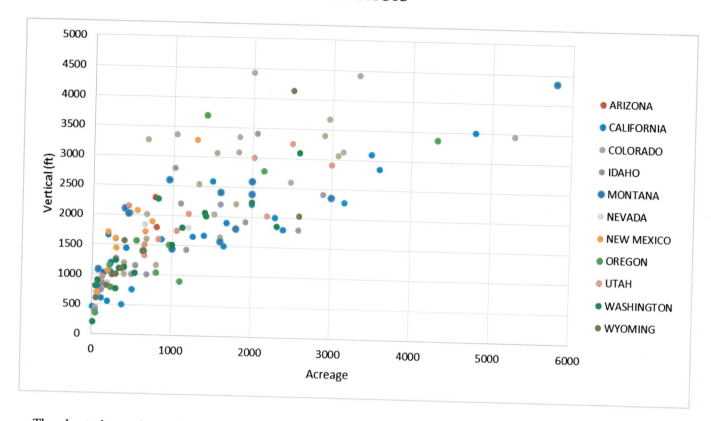

The chart above shows how a ski area's size relates to the amount of vertical drop one can experience on the slopes. The chart below shows how the acreage relates to ticket price (or not). Two ski areas were off the chart in size (Park City and Powder Mountain – both in Utah), which would have skewed the chart and made it difficult to see the trend.

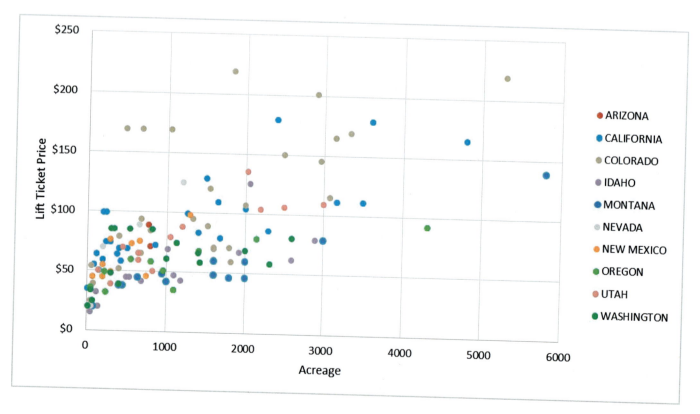

Montana

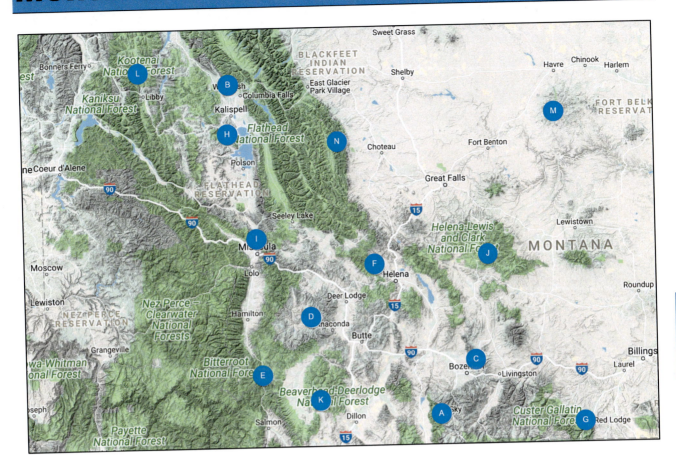

		Page
A.	Big Sky Resort	154
B.	Whitefish	156
C.	Bridger Bowl	158
D.	Discovery Ski Area	160
E.	Lost Trail Powder Mountain	162
F.	Great Divide	164
G.	Red Lodge Mountain	166
H.	Blacktail Mountain	168
I.	Snowbowl	170
J.	Showdown Montana	172
K.	Maverick Mountain	174
L.	Turner Mountain	175
M.	Bear Paw Ski Bowl	176
N.	Teton Pass (closed for 2017-2018)	

Big Sky Resort

Established: 1973	Acres: 5800	Vertical: 4350'	Annual Snowfall: 400"

Biggest Skiing in America - Big Sky Resort offers more than 5,800 seamless skiable acres with 4,350' vertical drop and about 2 acres per skier, that's more than a football field of room per skier.

More Slope Time – Ski more lines by not waiting in line. An average of 3,000 skiers per day, which is a fraction of skiers at metropolitan resorts of similar size.

Consistent Snowfall – Powder stashes are continually found throughout Big Sky due to the consistent snowfall (~400" annually) in the Northern Rockies with a natural fall-line back to the village base.

Terrain Variety – The best mix of beginners (15%), intermediate (25%), advanced (42%), and expert (18%) terrain for seamless skiing between four mountains served by 34 lifts with more than 300 runs. Plus, new runs are added every year.

Big Sky is part of the Ikon Pass.

LONE PEAK

Big Sky Resort, and its iconic, Matterhorn-like peak, have long stood alone on the mountain resort landscape, offering a ski experience that is, like Lone Peak, both unique and exceptional in the United States. Lone Peak presents over 300 degrees of aerial tram-served high alpine terrain dropping 4,350 vertical feet. From the 11,166ft summit of Lone Peak you can see two national parks and three states. After soaking in the view, discover nearly endless acres of chutes and pristine powder bowls opening into glades and groomers.

VILLAGE

The Mountain Village has lodging, dining, shopping, and rental shops. Savor American Alpine Fare and spectacular views at Everett's 8,800. Try a taste of Tuscany in the chic Andiamo Italian Grille. Or relax with nightly live entertainment, craft burgers, and local brews at Montana Jack. With over 30 options in and around the Mountain Village, one is sure to find something to satisfy one's appetite.

Whitefish

| Established: 1947 | Acres: 3000 | Vertical: 2353' | Annual Snowfall: 300" |

Whitefish Mountain Resort overlooks Glacier National Park and the Canadian Rockies. Snow falls more than half the time and lasts longer due to cloud cover and a lack of crowds. The people who ski here, half of them live here, and they ski a lot. So there's a difference when you meet someone on the lift, share a table at lunch or over a beer after skiing in the Bierstube—here they will talk to you more casually, naturally and connect as if you were an old friend.

Whitefish maintains its reputation for delivering outstanding service while keeping the ski experience affordable. This is evident in the ski magazine rankings which consistently place Whitefish in or near the top 10 in service and value. Whitefish is independently owned and operated which explains the affordable lift tickets ($79/day per adult – less if you ski 2 days).

Whitefish Mountain Resort is located only 8 miles from the town of Whitefish. A convenient and free snow bus runs a shuttle between the town and resort all day and into the evening.

AMBASSADOR TOURS

Yes, Whitefish Mountain Resort is BIG. There are 4 sides to the mountain which offers huge amounts of terrain for every level of skier or boarder. At Whitefish Mountain Resort, Ambassadors' primary goal is to orient you to the Mountain. You will find your dream terrain and have the time of your life! Complimentary tours at 10:30 am and 1:30 pm.

NIGHT SKIING

What better way to après ski than to keep skiing? Skiing under the lights is a fun way to extend your day on the slopes and is offered Friday and Saturday nights early January to the start of March and over the holidays between Christmas and New Years + Valentine's Day. There are three lifts serving beginner and intermediate terrain as well as the Fishbowl terrain parks.

Night Skiing Photo Courtesy of Brian Schott

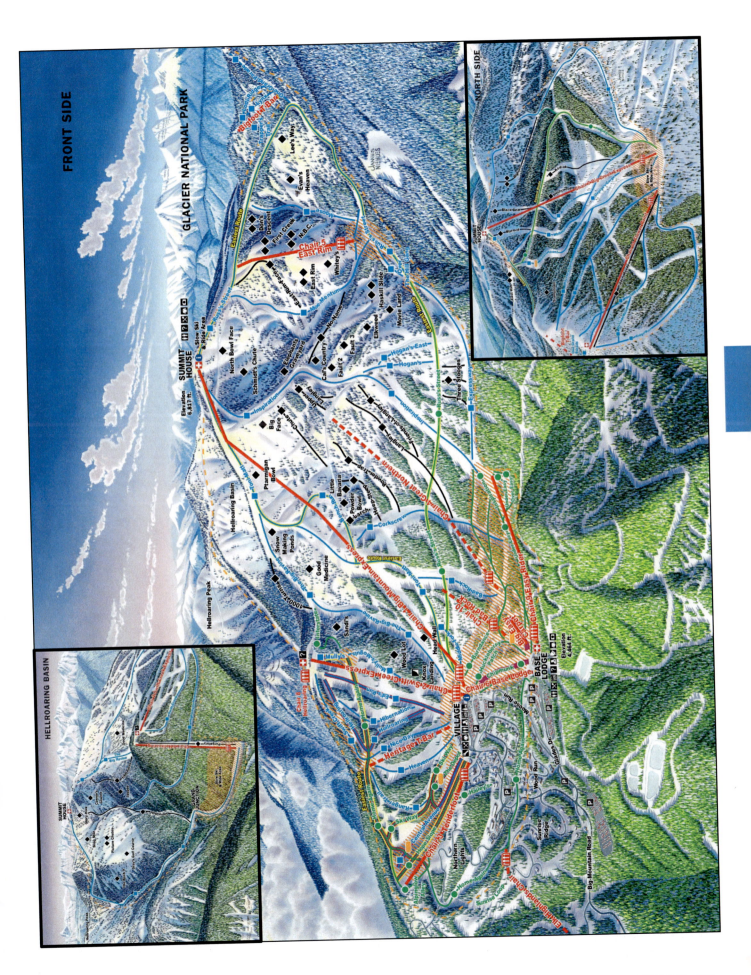

FRONT SIDE

GLACIER NATIONAL PARK

NORTH SIDE

HELLROARING BASIN

SUMMIT HOUSE
Elevation
6,817 ft.

BASE LODGE
Elevation
4,464 ft.

VILLAGE

Bridger Bowl

Established: 1955	Acres: 2000	Vertical: 2600'	Annual Snowfall: 350"

Bridger Bowl is one of those mountains a skier loves to discover. Though this Bozeman, Montana community ski area has been around for over 60 years, its coveted status as a local favorite has kept it off the ski resort radar in mainstream media. Only 16 miles from town, this nonprofit ski hill has stayed out of the resort development business and focused solely on their organizational charter to provide a quality ski experience at an affordable price. With ticket prices similar to mid-western ski hills offering a tenth of the vertical that Bridger has (2,600') to offer, this mountain, arguably, provides the best value for the dollar to ski in North America. Add in the fact that Bozeman has been highly accoladed as one of the best ski towns in the world, providing a wide selection of affordable lodging options, you've got a destination ski experience not to miss. Plus, this university town is loaded with great restaurants, micro-brew pubs and music for great evening fun.

The ski area is located on the east slope of the Bridger Mountain Range. Named for the four large bowls within their boundaries, Bridger offers exciting terrain with a variety of landscapes including long, wide-open slopes with groomed runs, glades, chutes and gullies. The mountain lays out in a large funnel or "V" shape expanding from a few hundred yards in width across the base area to nearly 2 miles wide at the ridge top.

Bridger Bowl has a first-class beginners area with conveyor lifts and a dedicated beginner chair for first time skiers and snowboarders. About 50% of the mountain is great for family and friends of beginner and intermediate skill levels. Plus, much of that terrain is some of the most beautiful on the mountain with exceptional views throughout. If you're an expert skier or rider, you are in for some of the best in-bounds, steep and deep skiing found in the Rockies.

Bridger Bowl's Ridge terrain presents some of the most challenging skiing and riding within any ski area boundary. This area has no marked trails and requires an avalanche transceiver to access. Ridge terrain is defined by steep chutes, rock cliffs, and big snowfields, some that may end in cliffs with no hazard warnings.

For newcomers to the area, Bridger's Ridge is best experienced with a guide through Bridger Bowl Snowsports. Take the 20 minute hike to the top from Bridger Lift or the Schlasman's Lift and enjoy all types of terrain with an instructor who knows the way.

LEGEND

● Easiest	☐ Slow Area
■ More Difficult	☐ Terrain Park
◆ Most Difficult	● Lift
◆◆ Expert Only	--- Backcountry Access Zone
— Road	‑‑‑ Closed Ski Area Boundary

The rating of trails for difficulty is relative only to the trails at Bridger Bowl. The degree of difficulty indicated is for the listed trail only and does not apply to adjacent off trail areas. Degree of difficulty can vary with changing snow and weather conditions.

Yellow shaded areas on the lower mountain indicate slow speed zones.

✚ Ski Patrol	Ⓟ Program Rental
Ⓣ Tickets/Passes	Ⓟ Playcare
⌗ Restaurant	Ⓡ Ski Rental
🚻 Restrooms	Ⓧ Ridge Terrain Access — Avalanche Transceiver Required
Ⓢ Snowsports	⚞ Backcountry Access Point

RIDGE TERRAIN

RESTRICTED ACCESS
AVALANCHE TRANSCEIVER REQUIRED
PARTNER AND SHOVEL
STRONGLY RECOMMENDED

★ WARNING ★

INCREASED RISK OF AVALANCHE
EXPERTS RO ONLY
STEEP CHUTES
UNMARKED CLIFFS

SKI AND RIDE WITH CAUTION
NO EASY WAY DOWN
NO GROOMING
NO HAZARD MARKING
NO MARKED TRAILS

PARK SMART

START SMALL
Work your way up. Build your skills.
MAKE A PLAN
Every feature. Every time.
ALWAYS LOOK
Before you drop.
RESPECT
The features and other users.
TAKE IT EASY
Know your limits. Land on your feet.

SKI AREA BOUNDARY NOTICE

SKI AREA BOUNDARIES ARE CLOSED EXCEPT AT DESIGNATED
FOREST SERVICE BACKCOUNTRY GATES AND ACCESS ZONES

‑‑‑ FOREST SERVICE BACKCOUNTRY ACCESS
‑‑‑ CLOSED SKI AREA BOUNDARY

★ DANGER ★

AVALANCHE DANGER AND OTHER LIFE THREATENING HAZARDS EXIST BEYOND
THE SKI AREA BOUNDARY. IF YOU CHOOSE TO LEAVE THE SKI AREA BOUNDARY
YOU ARE SOLELY RESPONSIBLE FOR YOUR SAFETY AND WELFARE. NO SKI PATROL
SERVICES OR AVALANCHE HAZARD REDUCTION. RESCUE BY GALLATIN COUNTY
SEARCH AND RESCUE - CALL 911
RESCUE MAY BE PROLONGED - BE PREPARED TO SURVIVE THE NIGHT

Summit Elevation: 8,800'
Base Elevation: 6,100'

EXTREME AVALANCHE POTENTIAL OUTSIDE THE SKI AREA BOUNDARY
IN-BOUNDS HAZARD REDUCTION REDUCES BUT DOES NOT ELIMINATE THE RISK OF AVALANCHE

Ski The Cold Smoke
BRIDGER BOWL

Custer Gallatin National Forest

XC Ski Center
3/4 mile North of Bridger Bowl

BASE AREA

Sunnyside
Virginia City
Jim Bridger Lodge
Saddle Peak Lodge
Eagle Mount Adaptive Program
Glenn's Glade
Sundog
Flurry
Hickey's Hollow
Snowflake
Snowflake Hut

Discovery Ski Area

Established: 1973	Acres: 2000	Vertical: 2388'	Annual Snowfall: 215"

An expert's brand of thrills served up in a local's hangout, Discovery is a terrific find that will remind you what skiing in Montana is all about! The north-facing Limelight lift offers some of the steepest lift-served terrain around, while the variety of beginner and intermediate runs on the Anaconda and north-facing Granite lifts provide great skiing for all abilities. Easily reached from Missoula, Butte and Helena, they have beautiful views and uncrowded slopes with enough tree skiing, powder bowls, groomed trails and mogul runs for all tastes.

Discovery has three faces. The front face is the perfect blend of gently sloping runs and more advanced groomed cruisers. Off the Granite Chair, things step up a notch with steeper groomed runs and mogul skiing. And the backside? Well, imagine the Chugach without the costly helicopter ride. It has some of Montana's steepest lift-served runs - 40° with 1,000 ft vertical drop.

Discovery also offers a lot of downhill thrills during the summer months at the Discovery Bike Park from June 18th through October. The trails are intermediate to advanced, with loads of features for downhill riders to enjoy.

Discovery is a family resort with an emphasis on great skiing, a fun atmosphere and friendly service. So while you won't find a timber frame Taj Mahal or a $40 bison tenderloin, you'll discover pretty much everything you need for a great ski day or trip. The Discovery Day Lodge is where you'll find the café and the Tap 'Er Lite Bar. The Lodge also houses the rental shop, retail shop, and the ski school.

8,150 ft.

Claim Jumper

Mills Road

7,650 ft.

Red Lion

Silver Bow

Southern Cross

Sapphire

Sluice Box

Gold Rush

Platinum

Gold Bug

Atlantic Cable

Berkeley

Tenderfoot

Anaconda

Rumsey

Jubilee

Northern Lights

JAMES
NIEHUES

Mungas

Tenderfoot

Easy

Britton

Lums Run

Totemoff

Ski Discovery is Located in
Beaverhead-Deerlodge
National Forest

Base 6850 ft.

LEGEND

◆◆ Experts Only   ✚ Ski Patrol
◆ Most Difficult   ▨ Slow Skiing
■ More Difficult   ╌╌ Ski Area
● Easier   Boundary
▬ Terrain Park
Emergency Communication located at all lift stations.

Rumsey Mountain

8,000 ft.

8,150 ft.

Burning Forest

Terminator

Snaggle Tooth

Spooky Hollow

Christmas Park

Mother Lode

Good Finger

Bad Finger

Winning Ridge

Maverick

Catchweave

Alax

Manhattan

The Pitch

Guns & Roses

Little Finger

Medicine Ridge

Tor / Lite

Center Stage

Orphan Girl

Meyer's West

Boiler Maker

Stage Right

Trinity

Russell

Limelight

Old # 1

Head Frame

Granite

Grouse

Winning Ridge

Kaxl's

Mine

Yosea Guys

6,785 ft.

Reacer

The Way West

Base 7,000 ft.

Thrashiker

Black Moon

JAMES
NIEHUES

Burro Alley

Base 6,480 ft.

The Wright Stuff

E Miller

Exhibition

Little Darling

Ski Discovery is Located in
Beaverhead-Deerlodge
National Forest

Almost Famous

Rising Star

Colter's Escape

Lord's Retreat

Silver Cross

Base 5,770 ft.

LEGEND

◆◆ Experts Only   ✚ Ski Patrol
◆ Most Difficult   ▨ Slow Skiing
■ More Difficult   ▬ Chair Lift
● Easier
Emergency Communication located at all lift stations.

Lost Trail Powder Mountain

Established: 1938	Acres: 1800	Vertical: 1800'	Annual Snowfall: 325"

When you visit Lost Trail Powder Mountain you will enjoy the beauty and uncrowded slopes of the Rocky Mountains' hidden jewel that straddles the border of Montana and Idaho along the Continental Divide. Being a family-owned ski area, their focus is on a great family experience. But that doesn't mean they lack a diversity – Lost Trail Powder Mountain has something for everyone from beginners to double-black expert only terrain to bowls, tree skiing, cliffs, two terrain parks, long blue groomers (2.5 miles), and a great learning area.

Their snow is some of the best in the Northern Rockies. It is easy to score a powder stash since the snow can accumulate Monday through Wednesday until the ski area opens on Thursday (open Thursday – Sunday and holidays including extended days during Christmas break).

You'll find a relaxed atmosphere and friendly staff waiting to lend a helping hand on the slopes or in the base lodge. The lodge is also where you will find the rental shop, snowsports school, and cafeteria.

TERRAIN PARKS

Lost Trail Powder Mountain is continuously upgrading its parks year after year. Its diverse terrain welcomes many skiers and snowboarders, ranging from rails, tables, and wallrides to the more natural powder pillows and cliff lines. Lost Trail has something for everyone no matter what kind of slope style you're into.

Be sure to visit the website to find all the latest events throughout the season such as their Steak Fry, Rail Jams, Pond Skim, and Skiesta Party.

AVALANCHE HAZARDS MAY EXIST
SKI PATROL AVALANCHE HAZARD REDUCTION EFFORTS DO NOT
ELIMINATE THE RISK OF AVALANCHE
BE SMART AND CONTROL YOUR EXPOSURE TO THESE RISKS

LT LOST TRAIL SKI AREA www.LostTrail.com

Yellow Shaded Areas
Indicate Slow Zone
Respect Other Riders/Skiers
RIDE FAST-LOSE PASS

KNOW THE CODE: IT'S YOUR RESPONSIBILITY

1. Always stay in control, and be able to stop or avoid other people or objects.
2. People ahead of you have the right of way. It is your responsibility to avoid them.
3. You must not stop where you obstruct a trail, or are not visible from above.
4. Wherever starting downhill or merging into a trail, look uphill and yield to others.
5. Always use devices to help prevent runaway equipment.
6. Observe all posted signs and warnings. Keep off closed trails and out of closed areas.
7. Prior to using any lift, you must have the knowledge and ability to load, ride and unload safely.

Lost Trail Ski area operates under a special use permit from the Bitterroot National Forest located within the Bitterroot and Salmon-Challis National Forests.

THE WHITE HOUSE
Experts Only ◆◆

Services
🚻 restrooms
⛷ ski school
Ⓟ parking
✚ ski patrol

Trail Markings
● easy
■ moderate
◆ difficult
◆ expert
⬭ terrain park
⟋ out trails
⟋ easiest way to lodge
⬭ slow zone

Lifts
double chairlift
surface lift
state line
highway
area boundary

Snow Report:

406-821-3211

losttrail.com/conditions

facebook.com/LostTrail

GO FOR THE SNOW!

LT LOST TRAIL SKI AREA www.LostTrail.com

Great Divide

Established: 1941	Acres: 1600	Vertical: 1580'	Annual Snowfall: 180"

Great Divide is Montana's most progressive, affordable skiing & snowboarding mountain. Located just north of Marysville, Montana on Belmont Mountain, Great Divide is just 23 miles from Montana's Capital City of Helena. With a wide selection of terrain, from beginner to extreme and everything in between, it's a great place for the whole family to enjoy. With fun food and drink across the mountain and free wi-fi in the base lodge, you can hit the slopes without missing a beat.

The base lodge offers a great place to get out of the cold, get some good food and grab a cold beer or cup of hot chocolate. On sunny days you can enjoy BBQ and the company of friends on the Sundeck. The Base Lodge Grill serves up burgers, hot dogs, soups, fries and more. The Missing Lynx Saloon is a fully stocked bar, with beers from local breweries, along with the usual domestics, a variety of wines, plus a broad selection of cocktails including some veggie heavy bloody mary's and caesars.

The WildWest Cabin perched at 7000 ft near the top of the WildWest chairlift, offers incredible wilderness views. A great place to warm up in between laps, grab a drink and a bowl of chili and get back after it.

TERRAIN PARKS

If you like to ride parks, you have landed in the right place. Great Divide offers six different parks ranging from fun easy rollers and boxes, to the huge jumps, gaps and rails of RODEO. Great Divide offers freestyle terrain for all ages and abilities. When all 6 Parks are open, they have an amazing total of up to 90 fun features!

NIGHT SKIING

Enjoy skiing under the stars on Friday nights until 9 pm. (Only $10 tickets after 4 pm.) Five of the terrain parks are open at night so you can ride the features under the lights. Both the Good Luck and Meadow Mountain lifts service the night skiing terrain.

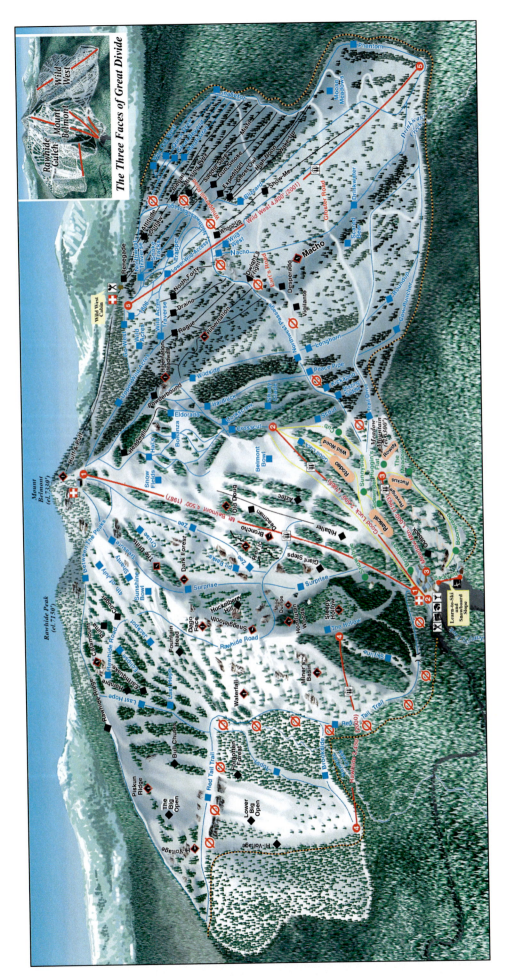

The Three Faces of Great Divide

Wild West

Mount Belmont

Rawhide Gulch

Red Lodge Mountain

Established: 1960	Acres: 1635	Vertical: 2400'	Annual Snowfall: 250"

Red Lodge Mountain is Montana Skiing, Pure and Simple. No lift lines, no attitude, no big prices. Just great snow, great people and an authentic experience in Montana's Rocky Mountains..

With amazing views from anywhere on the mountain, skiers and riders are sure to be just as excited on the lifts as they are on the slopes. The wide variety of terrain includes deep couloirs, groomers, glades, and even a whopping 2 ½ mile cruiser (Lazy M) to keep everyone challenged.

Red Lodge Mountain is a full-service ski area, offering several on-mountain dining options, a rental & repair shop, retail shop, and lessons from PSIA/AASI certified instructors. Two terrain parks let skiers and riders of all levels fine-tune skills on various jumps, rails, and other features.

Annually, a variety of events are hosted at Red Lodge Mountain, keeping the full spirit of the ski season around all winter. The Town Series Race League, Scrap Yard Terrain Park Series, and Winter Carnival (among others) are not to be missed and are full of fun and excitement for the whole family

THE TOWN

Red Lodge is located a short 7 miles from the ski area. The classic Western ski town offers gorgeous scenery and all the usual après ski options; dining, local craft brews, shopping, lodging, and live music to name a few. "Outside Magazine" considers Red Lodge one of the best places to live and play, and it doesn't take long for every visitor to understand why.

Only an hour's drive from Billings, Montana and Cody, Wyoming, it is easy to get to from all over the country with an easy flight and a quick, scenic drive. Road tripping is also a breeze with interstate highways close by..

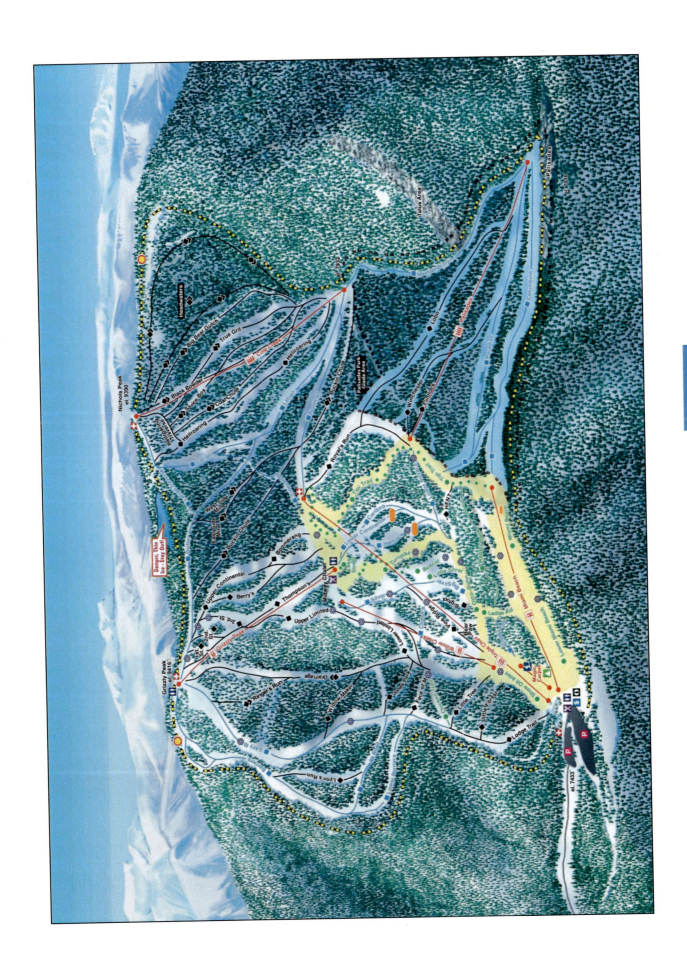

Blacktail Mountain

Established: 1998	Acres: 1000	Vertical: 1440'	Annual Snowfall: 250"

In driving to the mountain top, regardless of whether you are an expert or novice, skier or snowboarder, everyone starts at the top on Blacktail Mountain. Views from Flathead Lake to Glacier Park and of the Mission, Whitefish and Cabinet Ranges surround. On this "upside-down hill" you have a top to bottom run in before riding a chair.

By starting at the mountain top, one immediately experiences any possible wind condition. However, once skiers and boarders drop onto the north facing runs, they find Blacktail Mountain to be nearly wind free (a rarity). Most of the winds blow from the west and southwest, hitting the back side of the mountain, so the hill buffers the north side runs. There is seldom any fog, nor will you see snow ghosts or rime on chairlifts.

Most of the mountain is for trails but one terrain park exists with two medium jumps, a large jump, large box, shotgun rail, and a long rail.

Blacktail Lodge offers two options for hungry skiers. Fireplaces in both cafeteria and restaurant make taking a break a warm experience. Get a bite to eat, something to drink and enjoy the views! Check out delicious daily specials. Muley's Pub and Restaurant is a full menu sit down restaurant, with bar. Located on the third floor of the Lodge, this is a great place to meet for apres ski.

Upper Terminal Cafe on the second floor is cafeteria style, offers great lunches or bring your own and sit by the warm fireplace to enjoy a quick snack, hot beverage, or a visit with friends, before heading back out on the slopes.

The base lodge also houses the full-service rental shop and snow sports school where you can get lessons for all ages/skills.

BLACKTAIL
MOUNTAIN

NORTH

LODGE

West Ridge
Buck Snort
Cabinet View
West Ridge
Crystal Double Chair
White River
Tail Dragger
Blacktail Run
Independence Park
Clearcut
Blacktail Run
Short Branch
Cold Camp
Crossover
Willow Maker
Olympic Triple Chair
Easy Out
Never-ever
Tow
T bed
Emmons Ridge
Meadow
Damnation
Emmons Ridge
Radar
Snowblower
Meadow
Meadow
Thunderhead Double Chair
Lakeside Run
Snowslip
Pochelon's Powder
Bearpaw
Long Branch
The Glades
Lakeside Run

Snowbowl

snowbowl

Established: 1961	Acres: 950	Vertical: 2600'	Annual Snowfall: 300"

The base lodge also has ski rentals/repair shop that is equipped to handle all your needs. There is also a great ski school that offers lessons for all ages and skill levels.

Montana Snowbowl is the local hill for the college-town of Missoula – only 12 miles away. If you are looking for powder bowls and plenty of vertical, you've come to the right place. Snowbowl has a respectable 2,600 ft of vertical drop serviced by three double-chairlifts. Snowbowl is in the middle of a large expansion that will double the acreage and add over 20 new runs for 2018-2019.

GETTING THERE

Snowbowl is conveniently located a short 12 miles from Missoula, one of Montana's two university towns and the cultural hub for the western part of the state. Consistently mentioned in national rankings for its recreation opportunities and high quality of life standards, Missoula offers something for everyone with a wealth of dining, shopping, and night life options. To make it easy, take the shuttle bus that goes from in town directly to the hill.

Besides some of the most challenging runs around the Bowl is known for food, beverages and general great atmosphere at the base. There are two choices The Last Run and the The Double Diamond Cafe. How many ski areas do you know where folks just drive up for a pizza or just to hang out?

Showdown Montana

Established: 1936	Acres: 640	Vertical: 1400'	Annual Snowfall: 240"

Showdown Montana is nestled in the Little Belt Mountains at a base elevation of 6800-feet. The high location means it gets the best snow and keeps it longer than most areas. With non-existent lift lines and plenty of terrain to explore, Showdown has a variety of terrain for every type of type. 1400 feet of vertical over 600 acres means there is plenty to explore, all serviced with just three lifts.

But it wasn't always that easy. 81 years ago at Showdown Montana, known then as "King's Hill," you wouldn't find a bar with live music and hot drinks, a rental shop full of skis and boots, or a ski school where on any given Saturday about 150 kids can be found in different lessons. Instead, you would find a rope tow with a gas powered engine to get people up the hill. It was a difficult rope tow at that - one with a telephone pole and a tire rim to keep the rope off the ground. Lift tickets were 50 cents and people earned their turns. Showdown is the oldest continually operating ski area in Montana.

Today, after a day of skiing, take in some of the local flavor at the King's Hill Grille, which offers hot food and drinks until closing. Be sure to take in the atmosphere of the Hole in the Wall Saloon (open until 6:30 pm).

New for 2017-2018, Showdown is offering a $10 season pass to 4th and 5th graders! It's part of their effort to keep skiing affordable and get more kids and families involved in this great sport that makes Winter fun!

Showdown is 66 miles from Great Falls and 107 miles from Helena, Montana. The remote nature preserves the lift lines and tree stashes.

LESSONS

Showdown offers several beginner lesson packages for as low as $37 for lift ticket, rental equipment, and lesson. Or if you are not a beginner but would still like a lesson, just rent the gear, buy your ticket, then the lesson is only $15. Besides taking ski or snowboarding lessons, Showdown is one of the few mountains that also teaches Snowbike.

Showdown Trail Map

MOUNTAIN STATS

- 8,200 ft summit & 6,800 ft base elevation
- 255 average inches of snow per year
- 1,400 vertical feet
- 36 runs on 640 skiable acres
- 3 chairlifts, 1 learning conveyor
- Full service lodge and rental shop
- Terrain Park

SERVICES

✚ Ski Patrol	✗ Grill
🔔 Snow School	🥄 Ski Shop
SKI Ticket Office	R Rental Shop
Saloon	N Nursery

LIFT INFORMATION

		Vertical	Travel	Length	Close
A	Prospector	1,400ft	12.5min	6,700ft	3:30pm
B	Payload	1,100ft	9min	4,400ft	4:00pm
C	Sluice Goose Caboose	650ft	7.5min	3,150ft	4:00pm
D	Learning Conveyor	95ft	3.5 min	400ft	4:00pm

TRAIL MARKINGS

- 🟢 Easier
- 🟦 More Difficult
- ◇ Most Difficult
- ┄ Easier Way Down
- Terrain Park
- 🟧 Midway
- Slow Skiing Area
- ⋯ Uphill Ski Route
- Snow Shoe Route

Maverick Mt

Established: 1936	Acres: 450	Vertical: 2020'	Annual Snowfall: 200"

Hidden away in the mountains of southwest Montana, you'll find Maverick Mountain, one of Montana skiers' best-kept secrets. Maverick is a big mountain with 2,000 feet of superb snow and uncrowded trails offering exciting skiing for every level of skier. Although they only have one lift, you can ski over mile-long runs with consistent fall lines (24 trails to choose from). It is rare to find 450 acres so well served by a single lift.

Maverick has a day lodge that houses the Cowboy Café for daytime dining. Your day is not complete without a stop at the Thunder Bar (open until 9 pm), which serves a variety of microbrews on tap (including four local brews from Beaverhead Brewery). The lodge also has the ski rental shop and ski school.

Maverick is open Thursdays through Sunday and holidays.

Maverick Mountain is 41 miles outside of Dillon, Montana.

Turner Mountain

Established: 1961	Acres: 400	Vertical: 2100'	Annual Snowfall: 250"

With the finest snow conditions, wide-open slopes, fabulous scenery, no crowds and inexpensive lift tickets, Turner Mountain is truly the ideal place for the skier/snowboarder who desires the most from their skiing experience. Turner Mountain offers challenging terrain on a local hill outside of Libby, Montana. With just a single two-seater lift, you can access 400 acres of mostly black diamond runs that take you down 2000+ feet of vertical. With a single base lodge, Turner is able to house a full service snack bar, rental shop, and ski school.

The mountain is only open to the public on Friday through Sunday, but the best part is that you can rent the whole mountain (lift, lodge, parking) for a reasonable price Monday through Thursday.

Bear Paw Ski Bowl

| Established: 1960 | Acres: 80 | Vertical: 1079' | Annual Snowfall: 140" |

Bear Paw Ski Bowl, the "Last Best Ski Hill," offers an inexpensive, old-fashioned, friendly ski hill experience. They are managed and operated by an all-volunteer group of local skiers. Skiers and riders at Bear Paw will find a nostalgic and rustic trip back to a time when skiing was the emphasis and accommodations were provided by good neighbors with a smile.

A double chairlift services the whole hill with 24 runs to choose from. You won't find a fancy base lodge but you will enjoy a fun local mountain.

Check the website for hours of operation. Usually the ski area is only open on weekends.

Nevada

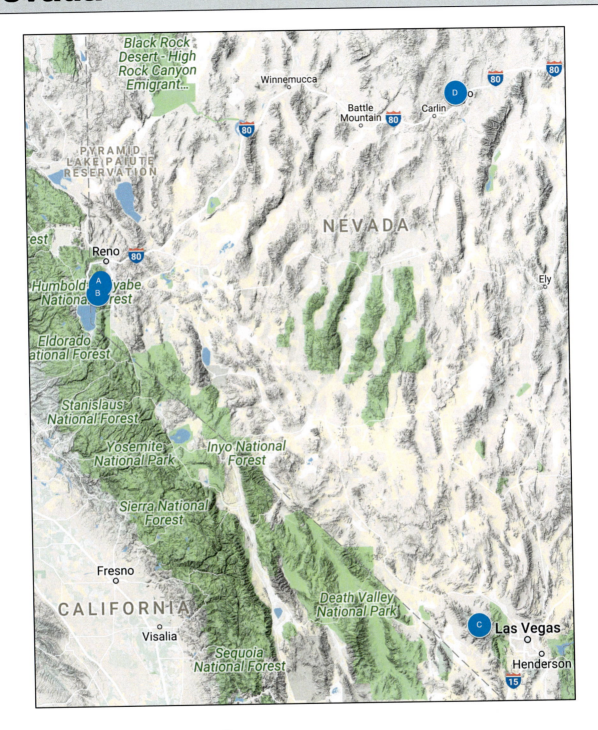

		Page
A.	Mt. Rose – Ski Tahoe	178
B.	Diamond Peak	180
C.	Lee Canyon	182
D.	Elko Snobowl	184

Mt. Rose – Ski Tahoe

Established: 1964	Acres: 1200	Vertical: 1800'	Annual Snowfall: 350"

Tahoe's Closest Skiing to Reno - Of all Lake Tahoe ski resorts, Mt. Rose is the closest to Reno - only 25 minutes from the Reno-Tahoe International airport and 15 minutes from North Lake Tahoe. It's also one of the first to open every year. Mt. Rose features 60+ trails with terrain to suit any type of skier or snowboarder. The high base elevation of Mt. Rose ensures supreme snow conditions, which is accessed by dual high-speed, six-passenger chairlifts that serve over 1200 acres of terrain.

EXPANSIVE LODGING OPTIONS

Reno is home to 9,000+ unbelievably affordable hotel rooms, many in luxury casino properties with top rated amenities. Quite simply, with Mt. Rose a mere 25 minutes away, a ski getaway out of Reno is the best value skip trip anywhere in the world! Even closer is Incline Village on Lake Tahoe's north shore providing abundant condo choices in addition to premier hotels.

CLOSE PARKING / EASY ACCESS

Get to the slopes and start skiing right away! Skip the exhaustive hikes through villages and avoid the mandatory shuttles from distant parking lots. At Mt. Rose they continue to keep the process simple and easy with convenient park lots close to the lifts.

TERRAIN

Mt. Rose has the all the terrain you need to fit the needs of everyone in your crew. From the ideal beginner slopes in their Enchanted Forest zone, novice skiers and riders will quickly advance to the expansive groomers accessible from both Summit six pack lifts in the Slide Bowl. Cap it off with the adrenaline charged steeps of The Chutes, offering some of the most accessible extreme terrain in Lake Tahoe, not to mention the longest continuous vertical in North America.

GREAT SNOW

Never to be overlooked is the fact that Mt. Rose offers Tahoe's highest base skiing and snowboarding. At 8,260' the parking lots are higher than some resorts peaks ensuring the most supreme snow conditions throughout the season, even on the warmest spring days.

Diamond Peak

Established: 1966	Acres: 655	Vertical: 1840'	Annual Snowfall: 300"

Come explore North Lake Tahoe's hidden gem – Diamond Peak. Located in Nevada's Incline Village, the affordable, family friendly resort offers breathtaking views of Lake Tahoe, a summit elevation of 8,540-feet and a 1,840-foot vertical drop. Skiers and boarders can experience 655 acres of beginner to expert-level terrain including some of the best tree skiing in the Tahoe Basin.

FOR FAMILIES

Diamond Peak is Tahoe's best ski resort for families, with free tickets for kids 6 and under, interchangeable parent tickets, slope-side parking lots just steps from the lifts, lesson options for kids 3+, uncrowded slopes, beginner terrain parks, and beautiful views of Lake Tahoe for the whole family to enjoy.

TERRAIN PARKS

Diamond Peak offers three terrain parks for all skill levels: the progression-oriented Lakeview and Popular parks and the Spillway Park which has bigger features. Features are constantly evolving and being added throughout the season so come back often to check it out.

LESSONS

Diamond Peak's professional instructors, low student-to-instructor ratio, dedicated children's learning area, gentle slopes, and a friendly environment provide an ideal place for first-time skiers and snowboarders and those looking to improve their skills and confidence.

Diamond Peak integrates Terrain Based Teaching into all beginner lessons, a method that has proven successful throughout the industry. Terrain Based Teaching involves incorporating small terrain features as part of the learning progression, which amps up the fun factor and helps beginners gain confidence and learn the skills they will need once they graduate from the beginner slopes. Features such as a mini halfpipe, rollers or spines help students develop specific skills and experience the sensation that more advanced skiers and riders know and love.

Diamond Peak
INCLINE VILLAGE LAKE TAHOE

DIAMOND PEAK 8,540 FT.

LAKE TAHOE

To South Lake Tahoe
25 MILES
VIA HWY 28

To Reno
27 MILES
VIA HWY 431

Snowflake Lodge
ELEVATION 7,400 FT.

BASE ELEVATION
6,700 FT.

Skier Services Building

Base Lodge

OUT OF BOUNDS
ILLEGAL TO CROSS
VIOLATORS WILL BE PROSECUTED

HIGH SPEED QUAD

SOLITUDE CANYON

GOLDEN EAGLE BOWL

THE GLADES

THE GREAT FLUME

CRYSTAL EXPRESS

CRYSTAL RIDGE

THUNDER

LIGHTNING

DIAMONDBACK

BATTLEBORN

SPILLWAY

SUNNYSIDE

POWDER

LAKEVIEW

RIDGE

LUGGI'S

DUSTY'S DELIGHT

PENGUIN

FREEWAY

WIGGLE

POPULAR

LOWER SHOWOFF

CAPPY'S CORNER

LODGEPOLE

LODGEPOLE GROUP

POPULAR

SCHOOL YARD

SCHOOLHOUSE

UPPER SHOWOFF

CHUTE

F.I.S.

CORKSCREW

SLALOM GLADE

LAKEVIEW QUAD

RIDGE RUN

O. GOD

G.S.

TRAIL PROGRESSION
Trails ranked in order of difficulty based on slope and typical snow conditions. This is a guide. Conditions, snow, and grooming can alter this order.

EASIER
School Yard
Lodge Pole

MORE DIFFICULT
Ridge Run to Freeway
Popular
Penguin
Lakeview
Wiggle
Dusty's Delight
Lower Showoff
Crystal Ridge
Sunnyside
Great Flume
Golden Eagle Bowl
Cappy's Corner

MOST DIFFICULT
Upper Showoff
Chute
F.I.S.
Corkscrew
Slalom Glade
Powder
Luggi's
Lightning
Diamondback
Battle Born
Thunder
G.S.
O God
The Glades
Solitude Canyon

Lee Canyon

| Established: 1963 | Acres: 195 | Vertical: 860' | Annual Snowfall: 161" |

Lee Canyon is located approximately one hour from downtown Las Vegas in the Humboldt-Toiyabe National Forest. Established in 1963, Lee Canyon offers guests 195 acres of terrain, 27 trails accessed via three chairlifts, 250 acres of hike-to terrain, a lift-served tubing hill, and a Nordic trail for snowshoeing. Averaging 161 inches of snowfall annually, Lee Canyon offers ski and snowboard coaching, terrain parks, a snowshoeing trail, and lodge amenities such as dining and retail, as well as a host of summer activities. Lee Canyon is part of the POWDR Adventure Lifestyle Co. portfolio.

SNOW CABANA

Be a slope-side V.I.P. with Lee Canyon's private Snow Cabana! It is the perfect mountain get away for the day. Ski in and out of the Cabana on the slopes for easy access to the lifts and use your own private staircase to the Main Lodge. The Cabana features plush couches, cable television, adjustable heat, and music station to plug in your tunes. Relax inside after riding while they deliver your food and drinks.

TERRAIN PARKS

Lee Canyon has terrain parks that cover a variety of abilities to accommodate progression. From beginner to freestyle pro, the terrain parks feature a variety of jibs, jumps, and assorted rails for everyone to practice or session all day.

TUBING HILL

Enjoy a designated tubing area with two lanes and enjoy the 90 minutes session to your heart's content. Tubes are included. Don't worry about hiking back up the hill as their tubing lift pulls you back up to the top with you still on your tube.

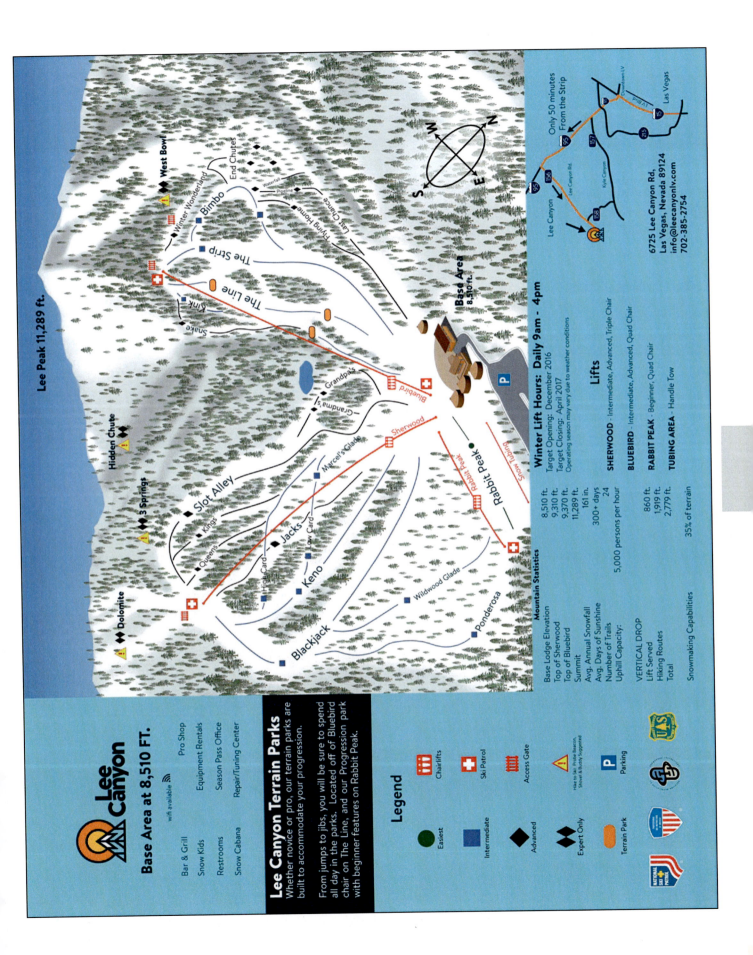

Lee Canyon

Base Area at 8,510 FT.

wifi available

Bar & Grill
Snow Kids
Restrooms
Snow Cabana

Pro Shop
Equipment Rentals
Season Pass Office
Repair/Tuning Center

Lee Canyon Terrain Parks

Whether novice or pro, our terrain parks are built to accommodate your progression.

From jumps to jibs, you will be sure to spend all day in the parks. Located off of Bluebird chair on The Line, and our Progression park with beginner features on Rabbit Peak.

Legend

● Easiest
■ Intermediate
◆ Advanced
◆◆ Expert Only
🟠 Terrain Park

🎿 Charlifts
➕ Ski Patrol
🚪 Access Gate
⚠️ Hike to Ski: Probe Beacon, Shovel & Buddy Suggested
🅿️ Parking

Lee Peak 11,289 ft.

West Bowl

End Chutes

Winter Wonderland

Bimbo

Waterfall

Pipeline

The Strip

Flying Home

Last Chance

The Line

Kink

Snake

Grandpa's

Grandma's

Bluebird

Sherwood

Hidden Chute

3 Springs

Slot Alley

Marcel's Glade

Kings

Queens

Jacks

Low Card

High Card

Keno

Blackjack

Wildwood Glade

Ponderosa

Rabbit Peak

Snow Tubing

Base Area
8,510 ft.

Dolomite

N / S / E / W (compass)

Mountain Statistics

Base Lodge Elevation	8,510 ft.
Top of Sherwood	9,310 ft.
Top of Bluebird	9,370 ft.
Summit	11,289 ft.
Avg. Annual Snowfall	161 in.
Avg. Days of Sunshine	300+ days
Number of Trails	24
Uphill Capacity:	5,000 persons per hour

VERTICAL DROP

Lift Served	860 ft.
Hiking Routes	1,919 ft.
Total	2,779 ft.

Snowmaking Capabilities   35% of terrain

Winter Lift Hours: Daily 9am - 4pm

Target Opening: December 2016
Target Closing: April 2017
Operating season may vary due to weather conditions

Lifts

SHERWOOD - Intermediate, Advanced, Triple Chair

BLUEBIRD - Intermediate, Advanced, Quad Chair

RABBIT PEAK - Beginner, Quad Chair

TUBING AREA - Handle Tow

Only 50 minutes From the Strip

Las Vegas

Lee Canyon

Lee Canyon Rd.

Kyle Canyon

6725 Lee Canyon Rd,
Las Vegas, Nevada 89124
info@leecanyonlv.com
702-385-2754

Elko Snobowl

| Established: 1996 | Acres: 60 | Vertical: 700' | Annual Snowfall: 42" |

SnoBowl is a 501 (c) (3) Not-for-Profit, Community Ski and Snowboard Area, owned and operated by the city of Elko. It first began operations in 1992, and is one of the most enjoyable winter recreation options that Elko has to offer. SnoBowl also offers lift-served mountain bike terrain for area riders, as well as cross country mountain bike and hiking trails for enjoyment when the lift isn't running.

SnoBowl features a 99-chair, 700 vertical foot double chairlift, with a peak elevation of 7,000 feet above sea level. It also has a rope tow for beginning skiers and a multitude of other outdoor options for people who are more inclined to hiking, sledding or snow-shoeing.

Snobowl is in the process of developing their terrain parks, and will be offering several features that were donated by Mammoth Mountain and transported by Thiessen Team, and Mountain West Valve, who have been great contributors to Snobowl and the local area.

New Mexico

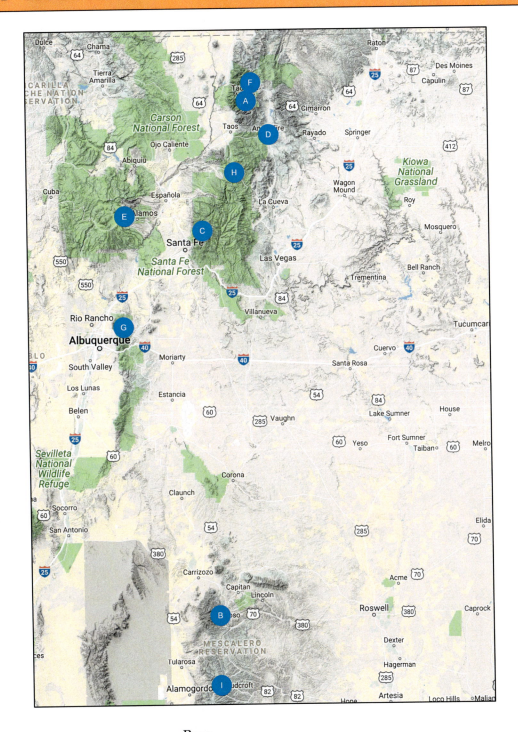

		Page
A.	Taos	186
B.	Ski Apache	188
C.	Ski Sante Fe	190
D.	Angel Fire	192
E.	Pajarito Mountain	194
F.	Red River	196
G.	Sandia Peak	198
H.	Sipapu	200
I.	Ski Cloudcroft	202

Taos

Established: 1955	Acres: 1294	Vertical: 3274'	Annual Snowfall: 300"

Nestled among the pristine peaks of northern New Mexico, Taos Ski Valley is undergoing a $300 million renaissance making it one of North America's premier vacation and adventure destinations. With over 300 inches of average annual snowfall, 300 days of sunshine and more than 1,200 skiable acres, Taos Ski Valley offers a relaxed, friendly atmosphere, breathtaking scenery and exhilarating terrain for every ability level for a spirited mountain experience unlike any other.

Taos Ski Valley is the only ski resort in the world to be B Corporation certified, meaning it has an unprecedented, verified commitment to environmental, social and economic justice. From its award-winning Taos Verde initiative, which is the cornerstone of its environmental efforts; its significant investment in the surrounding community for better economic prosperity for all; and its commitment to fair wages and a positive work environment for all employees, Taos Ski Valley is forging a new path of ethical business practices in the industry.

LODGING

The resort is maintaining its authentic charm while investing in new amenities both on-mountain and in the base area. The premier lodging experience is the new slopeside Blake Hotel at Taos Ski Valley, which opened in 2017. With its exquisite art collection and decor, sophisticated rooms, inspired spa, and attentive customer service, the Blake provides visitors to Taos Ski Valley with an unparalleled experience.

DINING

Dining options include 192 at The Blake, which offers an array of chef-driven cuisine and the Ski Valley's best wine list. The authentic Bavarian Lodge has the Valley's best slopeside deck and brings the European roots of the Ski Valley to life with its German fare and beer steins. Casual diners can select Stray Dog Cantina which offers a blend of Northern New Mexican flavors along town favorites including the Frito Pie.

LESSONS

Taos Ski Valley is home to the world-renowned Ernie Blake Snowsports School. Additionally, in 2017, Taos Ski Valley renovated in Children's Center, provided an enhanced and streamlined experience for families.

Taos is part of the Ikon Pass.

Ski Apache

Established: 1961	Acres: 750	Vertical: 1900'	Annual Snowfall: 185"

Ski Apache is the second largest ski area in New Mexico. It is known for its casual and welcoming atmosphere. Owned and operated by the Mescalero Apache Tribe, Ski Apache offers a mix of wide beginner slopes, tough bump runs along with nice cruising runs. A terrain park features jumps, tubes and rails. Ski Apache offers the best warm-weather powder skiing in the world with snowmaking on 33% of the mountain.

GONDOLA

Ski Apache is home to New Mexico's only eight-passenger gondola and has the most lift capacity of any resort in the state, allowing 5,600 guests to explore the mountain's runs and 1,900 foot vertical drop every hour. With more than 750 skiable acres, Ski Apache is the perfect location for skiers and snow boarders looking for a challenge or a relaxed day on the slopes.

Ski Apache has two base lodges, a mid-mountain restaurant and a mountain-top restaurant to satisfy all your dining needs.

ZIPTOUR (YEAR-ROUND)

Take your vacation above and beyond with the zip tour. This beautiful, stunning adventure rises over 11,000 feet. Parallel cables allow riders to glide down the mountain side-by-side. The adrenaline pumping, three part zip tour reaches over 8,900 feet in length, making it one of the longest in the world while offering a thrilling and unforgettable experience.

ADVENTURE CENTER

Families will appreciate the Adventure Center just for kids. The Adventure Center at Ski Apache offers a full day of fun activities for young skiers between the ages of 4 and 12 years old. Indoor and outdoor activities are available to ensure the children's safety and comfort. The experienced staff will keep children entertained and help them become the next generation of great skiers.

SKI AREA BOUNDARY

WHITE SANDS 4,100'

ELEV. 11,400'

ELEV. 11,500'

SIERRA BLANCA PEAK 12,005'

MOONSHINE GULCH

BURGER

TRENCH

AMBUSH
CHINO
MEADOWS
EAST MEADOWS
EAS TOF EAST
GERONIMO
CHAIR-LIFT LINE
SIERRA BLANCA TRAIL
OVER-WILD ONION
EAGLE
TRIPLE CHAIR #1
CHUTE
PEEBLES
LOWER MOONSHINE
LOWER SPRUCE

SCREAMING EAGLE
DEAD END
TERRIBLE
INCREDIBLE
MESCALERO
LOWER PEEBLES
UPPER PEEBLES
CALIENTE
ROY'S RUN
SBT
SBT
TRIPLE CHAIR #3
TRIPLE CHAIR LIFT LINE

SOUTH FACE
THE FACE
UPPER TRIPLE CHAIR #2
UPPER SPRUCE
UPPER SNOW PARK
LOWER SNOW PARK
SNOW PARK

TRIPLE CHAIR #6
APACHE BOWL
APACHE BOWL
APACHE BOWL
LINCOLN TRIPLE LIFT LINE
LINCOLN LIFT LINE
SMOKEY BEAR TRAIL
MIDWAY LINCOLN
APACHE ARROW GONDOLA
QUAD CHAIR #7
EASY STREET
ROPE TOW
GONDOLA

UPPER DEEP FREEZE
UPPER SPRUCE
LOWER DEEP FREEZE
CAPITAN HEAVY
COMPETITION PARK
CAPITAN QUAD-CHAIR #4
CAPITAN UTE
TOP
NOTCH
CATWALK
GAME TRAIL
RING TAIL

SUNNY SIDE
ELK RIDGE
BUCKHORN
TRIPLE CHAIR #5
BUNNY

OSCAR'S
ELK LIFT LINE
BEAR
BABY BEAR
CLIFF
BLU-RUN
BAMBI

ELK QUAD CHAIR #8
SKI AREA BOUNDARY

MAIN DAY LODGE

EASY STREET TERRAIN PARK

ELK LODGE

MOUNTAINTOP WARMING HUT

Ski Sante Fe

Established: 1946	Acres: 660	Vertical: 1725'	Annual Snowfall: 225"

With a base elevation of 10,350 feet, Ski Santa Fe is the launching point for a ski experience your family will never forget. Located just minutes from the heart of Santa Fe, a city rich in culture, fine arts and exceptional cuisine, this is one of the country's most diverse and unique ski destinations.

7 lifts take you up another 1,725 vertical feet to a summit elevation of 12,075 feet and some of the greatest skiing on 83 trails and breathtaking views in the Southwest.

Come Ski & Ride with us soon for a ski vacation that is sure to fulfill your family's desire for fun and adventure!

LESSONS & KIDS CENTER

Their certified snow sports school offers daily lessons for skiers & boarders including a Burton

Learn to Ride Center. Chipmunk Corner Children's Center is a fun safe environment with lessons, snowplay & day care.

DINING

The expanded & renovated La Casa Lodge features a full service ski & snowboard rental shop, La Casa Food Court & Baz Coffee Bar and the Ski Santa Fe Sports Shop.

TERRAIN PARK

Ski Santa Fe's Freestyle Terrain Park, "The Bone Yard," offers eight features for beginner to intermediate challenges. The Bone Yard is located on lower Gayway and will be open from 9:30am to 3:30pm daily.

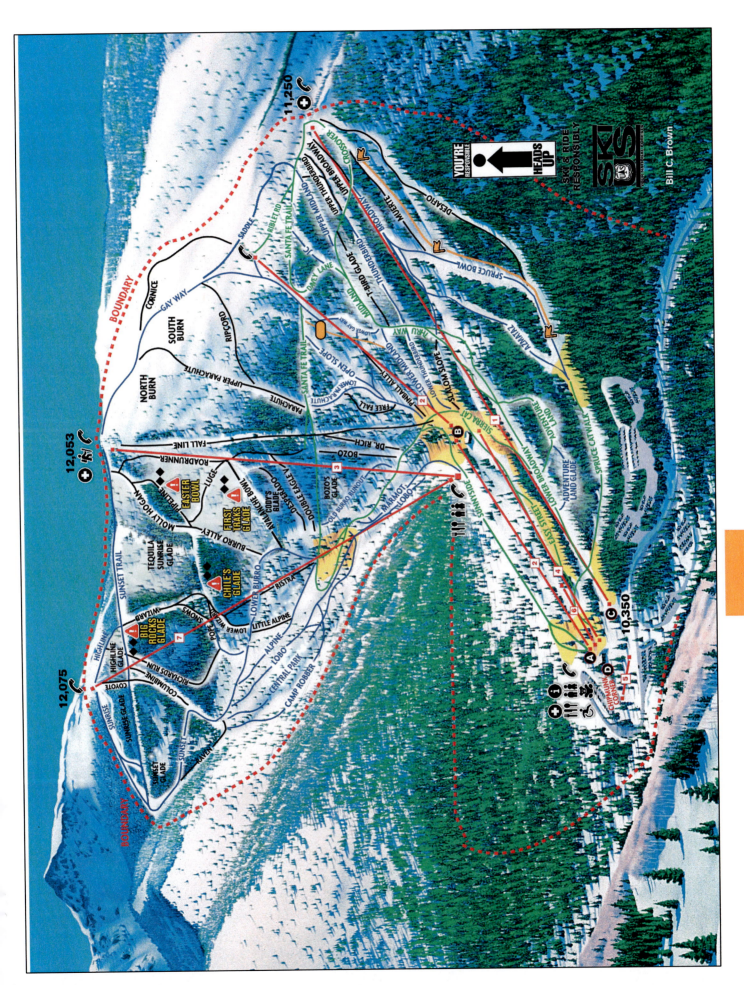

11,250

UPPER BROADWAY
UPPER BROADWAY
CROSSOVER
RIBLET RD.
SANTA FE TRAIL
DAVEY LANE
UPPER MIDLAND
UPPER THUNDERBIRD
T-BIRD GLADE
MIDLAND
MUERTE
BROADWAY
DESARIO
SPRUCE BOWL
ADMIRAL
SADDLE
CORNICE
GAY WAY
SOUTH BURN
RIPCORD
LOWER GAY WAY
OPEN SLOPE
SANTA FE TRAIL
LOWER MIDLAND
LOWER THUNDERBIRD
THRU WAY
SLALOM SLOPE
BOUNDARY
NORTH BURN
UPPER PARACHUTE
PARACHUTE
LOWER PARACHUTE
FREE FALL
PINBALL ALLEY
SIERRA CAT
LOWER BROADWAY
ADVENTURE LAND
ADVENTURE LAND GLADE
SPRUCE CAT WALK
12,053
FALL LINE
FALL LINE
DR. RICH
BOZO
ROADRUNNER
LUGE
BOZO'S GLADE
MARMOT
LOBO
EAST STREET
EASIER BOWL
DOUBLE EAGLE V
AVALANCHE BOWL
CODY'S GLADE
DESPERADO
SUNNYSIDE
PIPELINE
FIRST TRAK'S GLADE
BURRO ALLEY
LOST BURRO RUNOUT
LOWER BURRO
RISTRA
TEQUILA SUNRISE GLADE
MOLLY HOGAN
CHILE'S GLADE
LITTLE ALPINE
SUNSET TRAIL
LOWER WIZARD
POPE
SNOWS
WIZARD
BIG ROCKS GLADE
ALPINE
LOBO
10,350
CHIPMUNK CORNER
HIGHLINE
HIGHLINE GLADE
COLUMBINE
RICHARDS RUN
COYOTE
CENTRAL PARK
CAMP ROBBER
12,075
SUNRISE
SUNRISE GLADE
SUNSET GLADE
SUNSET
RAVEN
BOUNDARY

HEADS UP
YOU'RE RESPONSIBLE
SKI & RIDE RESPONSIBLY
SKI US

Bill C. Brown

Angel Fire

Established: 1966	Acres: 560	Vertical: 2077'	Annual Snowfall: 210"

Angel Fire Resort is located in the Southern Rockies of Northern New Mexico – a 3-hour drive from Albuquerque & an hour and a half from Santa Fe. Averaging 210 inches of snow annually, Angel Fire Resort is known as the most family-friendly resort in the southwest.

Angel Fire Resort has created the ideal learning environment for those new to skiing and snowboarding, as well as offering the best groomed black diamond slopes for the experts. Angel Fire Resort features 81 trails, 7 lifts, 3 terrain parks and a vertical drop of 2,077 feet. Liberation Park, one of Angel Fire's most recently redesigned areas creates New Mexico's first terrain park with dedicated chairlift access.

Offering a wide selection of lodging options, dining choices and off and on-mountain activities, Angel Fire Resort was named "America's Most Affordable Ski Town" by Realtor.com and ranked a Top 25 "Best Family Ski Resort in North America" by Dream Vacation Magazine.

The resort is located 8,600-feet above sea level in the Southern Rockies and has views of Wheeler Peak, the highest point in New Mexico.

In winter, visitors can enjoy:

- Skiing and Snowboarding
- Night Skiing and Snowboarding
- Tubing and Sledding
- Nordic Skiing
- Snow Blades
- Après style Lodging and Dining

MOUNTAIN TOURS

Angel Fire offers complimentary Mountain Tours beginning 11:00 a.m. Friday, Saturday, and Sundays. Tours last approximately 1 1/2 hours. Ski with experienced, local guides. Learn how Angel Fire Ski Resort was born. Wild West Legends Annie Oakley, Buffalo "Bill" Cody, Jesse James and more.

FIRST TRACKS

Guests can sign-up for the First Tracks program which allows you to load the lift at 8 a.m. – a whole hour before the mountain opens.

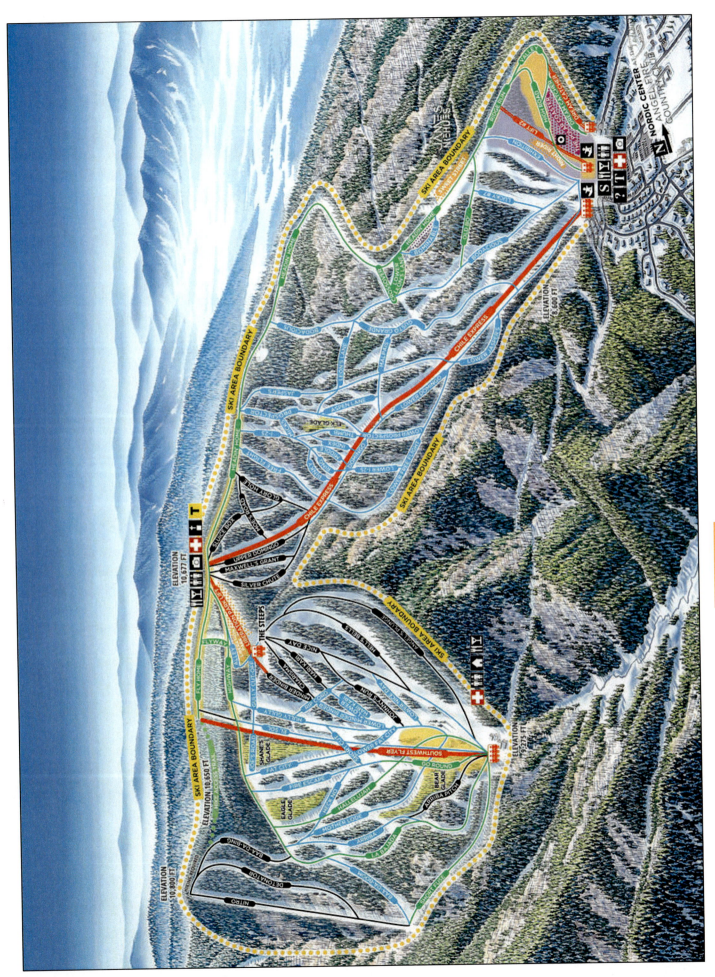

Pajarito Mountain

| Established: 1957 | Acres: 300 | Vertical: 1440' | Annual Snowfall: 163" |

Pajarito Mountain is located on the eastern edge of the Jemez Mountains in north central New Mexico, 5 miles west of Los Alamos. It comprises of approximately 750 acres of land, originally developed as a ski area in the late 1950's. Pajarito is open to the public for skiing and snowboarding from late November to end of March, weather permitting. The mountain has great views to the east over the Rio Grande Valley towards the Sangre de Cristo Mountains, and from the top, to the west over the Valle Grande.

Pajarito Mountain currently has over 300 acres of skiable terrain, with some excellent tree skiing. Pajarito is known for some of the best bump skiing in the state. With a summit elevation of 10,440 feet and a 1,440 foot vertical drop, Pajarito offers incredible fall-line skiing. For the advanced skiers, the mountain offers black-diamond plunges that will provide a good challenge. It's rarely crowded, and is noted for its lack of lift lines. Although there is no lodging at the mountain, there are several hotels and other lodging options available in Los Alamos and Santa Fe.

Pajarito features a ski and snowboard school, café, and rental facility and a large volunteer ski patrol. New this winter (2018), Pajarito is adding a new magic carpet to replace the old Mitey Mite, offering beginners an easier way to learn how to ski and ride.

National Geographic named Pajarito one of their "Best Secret Ski Towns". For years, Los Alamos was shrouded in secrecy during the Manhattan Project, and the town's ski area was also considered somewhat hush-hush. Now Pajarito is making this unique ski area more well known, while also preserving and celebrating the rich history behind it.

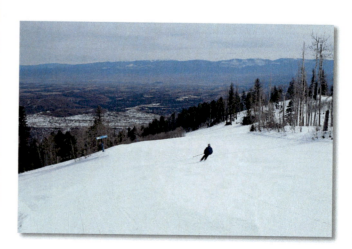

LEGEND

- 🟢 Easiest
- 🟦 More Difficult
- ◆ Most Difficult
- ◆◆ Experts Only
- Lift
- Ski Area Boundary
- Ski Patrol
- SLOW skiing zone
- Terrain Park
- Snow Sports School
- 🅟 Picnic Area

LIFTS

1. Spruce   (double)   907' vertical
2. Mother   (double)   1,180' vertical
3. Beginner   (double)   270' vertical
4. Aspen   (triple)   1,107' vertical
5. Townsight   (quad)   1,020' vertical
6. Magic Carpet (surface lift)

WWW.PAJARITO.SKI

ON THE MOUNTAIN

HOURS OF OPERATION:
9 am - 4 pm

Pajarito Mountain Cafe
in the Main Lodge
Full Menu, Open 8 am - 3 pm

Snow Sports School
*Learn Alpine skiing,
snowboarding or telemarking
with our experts.*

SKI PATROL:
(505) 662-1991

MAIN OFFICE:
(505) 662-5725

Rental & Tuning Shop
in the Main Lodge, Lower Level
*Get rental gear or a tune up on
your gear.*

Gifts & Accessories in the
Old Lodge
*Goggles, gloves, logowear and
more!*

PAJARITO MOUNTAIN

Red River

Established: 1959	Acres: 290	Vertical: 1600'	Annual Snowfall: 214"

In the old days people came to Red River in search of gold. Now people come to town in search of different treasures the beauty of nature, memorable times with family and friends, a slower pace, and four seasons of fantastic outdoor adventure. The Red River ski area is right in town so you can walk to the lifts.

Red River has something for everyone – long groomers for the intermediate skier, numerous tree runs for the more adventurous, a mellow learners area near the base, and terrain parks that crave air time. The slopes are always ready thanks to advanced snow-making technology.

TERRAIN PARKS

Red River Ski & Summer Area is home to three terrain parks for every riding ability. Looking to show off? Then head to Hollywood, their main park home to the largest jumps, jibs, and hits. Their dedicated park staff is serious about building the best parks in the state.

DINING & LODGING

Red River has a mountain-top restaurant (Ski Top) and a base lodge with several dining options. There are even Snow Coach Dinner Tours in which guests leave the base of the mountain from The Lift House après ski to be transported via heated coach up the mountain to the Tip Restaurant where they are served a 3-course meal at 10,350 feet.

Sandia Peak

Established: 1937	Acres: 200	Vertical: 1700'	Annual Snowfall: 100"

The Sandia Peak Ski Area is located in the Cibola National Forest, approximately 30 minutes from the Albuquerque Metro area and fully equipped for a fun day on the slopes. Here you find Sandia Peak's certified snow sports school, a complete rental shop, skiers' cafe, and the Sandia Peak Sports Shop. The ski area offers an excellent learning environment for the novice skier as well as some of the longest cruising terrain available in New Mexico. The ski area offers 30 trails serviced by four chairlifts and a children's mitey mite.

For the freestylers, there is the "Scrapyard" terrain park with rails and fun boxes when snowfall permits. Or for those that are looking for Nordic skiing, there is a vast network of 47 km of trails at the top of the mountain.

Sandia Peak's ski season is mid-December through mid-March. Open daily 9 am – 4 pm opening day through the New Year's Holiday, then Friday – Sunday for the remainder of the season.

SCENIC TRAMWAY

Skiers can also access the ski area from the western slope of the Sandias (city side) via the scenic tramway. A trip on the Sandia Peak Aerial Tramway transports you above deep canyons and breathtaking terrain a distance of 2.7 miles. See some of nature's more dramatic beauty unfold before you. At sunset the desert skies produce a spectacular array of color, and your vantage point from the observation deck atop 10,378 foot Sandia Peak in the Cibola National Forest affords an 11,000 square-mile panoramic view of the Rio Grande Valley and the Land of Enchantment.

DINING

At the top of the mountain, a new state of the art restaurant is under construction with a projected opening of 2019. The restaurant will feature spectacular views of the Rio Grande Valley to the west and views to the east of the ski area overlooking the Estancia Valley. At the base lodge is The Café which serves breakfast and lunch. On the other side of the mountain at the base of the tram is Sandiago's Grill at the Tram. Whether it's a family dinner or a carefully planned event, Sandiago's is a perfect place to enjoy great food with an incredible view.

SKI TRAILS

Elevation 10,378 ft.

Cibola National Forest
Four Seasons Visitors Center

Upper Tram Terminal
RESTAURANT

SERVICE ROAD

YOU'RE RESPONSIBLE

HEADS UP

SKI & RIDE RESPONSIBLY

ROB'S RUN
LA MADERA
FRED'S RUN
PROHIBITION
SANDIA
EXHIBITION
INHIBITION
ASPEN
DOUBLE EAGLE
DIABLO
CIBOLA
GO DROP INN
ASPEN BOWL
TO CHAIR 2
FOSTER MURPHY
ASPEN NARROWS
CIBOLA CUT OFF
CIBOLA
SHORT SWING
DIPSEY
DOUBLE EAGLE II
SKI CLUB
CIBOLA NATIONAL FOREST
SLALOM
LOWER SLALOM
SILVER ARROW
SLALOM
HUPS
BURN
RACE ARENA
CIBOLA
GREG S
CIBOLA RIDGE
LITTLE SUICIDE
CUBBY CORNER
SUICIDE
DOUBLE EAGLE II DAY LODGE
HUPS

SANDIA PEAK LEGEND

LIFTS INDICATED IN RED:

	LENGTH	RISE
1- Chairlift #1	7,500 ft.	1,700 ft.
2- Chairlift #2	4,000 ft.	1,000 ft.
3- Chairlift #3	7,500 ft.	1,700 ft.
4- Beginner Chairlift #4	1,500 ft.	300 ft.
5- Children's Mitey Mite	200 ft.	50 ft.
(Snow school participants only)		

Base Area Elevation: 8,678 ft.   Peak Elevation: 10,378 ft.
Vertical Rise: 1,700 ft.   Chairlift Service: 10,350 ft.

- 🟢 Easiest
- 🟦 More Difficult
- ◆ Most Difficult
- Slow Skiing Zone
- ⚠️ Caution
- ✚ Ski Patrol
- ⋯⋯ Ski Area Boundary
- 🔴 Terrain Park

- 📞 Emergency Phone
- 🚻 Restrooms
- 🍴 Food Service
- ❓ Information
- Ski Rental & Snowboard
- Snow Sports School
- 🎫 Ski Tickets
- ♿ Adaptive Ski Program

Please ski safely and in control at all times. Snowmaking activities are routinely in progress on slopes and trails. Snow maintenance vehicles and other over-snow vehicles such as snowmobiles may be present on any terrain at any time. Ski defensively. Look ahead and be prepared to stop.

YOUR RESPONSIBILITY CODE

Skiing can be enjoyed in many ways. At ski areas you may see people using alpine, snowboard, telemark, cross country or other specialized ski equipment, such as that used by disabled or other skiers. Regardless of how you decide to enjoy the slopes, always show courtesy to others and be aware that there are elements of risk in skiing that common sense and personal awareness can help reduce. Observe the code listed below and share with other skiers the responsibility for a great skiing experience.

1. Always stay in control, and be able to stop or avoid other people or objects.
2. People ahead of you have the right of way. It is your responsibility to avoid them.
3. You must not stop where you obstruct a trail, or are not visible from above.
4. Whenever starting downhill or merging into a trail, look uphill and yield to others.
5. Always use devices to help prevent runaway equipment.
6. Observe all posted signs and warnings. Keep off closed trails and out of closed areas.
7. Prior to using any lift, you must have the knowledge and ability to load, ride and unload safely.

Know the Code. It's Your Responsibility.

This is a partial list. Be safety conscious. Officially endorsed by: National Ski Areas Association, National Ski Patrol and Professional Ski Instructors of America.

SKI US YOUR NATIONAL FORESTS

LOCATION
Sandia Crest Scenic
Hwy 536, mile marker 6

TRAMWAY ROAD
PASEO DEL NORTE
Montano
MONTGOMERY
Downtown
CENTRAL AVE.
SUNPORT BLVD.
I-25
I-40
Sandia Peak Tramway Base Terminal
Sandia Peak Ski Area
Sandia Mountains
Hwy 536
Cedar Crest
Tijeras
TRAMWAY BLVD.

Sipapu

Established: 1952	Acres: 200	Vertical: 1055'	Annual Snowfall: 190"

Home to the longest ski season in New Mexico, Sipapu Ski and Summer Resort offers more than 43 trails, and family fun for all ability levels. From green and blue groomed cruisers to the steeps and powder stashes found above Lift 1, this mountain has something for everyone. What's more is that you can access it all without waiting in a lift line nearly all season long.

Sipapu's philosophy is to be the most family-friendly resort in the Rockies, and guests have been skiing the mountain since 1952. The resort is small enough so that kids won't get lost, and the laid-back style is perfect for families looking to enjoy a fun and affordable ski vacation.

Sipapu's newly renovated base lodge opens this winter with a new rental shop, ticket office, gathering space and more. Sipapu offers slopeside lodging, plus new cabins this season, and features the Riverside Café in the day lodge.

TERRAIN PARKS

Sipapu has four distinct terrain parks, including the only organic terrain parks in the state. Playground and Flight School are built entirely from resources found on the mountain and in the surrounding Sangre de Cristo Mountains.

Sipapu's terrain parks offer features for all skill levels. Advanced skiers and riders will find over a dozen features - including a triple combo on Don Diego, Sipapu's biggest terrain park. Pedro's Park offers beginner features where you can learn your first jump or take your tricks to the next level. Don't miss C-Wall on Playground, their 30-foot wall ride. And Flight School is all about airtime.

FREE LESSONS FOR FIRST TIMERS

Sipapu provides the perfect place to learn to ski, snowboard and more. For first-time skiers and snowboarders (ages 7 and older), receive up to three FREE lessons with the purchase of one full-day, full-price lift ticket. Sipapu's ski and ride instructors teach the fundamentals of skiing and snowboarding in a fun learning environment.

Sipapu is located 20 miles southeast of Taos, and two hours north of Albuquerque.

Ski Cloudcroft

Established: 1963	Acres: 74	Vertical: 700'	Annual Snowfall: 70"

Ski Cloudcroft is a small family owned and operated ski resort originally opening in 1963. It is a small family and beginner oriented resort focused on creating a positive introduction to the sport for those that are new to it. Cloudcroft is the Southern most ski resort in New Mexico, and second only to Mount Lemmon in Tucson. Being this far south, Mother Nature is often a bit unpredictable. The snowmaking system was rebuilt in 2016 with a series of SMI Super Polecats.

The mountain itself is serviced by one double chairlift, and in the bottom area there is a surface lift for the beginner slope, and a handle tow for the tubing area.

The tubing run is the longest in New Mexico, and which will be doubling in size in 2018.

The mountain is small with 705' of vertical, and roughly 33% beginner, 33% intermediate, and 33% advanced runs. Cloudcroft offers one of the cheapest lift tickets in the country, and when Mother Nature does cooperate, the mountain is a lot of fun! You can ski more vertical feet here in a day than you can most of the bigger resorts in New Mexico due to the lift speed and no lift lines.

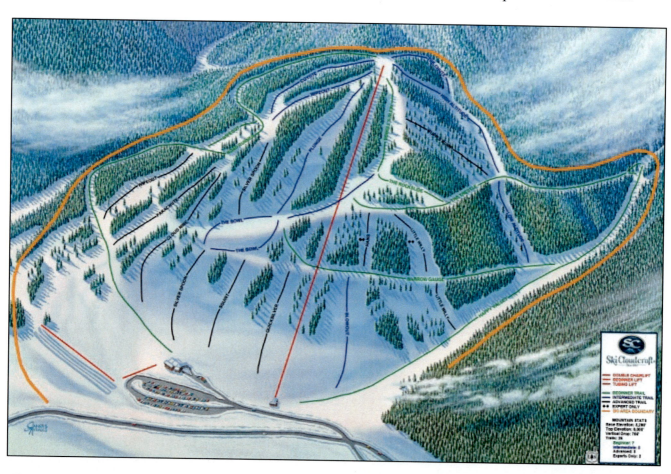

Oregon

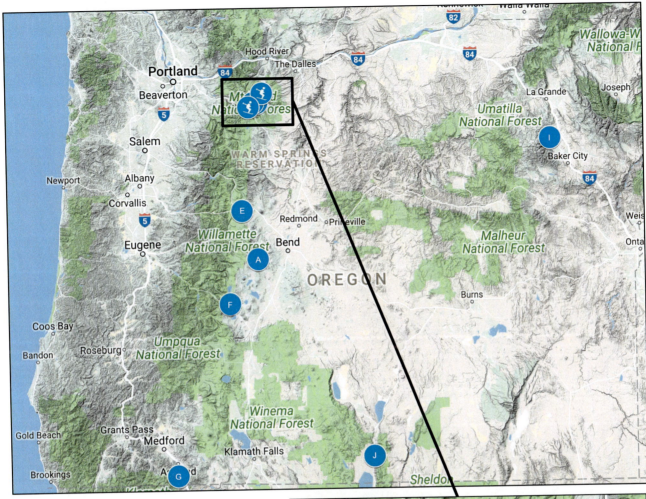

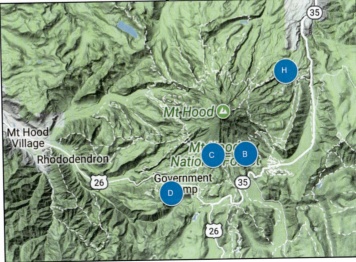

		Page
A.	Mt. Bachelor	204
B.	Mt. Hood Meadows	206
C.	Timberline	208
D.	Mt. Hood Skibowl	210
E.	Hoodoo	212
F.	Willamette Pass	214
G.	Mt. Ashland	216
H.	Cooper Spur	218
I.	Anthony Lakes	219
J.	Warner Canyon Ski Area	220

Mt. Bachelor

Established: 1958	Acres: 4318	Vertical: 3365'	Annual Snowfall: 462"

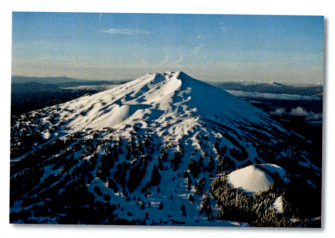

With over 4,300 acres of lift-accessible terrain, you won't want to pass up a trip to the ski resort with the highest skiable elevation in all of Oregon and Washington. Mt. Bachelor, located on the eastern flanks of Oregon's Central Cascades, is known for its light, dry snow, diverse terrain, family-friendliness and long seasons.

Bill Healy founded Mt. Bachelor Ski Area December 19, 1958 with a rope tow and a single lift. Mt. Bachelor has since grown to be one of the largest ski resorts in the U.S. The resort boasts a wide variety of terrain. Guests can ski or ride 360 degrees off the summit, hike the adjoining cinder cone for a thrilling run down, or, ski the trees to find that great cache of powder!

Not only is Mt. Bachelor a great place for expert skiers and riders to get that burn, it is also a fantastic place to learn a snow sport or take the family for an exciting day out. Carrousel, their free beginners lift, offers an easy ride up and gentle slope down. There are also numerous lesson packages to choose from.

You won't find any slopeside lodging, fancy base villages, or condo developments. And Mt. Bachelor is proud of that. The focus is on pure enjoyment of the mountain, with no distractions

SLED DOG RIDES

Add a wild, magical experience to your Mt. Bachelor get-away with a ride behind a real dog sled team! Stay snug and warm in the sled while the team, along with a professional musher, takes you on an exciting adventure.

SNOWBLAST TUBING

Located between the Mountain Gateway building and the bottom of Red Chair, experience the snow like never before! Snowblast Tubing Park, where the rubber meets the snow, is full of fun with an 800 foot ride full of rollers. Plus, surface lifts pull you up the slope comfortably and quickly.

GETTING THERE

Conveniently located just 22 miles west of Bend, Mt. Bachelor's season is one of the longest in the Northwest, usually starting in November by Thanksgiving and lasting well into May. Surrounded by the tall hemlocks and pines of the Deschutes National Forest and breathtaking views of the Three Sisters and other Cascade peaks, you are sure to enjoy that authentic Oregon experience you seek at Mt. Bachelor!

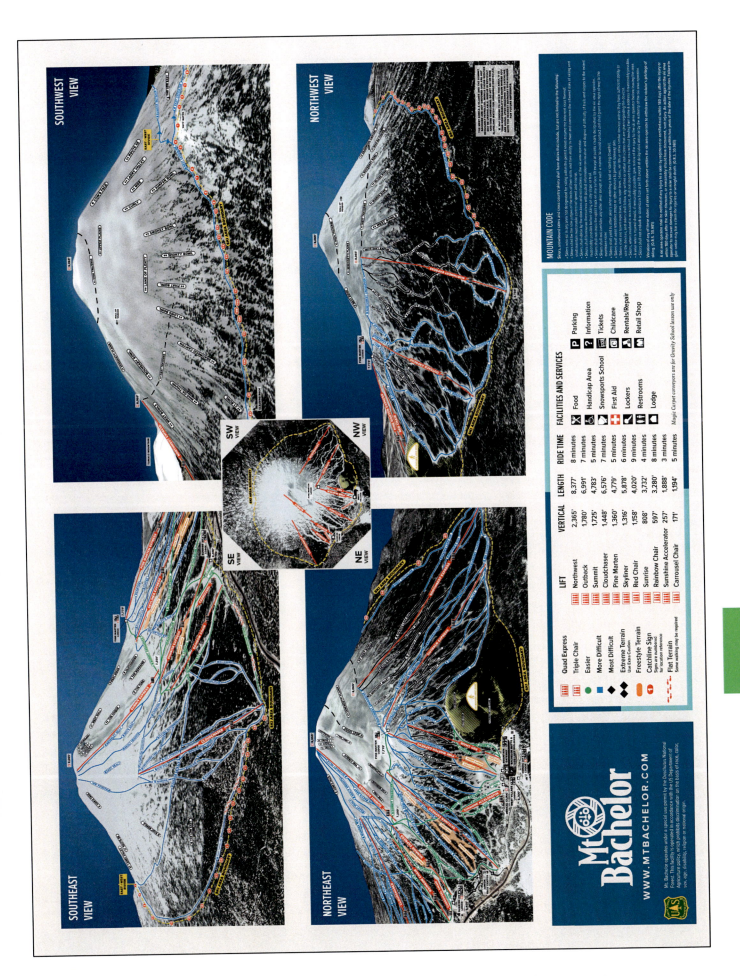

SOUTHWEST VIEW

NORTHWEST VIEW

SOUTHEAST VIEW

NORTHEAST VIEW

SW VIEW

NW VIEW

SE VIEW

NE VIEW

Mt Bachelor

WWW.MTBACHELOR.COM

LIFT		VERTICAL	LENGTH	RIDE TIME
Northwest		2,365'	8,377'	8 minutes
Outback		1,780'	6,991'	7 minutes
Summit		1,725'	4,783'	5 minutes
Cloudchaser		1,448'	6,576'	7 minutes
Pine Marten		1,360'	4,779'	5 minutes
Skyliner		1,316'	5,878'	6 minutes
Red Chair		1,158'	4,020'	9 minutes
Sunrise		808'	3,732'	4 minutes
Rainbow Chair		597'	3,280'	8 minutes
Sunshine Accelerator		257'	1,888'	3 minutes
Carrousel Chair		171'	1,194'	5 minutes

Magic Carpet conveyors are for Gravity School lesson use only

Quad Express
Triple Chair
Easier
More Difficult
Most Difficult
Extreme Terrain Use Extra Caution
Freestyle Terrain
Catchline Sign Signs are numbered for location reference
Flat Terrain Some walking may be required

FACILITIES AND SERVICES

Food
Handicap Area
Snowsports School
First Aid
Lockers
Restrooms
Lodge

Parking
Information
Tickets
Childcare
Rentals/Repair
Retail Shop

MOUNTAIN CODE

Mount Hood Meadows

| Established: 1968 | Acres: 2150 | Vertical: 2777' | Annual Snowfall: 430" |

Mt. Hood Meadows offers some of the most spectacular skiing and snowboarding in the Northwest! The resort is close to Portland - just 90 minutes away - but delivers a big mountain experience you'd expect to travel much farther to enjoy. Mt. Hood Meadows Ski Resort sprawls across Mt. Hood's southeast flank, the sunny, wind-protected side of Mt. Hood. Meadows' playful terrain welcomes and challenges all levels of skiers and snowboarders. The entire staff is committed to providing you with a truly memorable and unique experience that is Mt. Hood Meadows.

From the steeps of the front side bowls to the gentle slopes of their beginner runs, Mt. Hood Meadows terrain is known for its diversity and playfulness. Voted by Oregonians for having the best cruising intermediate terrain in the state, Meadows offers more than 2,150 acres of pure enjoyment. Rising to its highest lift-served elevation of 7,300 feet, you'll feel like you're on the top of the world as you take in a panoramic view to the east and south.

Legendary Heather Canyon is like its own separate ski area - endlessly steep pitches of powder into the spectacular Canyon. There's an additional 1,700 vertical feet for hikers who want to drop into the double blacks of Super Bowl above Heather, bringing the total vertical available in just one run to almost 4,500 feet.

Access gates (experts only) into Private Reserve and S&R Cliffs provide extremely challenging, pulse-pounding gladed trails with cliff outcroppings. Those searching for the more open bowls of Elk and Yoda will be rewarded with epic runs and an experience you'll long remember and brag about. With 11 lifts, including five high-speed quads, the entire 2,150 acres of skiable terrain is easily accessed.

This is a big mountain experience, with enough acreage to keep you busy for days and enough character so you will respect and remember your time on these trails. "It's so much bigger than what I thought," is a common reaction of those hitting the slopes for the first time, knowing that they'll need to come back several times before they fully experience all Meadows has to offer.

NIGHT SKIING

Night skiing is offered from 3 to 9 PM Wednesday through Sunday for Meadows After Dark when conditions allow (typically in early to mid December through early March).

The Meadows has a main day lodge that includes several restaurants, the Ski & Snowboard School, the Rental Center, two retail shops and a Daycare Facility; and a newly remodeled skier services lodge with a restaurant, day lockers and ticket sales.

MT. HOOD MEADOWS

50 1968 – 2018

Your mountain home

MOUNTAIN STATISTICS

Top Cascade Express	7,305 Ft.
Bottom Hood River Express	4,523 Ft.
Vertical Rise	2,777 Ft.
Base Lodge Elevation	5,306 Ft.
Superpipe Skiing	1,700 Vert. Ft.
Longest Run	2,150
Skiable Acres	2,150
Night Runs	140
Annual Snowfall	430"

LIFT STATISTICS

LIFT	ELEVATION	VERTICAL RISE
Blue	5,378-6,555	1,177 Ft.
Buttercup	5,356-5,514	158 Ft.
Cascade Express	5,914-7,305	1,391 Ft.
Daisy	5,366-6,040	675 Ft.
Easy Rider	5,434-5,866	432 Ft.
Heather	5,255-5,958	705 Ft.
Hood River Express	4,528-5,928	1,400 Ft.
Mt. Hood Express	5,366-6,546	1,178 Ft.
Shooting Star Express	5,606-6,546	940 Ft.
Stadium Express	5,889-5,949	58 Ft.
Vista Express	5,450-6,571	1,121 Ft.

WE USE RFID GATES!

HEATHER CANYON, CLARK CANYON & PRIVATE RESERVE

◆◆ Heather Canyon, Clark Canyon & Private Reserve

Gate Access Only ◆◆

Access to Heather Canyon, Clark Canyon and Private Reserve is through access gates only. These areas are not patrolled on a regular basis and avalanche danger exists at all times. You may be entering tightly wooded and cliffed terrain. Beware of waterfalls, creek holes and other unmarked obstacles. Names shown are for reference only and are not designated trails or runs.

Skiing/Riding with a partner and carrying a beacon, probe and shovel are highly recommended. Closure violators will lose lift privileges and may be criminally trespassed.

Avalanche Mitigation Advisory
Mt. Hood Meadows uses several methods for avalanche reduction including remote delivery systems. Mitigation work may be in progress at any time.
Stay out of closed areas!

Meadows Parks

The Zoo	S
Fireweed	M/D
Superpipe	M/D
Minipipe	M/D
Shipyard	S/M/L
Barked Slalom	S/D
Forest Park	S
Vista Park	M/D

PARK SMART

Start Small — Work your way up. Build your skills.
Make a Plan — Every feature. Every time.
Always Look — Before you drop.
Respect — The features and other users.
Take it Easy — Know your limits. Land on your feet.

TRAIL MAP LEGEND

- Easier
- More Difficult
- Most Difficult
- Extremely Difficult
- Freestyle Terrain
- Night Runs
- Area Boundary
- Out of Bounds
- Access Gates
- Gated Access Boundary

- High Speed Quad
- Double Chair Lift
- Dining
- Restrooms
- First Aid Station
- Slow Zones
- Shuttle Pickup
- Recycling & Garbage
- Doggie Park

Timberline

| Established: 1937 | Acres: 1415 | Vertical: 3690' | Annual Snowfall: 550" |

Timberline offers the most vertical feet of skiing in the Pacific Northwest and the longest ski season in North America (all year round). It also has some of the country's most dependable snow, beautiful scenery, and progressive freestyle terrain. Seven chairlifts serve over 1,415 skiable acres and 41 trails for all ability levels. Snowcat skiing is offered high up on the mountain when conditions permit.

SUMMER SKIING

Timberline is home to the most energetic summer snow scene on the planet. Everyone from Olympic athletes to up-and-coming racers to freestyle enthusiasts descend on the Palmer Snowfield between the months of June and September. Much of the terrain is reserved by various camps and organizations, but they always maintain open areas to the public so everyone can enjoy summertime turns on the South slopes of Mt. Hood. Only the Palmer Snowfield is available in the summer, but with 1,500+ ft of vertical, that should be plenty. The historic Magic Mile lift brings skiers up to the Palmer lift, which is often only open for summer skiing. The Magic Mile was the 2nd lift in North America when it opened in 1939, ushering in the golden age of skiing on Mt. Hood.

TIMBERLINE LODGE

Constructed in 1937, Timberline Lodge stands on the south slope of Mt. Hood at an elevation of 6,000 feet above sea level. This beautiful 55,000 square-foot National Historic Landmark is still being used for its original intent – a magnificent ski lodge and mountain retreat for everyone to enjoy.

The lodge is an architectural dream with all of its craftsman details, artwork, and truly regional style known as Cascadian. There are even guided U.S. Forest Service tours of the lodge.

Besides providing slope-side lodging, Timberline Lodge also houses six restaurants, a fitness room, sauna, and outdoor hot tub by the pool.

Mt. Hood Skibowl

| Established: 1937 | Acres: 960 | Vertical: 1500' | Annual Snowfall: 300" |

When the snow starts to fall on Mt. Hood, snow enthusiasts eagerly await news of opening day at Skibowl, America's Largest Night Ski Area and the closest ski resort to Portland, Oregon. Skibowl offers the best skiing in Oregon for many reasons.

Skibowl provides snow riders with some of the best terrain in the Mt. Hood National Forest, featuring 34 fully lit runs, 65 runs total and a vertical drop of 1,500 feet. With the most Black Diamond runs of any resort in the state and two fully lit terrain parks, Skibowl draws accomplished snow riders as well as beginners and intermediate riders out for a great time.

NIGHT SKIING

Not only is Mt Hood Skibowl the best night skiing in Oregon, they also have the largest night skiing terrain in the country. All lifts, including the Lower Bowl, Upper Bowl, Multorpor and Cascade lifts have lighting, providing 34 lit runs for you to enjoy.

Mt Hood Skibowl is proud to provide one of the longest ski days. Watch the sun set on the beautiful Mount Hood while you get in a few more runs long after nearly all the other mountains close (3 pm to 10 or 11 pm). Liftopia even called Mt Hood Skibowl one of the "Top 5 Night Skiing Spots" in America.

Be sure to grab a large hot chocolate at Starlight Cafe or Multorpor Cafe or enjoy a winter warmer at the Beer Stube or 70 Meters Bar & Grill at the base of the mountain, or the historic Mid-Mountain Warming Hut.

SNOW TUBING

The Snow Tube and Adventure Park at Skibowl East is fun for all ages! Skibowl offers the only conveyor tube lifts on Mt. Hood. The fun begins as you ride one of two conveyors to the top of the main hill. Then it's a heart pounding ride to the bottom in a specially designed tube. Be sure to check out the world's only Cosmic Tubing®!

Hoodoo

| Established: 1938 | Acres: 806 | Vertical: 1035' | Annual Snowfall: 450" |

Hoodoo is a family-friendly ski area that is convenient to both sides of the Cascade Range and features more than 800 acres of terrain, 32 runs, five lifts, miles of cross country and snow shoe trails and The Autobahn, one of the largest tubing parks in the West. The ski area also offers half-hour lessons teaching the basics of snow biking, an extreme sport in which participants ride small bikes with seats, handlebars and small skis instead of wheels.

Hoodoo has a 60,000-square-foot lodge which houses a ski school, equipment rentals and a full-service restaurant on the first-level where guests can get breakfast, hot and cold menu items, snacks and hot chocolate to warm up with.

NIGHT SKIING

Central Oregon's only night skiing destination, Hoodoo lets you ski under the stars (and the lights) on Fridays and Saturdays until 9 pm.

TUBING

For a different type of excitement, try out the Autobahn tubing park. Seven lanes of tubing complete with a rope tow to bring up the tubes. Or there is a Snow Bunny Sledding Hill for only $5/day but bring your own sled.

RESPONSIBILITY CODE

1. ALWAYS STAY IN CONTROL, AND BE ABLE TO STOP OR AVOID OTHER PEOPLE OR OBJECTS.

2. PEOPLE AHEAD OF YOU HAVE THE RIGHT OF WAY. IT IS YOUR RESPONSIBILITY TO AVOID THEM.

3. YOU MUST NOT STOP WHERE YOU OBSTRUCT A TRAIL, OR ARE NOT VISIBLE FROM ABOVE.

4. WHENEVER STARTING DOWNHILL OR MERGING INTO A TRAIL, LOOK UPHILL AND YIELD TO OTHERS.

5. ALWAYS USE DEVICES TO HELP PREVENT RUNAWAY EQUIPMENT.

6. OBSERVE ALL POSTED SIGNS AND WARNINGS. KEEP OFF CLOSED TRAILS AND OUT OF CLOSED AREAS.

7. PRIOR TO USING ANY LIFT, YOU MUST HAVE THE KNOWLEDGE AND ABILITY TO LOAD, RIDE AND UNLOAD SAFELY.

SERVICES
- Food
- Restrooms
- P Parking
- Ski School
- Tubing Park
- Tickets
- R Rental Shop
- Ski Patrol
- Night Skiing

CHAIR LIFTS
- Quad Chairlift
- Triple Chairlift
- Double Chairlift
- Tube Lift

TRAIL MARKINGS
- Beginner
- Intermediate
- Expert
- Freestyle Terrain
- Patrolled Ski Area Boundary
- X.C Ski Trail

Trails: Leap Of Faith, Hodag's Horn, Dante's Vision, Hodag Chair, Impossible Dream, Rabbit Run, Hodag's Tail, Over Easy, Tiny's Tear, Mambo, Dive, Impossible Dream, Over Easy, Big Dipper, Frank's Flight, Blue Valley, Three Creeks, Hesitation, Over Easy, Red Road, Todd's Trees, Schuss Chute, Manzanita Chair, Good Ol' Big Wall, Big Dipper, Grandstand, Crater, Face, Midway, Big Green Machine, Powder Valley 3, Headwall, Easy Rider, Sled Hill, Gripper, Angel's Flight, Slalom Course, Doobie's Descent, Ed Chair, Red Valley, Midway, Powder Valley 2, Powder Valley 1, Home Run, Art's Alley

voodoo

Willamette Pass

| Established: 1941 | Acres: 555 | Vertical: 1562' | Annual Snowfall: 430" |

Willamette Pass is a hidden gem of Oregon, situated south between Eugene and Bend. It is a local hill with 555 acres of terrain for all levels, but mostly intermediate to advanced skiers. It has great tree skiing and the steepest developed run in the Pacific Northwest (RTS, 52° in places). The area referred to by locals as SDN (Steep Deep and Narrow) can hold its powder after the rest of the mountain has been tracked out because it is protected from sun exposure.

Beginners and intermediate skiers love the gentle, groomed terrain available from the Sleepy Hollow and Twilight lifts, while advanced and expert skiers appreciate the challenging steeps and high-speed cruisers available from the Eagle Peak and Peak 2 lifts. Regardless of your ability level, nearly every run boasts spectacular scenery. On a clear day you can see Waldo, Crescent, and Odell Lakes, and many Cascade peaks.

Being a local hill, the base day lodge is the hub of activity. It houses the restaurant, lounge, retail shop, ticket sales, ski, snowboard, Nordic and snowshoe rentals, and the ski and snowboard school.

TERRAIN PARK

Whether you're looking to have a little fun or just wanting to improve on your skills, Willamette Pass Resort features two terrain parks when conditions permit. The primary park is located on By George with a secondary park located on Timburr Glades. Both parks feature a variety of terrain park features to help improve your skills, including boxes, rails rollers and jumps.

OTHER SNOW ACTIVITIES

Try snowshoeing or cross-country skiing at Willamette Pass, while trekking along 20 kilometers of groomed trails in the Willamette National Forest. Or just head off into the more than 300 acres of ungroomed terrain within the ski area boundary for a backwoods experience. During scheduled operations the trails are groomed to offer great variety for all abilities.

Photos courtesy of Larry Turner

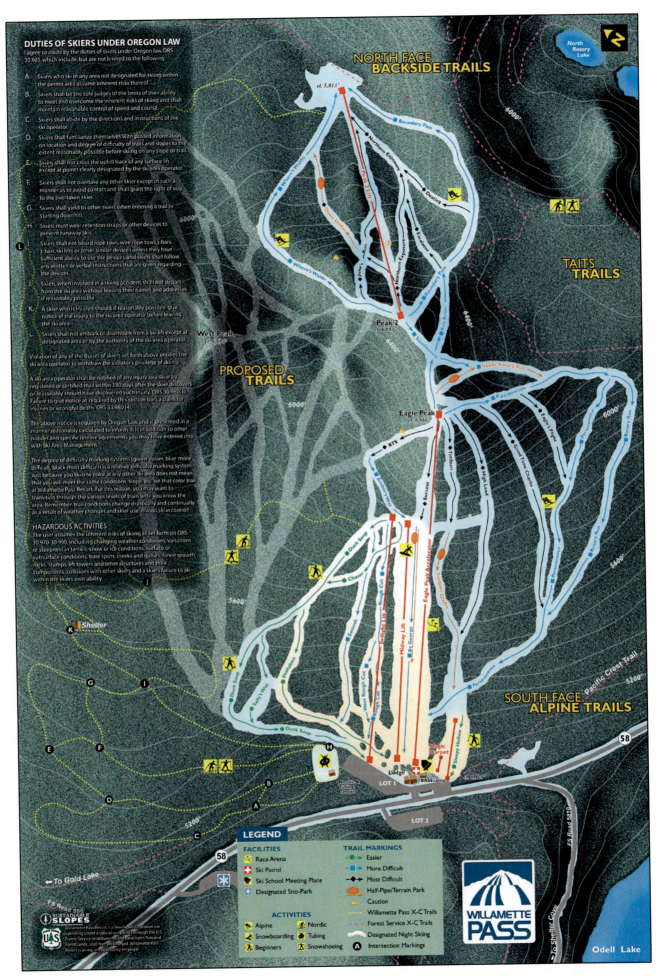

Mt. Ashland

Established: 1964	Acres: 220	Vertical: 1150'	Annual Snowfall: 256"

With a peak elevation of 7,533', Mt. Ashland ski area is situated at the highest point in the Siskiyou Mountain range, just minutes from downtown Ashland and Medford. Their terrain favors intermediate to advanced skiers and riders. However, beginners are also welcome and have their own learning area, low cost rentals and instruction programs.

Four chair lifts provide access to twenty-three ski trails plus open bowl skiing.

For the more adventurous, there are two terrain parks that have features for all levels of riders. All freestylers welcome!

At the base is a Tudor-style mountain lodge provides that has a food service, bar/lounge, ski school, retail and ticket sales. Ski and snowboard rentals are also available.

The ski area is a community-focused ski area operated by a nonprofit organization dedicated to providing an outstanding alpine recreation experience for people of all ages and skill levels. As an asset to the community, they remain true to their core values: it is a local ski hill with great snow, exciting terrain, providing access to a diverse alpine environment and a fun family atmosphere.

NIGHT SKIING

Twilight Skiing is from 4 to 9 p.m. every Thursday and Friday evening in January, February, and the first two weeks in March. Twilight skiing is a great way to experience Mt. Ashland. (40 acres are lit)

FREE SHUTTLE BUS

The 40-passenger Mt. Ashland Ski Hopper bus is scheduled to run when most people visit Mt. Ashland. Ride in style to and from the ski area on the Hopper bus, featuring reclining seats and three video screens. And it's free!

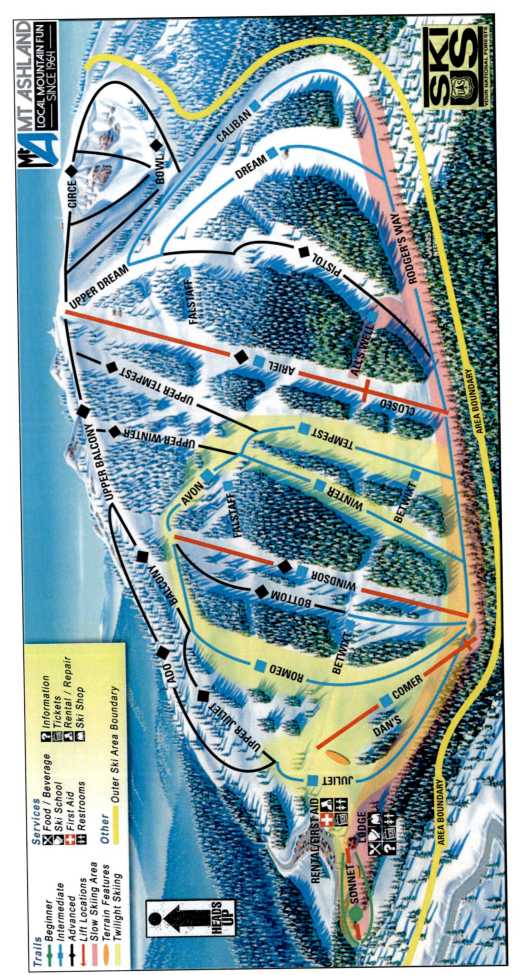

MT ASHLAND
LOCAL MOUNTAIN FUN
— SINCE 1964 —

SKI US

YOUR NATIONAL FORESTS

CALIBAN

DREAM

BOWL

CIRCE

UPPER DREAM

RODGER'S WAY

PISTOL

FALSTAFF

UPPER TEMPEST

ARIEL

ALL'S WELL

CLOSED

UPPER BALCONY

UPPER WINTER

TEMPEST

AVON

FALSTAFF

WINTER

BETWIXT

BALCONY

WINDSOR

BOTTOM

ADO

ROMEO

BETWIXT

UPPER JULIET

COMER

DAN'S

JULIET

RENTAL/FIRST AID

LODGE

SONNET

AREA BOUNDARY

AREA BOUNDARY

HEAD'S UP

Trails
- Beginner
- Intermediate
- Advanced
- Lift Locations
- Slow Skiing Area
- Terrain Features
- Twilight Skiing

Services
- Food / Beverage
- Ski School
- First Aid
- Restrooms
- Information
- Tickets
- Rental / Repair
- Ski Shop

Other
- Outer Ski Area Boundary

Cooper Spur

Established: 1953	Acres: 50	Vertical: 350'	Annual Snowfall: 100"

The Ski Area at Cooper Spur Mountain Resort offers skiing and snowboarding, instruction, cross country skiing and a tubing center. The ski area features a double chair lift and a rope tow servicing ten ski runs. As one of the oldest and longest continuously operating ski areas in Oregon, Cooper Spur provides the enchantment that comes from this charming small ski area.

Cooper Spur is perfect for families with little ones who just want to play in the snow. Snow tubing and a children's play area, as well as instruction designed to get kids up and sliding on skis and snowboards make for a great day on the mountain. Cooper Spur is a full service ski area, with equipment rentals, a ski and snowboard school, beginner rope tow and a double chairlift. The ten runs of fun provide variety, all within the watchful eye of mom and dad. So let 'em loose and have some fun!

The combination of affordable pricing, fun snow play activities, beginner to intermediate level terrain, and the manageable size of the ski area presents an ideal outing for families or groups.

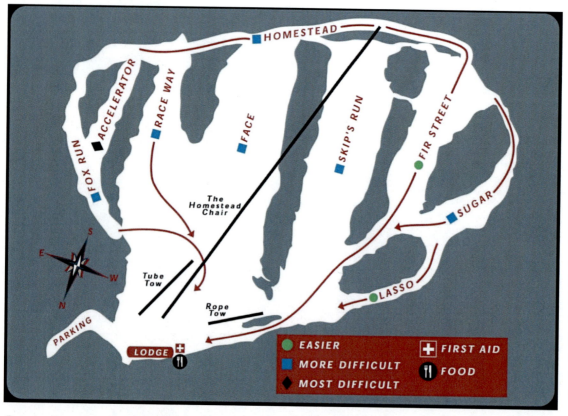

The charming alpine lodge provides a place to warm up and recharge, serving guests a delicious selection of great tasting food. The covered outdoor deck allows guests to soak up the sunshine, enjoy picnic lunches, and keep track of the rest of their party with an expansive view of almost the entire ski area.

Cooper Spur Mt. Resort offers cabins, condos and lodge hotel rooms, and a Nordic Center at the property.

Anthony Lakes

Established: 1963	Acres: 1100	Vertical: 900'	Annual Snowfall: 300"

Anthony Lakes is an incredible one lift, non-profit ski area. The Rock Garden Lift takes you to the top of the ridge. The in-bounds terrain serves up a variety of black diamonds, cliffs and some great tree skiing. Just outside of the ski area is some of the best sidecountry terrain in Oregon. With the couloir's, chutes and bowls right next to the ski area, it almost looks like an Oregon version of the Tetons.

Anthony Lakes offers one of the least expensive lift tickets. And if that wasn't enough, Thursdays are ½ price.

Anthony Lakes has the highest base elevation in Oregon at 7,100 ft, so while it could be raining elsewhere, it most certainly will be snowing here.

Warner Canyon Ski Area

Established: 1938	Acres: 240	Vertical: 780'	Annual Snowfall: 150"

The Warner Canyon Ski Area is one of the oldest ski areas in Oregon and offers 20 trails from a triple-seat lift. It's an amazing amount of varied terrain from one lift.

Their rustic, old-fashioned ski lodge provides all the necessary amenities with a small-town, family-friendly style. The wood stove provides a toasty warming area to lounge on couches and warm up in between powder runs. There are plenty of picnic tables for families or large groups to eat and to socialize. Large windows and a new deck dominate the southern side of the building adding lots of light and warm sunshine to bask in. The lodge has a full-service snack bar and grill. Lodging and ski rentals are available in the town of Lakeview, six miles away. Warner also offers free ski/snowboard lessons to children on Saturday mornings (Jan-Feb).

Only open on weekends, 9 am to 4 pm – check http://warnercanyon.org/ to see which holidays are also open.

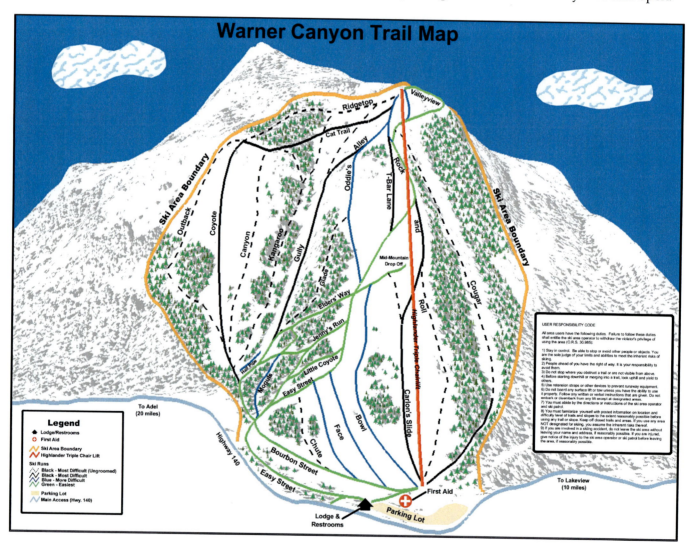

Utah

		Page
A.	Powder Mountain	222
B.	Park City	224
C.	Snowbasin	226
D.	Snowbird	228
E.	Alta	230
F.	Deer Valley	232
G.	Solitude	234
H.	Brighton	236
I.	Beaver Mountain	238
J.	Brian Head Resort	240
K.	Eagle Point	242
L.	Sundance	244
M.	Cherry Peak	246
N.	Nordic Valley	248

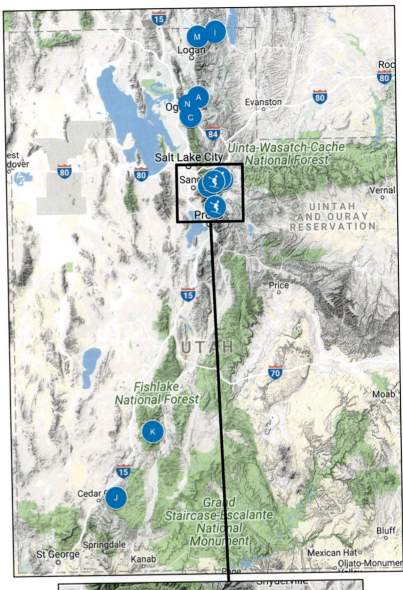

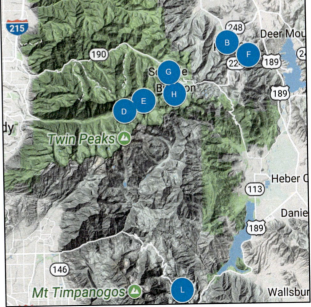

Powder Mountain

| Established: 1972 | Acres: 8464 | Vertical: 2205' | Annual Snowfall: 500" |

Powder Mountain is all about snow, and lots of it – 8,464 acres of skiable terrain. That is more than any other resort in the United States. Powder Mountain can boast of the lowest skier density of any major ski resort because they are one of the only resorts in the world to cap season passes (3,000) and day passes (1,500 daily), which translates to a minimum of 2 acres per skier. All this in just under an hour from Salt Lake City airport.

With so much acreage, it is wise to start with a complimentary mountain tour in which knowledgeable hosts introduce you to the mountain. Beginning at 10 am and 1 pm daily. Rendezvous outside the Mountain Adventure Yurt.

SNOWCAT TOURS

Powder Mountain offers two types of snowcat tours: The Powder Expedition which takes 12 guests with two guides out to untracked bowls, glades and nicely spaced treed terrain as far as the eye can see.

The other tour is a Sunset Expedition in which ten guests are taken up to see unobstructed views of the

Ogden Valley, Wasatch Mountains and beyond to the Unita's. Tours depart from the yurt prior to sunset, and will culminate with alfresco dining as the sun sets over the Wasatch Mountains. On the return trip, the moonlight transforms the snow covered slopes into a shimmering wonderland adding a romantic touch to the adventure, so don't forget the Tic Tacs.

NIGHT SKIING

The fun doesn't end at 4 pm. Night skiing is offered every night until 9 pm. The terrain includes runs from the main Sundown lift and the Sundown Terrain park.

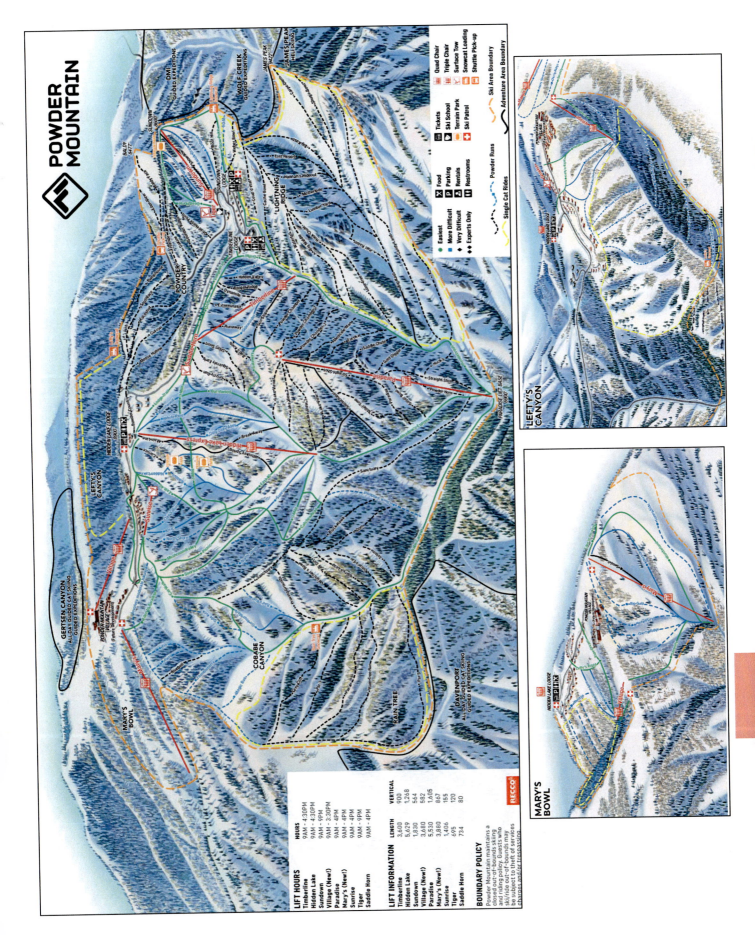

POWDER MOUNTAIN

LEFTY'S CANYON

MARY'S BOWL

Legend

Easiest	●	**Quad Chair**
More Difficult	■	**Triple Chair**
Very Difficult		**Surface Tow**
Experts Only	◆	**Snowcat Loading**
		Shuttle Pick-up

Food		**Tickets**
Parking		**Ski School**
Restrooms		**Rentals**
		Terrain Park
		Ski Patrol

Powder Runs
Single Cat Rides
Ski Area Boundary
Adventure Area Boundary

LIFT HOURS

	HOURS
Timberline	9AM - 4:30PM
Hidden Lake	9AM - 4:30PM
Sundown	9AM - 9PM
Village (New!)	9AM - 3:30PM
Paradise	9AM - 4PM
Mary's (New!)	9AM - 4PM
Sunrise	9AM - 4PM
Tiger	9AM - 9PM
Saddle Horn	9AM - 4PM

LIFT INFORMATION

	LENGTH	VERTICAL
Timberline	3,600	900
Hidden Lake	5,629	1,268
Sundown	1,830	564
Village (New!)	3,680	582
Paradise	5,530	1,605
Mary's (New!)	3,880	867
Sunrise	1,406	155
Tiger	695	120
Saddle Horn	734	80

BOUNDARY POLICY

Powder Mountain maintains a closed out-of-bounds skiing and riding policy. Guests who ski/ride out-of-bounds may be subject to theft of services charges and/or trespassing

RECCO

Park City

PARK CITY

Established: 1963	Acres: 7300	Vertical: 3200'	Annual Snowfall: 355"

Located in the heart of Park City, Utah, only a 35-minute drive from Salt Lake City International Airport, Park City is home to over 7,300 skiable acres with a good mix of beginner, intermediate and advanced terrain. During Summer 2015, the Resort undertook the largest resort improvement project in the history of American skiing, one that linked it with neighbor Canyons Resort via gondola to create the United States' largest ski area. Park City bustles with activities year-round with three distinct base areas, nine hotels, thrilling family adventures, and more than 16 restaurants.

With over 7,300 acres, 300+ trails, 41 lifts, eight terrain parks, 14 bowls, six natural half pipes, one super pipe and one mini pipe, plus many diverse ski-in/ski-out and village adjacent lodging properties, Park City is an easily accessible, world-class mountain destination located in an authentic & historic western town.

As North America's Leader in groomed terrain, over 750 acres (120 trails) are groomed nightly. They take pride in grooming wall-to-wall on most trails, laying fresh corduroy across the entire trail for an unrivaled skiing experience. Park City also excels at freestyle terrain - home to two of the Top Ten terrain parks in the US, with over 150 park features as well as a 22-ft pipe and 13-ft pipe.

Town Lift

Park City is the only resort with lift access directly to the town's historic Main Street. You can ski or ride down the Quit'N Time or Creole runs to the multitude of shops, restaurants, bars and galleries that give Park City its authentic mining town feel.

Dining

Enjoy fine dining at the award-winning Farm Restaurant at Canyons Village which debuts seasonal menus that celebrate locally sourced, sustainable cuisine. Check out the made-to-order Mediterranean station at Miners Camp. Indulge in fresh, homemade donuts, made-to-order items, and unparalleled views at 9,200' at Cloud Dine. Or, reserve a table at Lookout Cabin and savor the views along with the Chef's homemade cheese or chocolate fondue.

Winter Activities

For those that are looking for something off the slopes, there are sleigh rides, the Flying Eagle zip line, Alpine Coaster, snowmobile tours, and snowshoeing to name just a few.

Park City is part of the Epic Pass.

PARK CITY

Snowbasin

snowbasin

Established: 1940	Acres: 3000	Vertical: 2900'	Annual Snowfall: 300"

Snowbasin Resort is top rated by Ski Magazine in the categories of Service, On-Mountain Food, Lifts and Grooming, is located less than 35 miles North of Salt Lake City. It has one of the easiest drives from Salt Lake International Airport as well as quick access to the Park City Area and Downtown Ogden. With 3,000 skiable acres and 3,000 vertical feet, Snowbasin Resort is best known for wide-open bowls, gladed runs, pristine groomers, powder stashes days after a storm, three terrain parks, and excellent service.

Early access to the slopes via the gondola is available on the weekend for those that book a private lesson through the Snowsports school. (8am – 9am before it opens to the public.)

For those that don't ski but still want to enjoy the scenic views, they can take the Needles gondola to the top of the mountain where delicious dining awaits at the Needles Lodge. For the more adventurous non-skier, you can also ride the John Paul open chairlift to John Paul Lodge, then continue on the Allen Peak Tram to the top of the 2002 Olympic Men's Downhill course.

Snowbasin also offers 16 miles of groomed cross-country trails through beautiful glades and meadows under towering mountain peaks.

Discover why Snowbasin Resort is consistently recognized as one of the best family resorts in North America with wide open runs, great food, excellent Snowsports school, and convenient access. Snowbasin Resort is a member of the Grand America Hotels and Resorts family.

FREE ON-MOUNTAIN PHOTOGRAPHY

On-mountain photographers are stationed at several locations around the mountain ready to capture your best day ever! Show off your best turns as you pass them or ask them to take your family portrait! Go online to snowbasinphotos.com, enter the date the image was taken, find your image and download it for free!

FLY, SKI FOR FREE

Fly Alaska Airlines to Salt Lake City International airport on any of the direct flights from seven different cities between Monday and Wednesday and register at SkiOgden.com for your free lift ticket to Snowbasin Resort.

snowbasin

STRAWBERRY PEAK
9265'

DEMOISY PEAK
9370'

NEEDLES
9010'

MT. OGDEN
9570'

ALLEN PEAK
9465'

MOUNTAIN STATS

Top Elevation: 9,350 feet
Base Elevation: 6,450 feet
Vertical Rise: 2,900 feet
Avg Annual Snowfall: 300 inches
Skiable Area: 3,000 acres

BASE AREA MAP

UTAH 227

Snowbird

snowbird

Established: 1971	Acres: 2500	Vertical: 3240'	Annual Snowfall: 500"

It is tough to beat Snowbird's combination of dry Utah powder snow, vast terrain, and close proximity to Salt Lake City (only 29 miles away). And you have plenty of time to visit since Snowbird has the longest season of any ski area in Utah. Indulge yourself in on-mountain fine dining and ski in/out lodging. Snowbird has it all.

With 10 chairlifts and one aerial tram that holds 125, there is no shortage of uphill capacity (17,400 skiers/hour). Be sure to try the iconic Snowbird tram, it offers amazing views and a comfortable ride to the top. Just be sure to bring a snorkel, you may need it.

Snowbird is part of the Ikon Pass.

TOURS & GUIDES

Snowbird offers a guided backcountry tours, snowcat skiing, snowmobile tours, and mountain tours. The mountain tours are great for first-time visitors. Mountain hosts offer free, guided tours to acquaint guest with the resort's terrain.

THE SUMMIT

The Summit is Snowbird's newest year-round guest facility located atop Hidden Peak at 11,000 ft. Enjoy amazing 360 degree views of the surrounding Wasatch-Cache National Forest while enjoying masterful creations from a French-Rotisserie inspired menu designed by Snowbird Executive Chef George Lackey.

Alta

Established: 1938	Acres: 2200	Vertical: 2020'	Annual Snowfall: 551"

Whatever your ability, Alta has skiing terrain for you. Deep powder snow, soft groomers and spectacular scenery help to create a memorable skiing experience. Alta's best kept secret? While known for their expert powder slopes, Alta also has great beginner and intermediate terrain.

Alta became a ski area the winter season of 1938-39. A passionate group of local businessmen and relief from the tax burdens of a long-time Alta miner were the catalysts for the formation of Alta.

Alta was the first ski area in Utah to install a lift, two years behind Sun Valley, Idaho's installation in 1936. Alta grew slowly, building new lifts as the numbers of skiers grew and working with businesses in the area to provide day shelters and eventually lodging.

Alta has been referred to as a "skier's mountain" for many reasons. It is known for its scenery, diverse terrain and for the uncanny quality of snow that it receives season after season. Also, Alta does not allow other types of winter recreation other than skiing. It is a watershed, so no mechanized vehicles are allowed. The ski area has decided to be "just for skiers", so other snow-sliding equipment is not allowed. It is one of three areas in the United States that does not allow snowboarding.

There is a spirit to Alta. Perhaps it is because generations of skiers have been able to pass on their love for the mountain. It may be because there is a bit of a "purist's" feel for those who choose to ski here. Whatever the reasons, Alta is a place that many local and destination skiers choose to call home.

TOUR WITH A RANGER

For those interested in the natural wonders of Alta, there are complimentary tours with a volunteer naturalist. Topics covered on the tour include the fascinating local mining history, wildlife, public lands, the watershed and winter ecology.

BACKCOUNTRY

Alta offers several flavors of backcountry adventures of guided off-trail skiing on those superb powder days in the Grizzly Gulch Bowl: Snowcat tours, backcountry hike-in guided tours, and heli skiing.

Alta is part of the Ikon Pass.

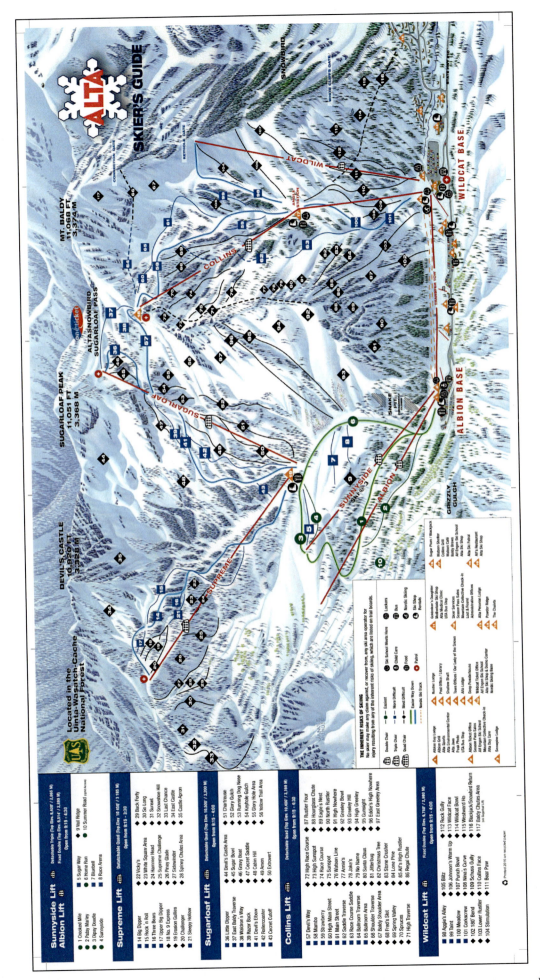

ALTA

SKIER'S GUIDE

Located in the
Uinta-Wasatch-Cache
National Forest

MT. BALDY
11,068 FT.
3,374 M

SUGARLOAF PEAK
11,051 FT.
3,368 M

DEVIL'S CASTLE
10,920 FT.
3,328 M

SNOWBIRD

ALTA/SNOWBIRD
SUGARLOAF PASS

COLLINS

SUGARLOAF

SUPREME

SUNNYSIDE

ALBION

GRIZZLY GULCH

WILDCAT

WILDCAT BASE

ALBION BASE

SNAKE PIT!

TRANSFER TOW

Sunnyside Lift / **Albion Lift**
Detachable Triple (Top Elev. 9,400' / 2,866 M)
Fixed Double (Top Elev. 8,514' / 2,591 M)
Open from 9:15 – 4:30

1 Crooked Mile
2 Patsy Marley
3 Dipsy Doodle
4 Sunnyside

5 Sugar Way
6 Home Run
7 Bluebell
8 Race Arena

9 Vail Ridge
10 Summer Road (open season)

Supreme Lift
Detachable Quad (Top Elev. 10,450' / 3,185 M)
Open from 9:15 – 3:30

14 Big Dipper
15 Rock 'n Roll
16 Three Bears
17 Upper Big Dipper
18 No. 9 Express
19 Erosion Gullies
20 Challenger
21 Sleepy Hollow

22 Vicky's
23 White Square Area
24 Hammer Head
25 Supreme Challenge
26 Piney Glade
27 Sidewinder
28 Spivey Chutes Area

29 Back Forty
30 So Long
31 Sunset
32 Snowshoe Hill
33 Last Chance
34 East Castle
35 Castle Apron

Sugarloaf Lift
Detachable Quad (Top Elev. 10,500' / 3,200 M)
Open from 9:15 – 4:00

36 Little Dipper
37 East Baldy Traverse
38 Waldron's Way
39 Razor Back
40 Ginny Boat
41 Devil's Elbow
42 Rollercoaster
43 Cecret Cutoff

44 Devil's Castle Area
45 Sugar Bowl
46 Ginny Boat
47 Cecret Saddle
48 Cabin Hill
49 Amen
50 Extrovert

51 Chartreuse
52 Glory Gulch
53 Running Dog Nose
54 Keyhole Gulch
55 Glory Hole Area
56 Yellow Trail Area

Collins Lift
Detachable Quad (Top Elev. 10,400' / 3,169 M)
Open from 9:15 – 4:30

57 Devil's Way
58 Mambo
59 Strawberry
60 High Main Street
61 Main Street
62 Saddle Traverse
63 Race Course Saddle
64 Ballroom Traverse
65 Ballroom Area
66 Shoulder Traverse
67 Baldy Shoulder Area
68 Fred's Slot
69 Spring Valley
70 Spruces
71 High Traverse

72 High Race Course
73 High Sunspot
74 Race Course
75 Sunspot
76 Watson Line
77 Annie's
78 Jake's
79 No Name
80 Santa Claus
81 Jitterbug
82 Christmas Tree
83 Stone Crusher
84 Lone Pine
85 Alf's High Rustler
86 Regal Chute

87 Rustler Four
88 Hourglass Chute
89 Eagle's Nest
90 North Rustler
91 High Nowhere
92 Greeley Bowl
93 Greeley Hill
94 High Greeley
95 Gunsight
96 Eddie's High Nowhere
97 East Greeley Area

Wildcat Lift
Fixed Double (Top Elev. 9,760' / 2,200 M)
Open from 9:15 – 4:00

98 Aggie's Alley
99 Taint
100 Meadow
101 Corkscrew
102 180 Bend
103 Lower Rustler
104 Stimulation

105 Blitz
106 Johnson's Warm Up
107 Punch Bowl
108 Nina's Curve
109 Schuss Gully
110 Collins Face
111 Bear Paw

112 Rock Gully
113 Wildcat Face
114 Wildcat Bowl
115 Westward Ho
116 Backpack/Snowbird Return (via Supreme Lift)
117 Baldy Chutes Area

THE INHERENT RISKS OF SKIING
No skier may make any claim against, or recover from, any ski area operator for injury resulting from any of the inherent risks of skiing, which are listed on trail boards.

Double Chair
Triple Chair
Quad Chair

Easiest
More Difficult
Most Difficult
Easiest Way Down
Nordic Ski Track

Ski School Meets Here
Child Care
Food
Patrol

Lockers
Bus
Nordic Skiing
Ski Shop
Rentals

Rustler Lodge
Post Office / Library
Shallow Shaft
Twins Offices / Our Lady of the Snows
Deep Powderhouse
Wildcat Ticket Office
Alf Engen Ski School
Alta Ski Shop & Demo Center
Nordic Skiing Base

Alta Environmental Center

Albion Guy Lodge
Albion Grill
Alta Sports
Alta Java
Alta Tram

Albion Ticket Office
Season Pass Sales
Alf Engen Ski School
Alta Ski School
Alta Java

Sugar Plum / Backpack
Watson Shelter
Collins Grill
Watson Café
Buddy Werner
Alf Engen Ski School
Alta Ski Shop

Goldminer's Daughter
Mountain Collective Check-in
Lost & Found
Administration Offices

Peruvian Lodge
Alta Ski Festival
Alta Ski Shop

Powder Ridge
Alf's Restaurant
The Chalets

Snowpine Lodge

Deer Valley

| Established: 1981 | Acres: 2026 | Vertical: 3000' | Annual Snowfall: 300" |

Deer Valley Resort has become known for revolutionizing ski area service and they never stop striving to better their guests' vacation experience. Since opening in 1981, Deer Valley has been committed to providing a level of care rarely found at a ski resort, delivering classic, consistent, quality service both on and off the mountain.

Deer Valley is also known for it's impeccably groomed runs. Every night, 32 groomers and 16 snowcats spend 266 collective man hours laying down the corduroy. That's why Deer Valley has been voted #1 for grooming in Ski magazine numerous years.

Besides plenty of groomed runs, Deer Valley also has bowl and glade skiing (over 930 acres of glades to enjoy).

The Deer Valley focuses on the skiing experience in several ways. The first is by keeping the crowds down to a reasonable size. Only 7,500 lucky guests are allowed on the slopes in a day. Another way to ensure more time is spent skiing is through the use of many lifts, 21 in total (12 high speed). This makes for an uphill capacity of 50,470 skiers per hour! Lastly, the skiing experience is preserved by not allowing snowboarders on the slopes. All of this translates into packing in the laps.

CUSTOMER SERVICE

Based on the foundation of first-class service, Deer Valley Resort was one of the first to offer ski valets to carry guests' ski gear from their cars to the slopes, provide free parking lot shuttles, design magnificent lodges in the vein of National Park buildings, refer to customers as "guests" as is done at fine hotels, have a state-licensed child care facility on site, uniform all its employees from kitchen staff to lift attendants, provide tissues in the lift lines, provide complimentary ski storage even overnight and much more.

FAMILY FRIENDLY

Deer Valley has one of the best ski schools, having been started by the legendary Stein Eriksen. Instructors are available for all ages and skill levels. Or if the kids aren't ready for skiing, there is a full-service children's center with fun activities.

Deer Valley is part of the Ikon Pass.

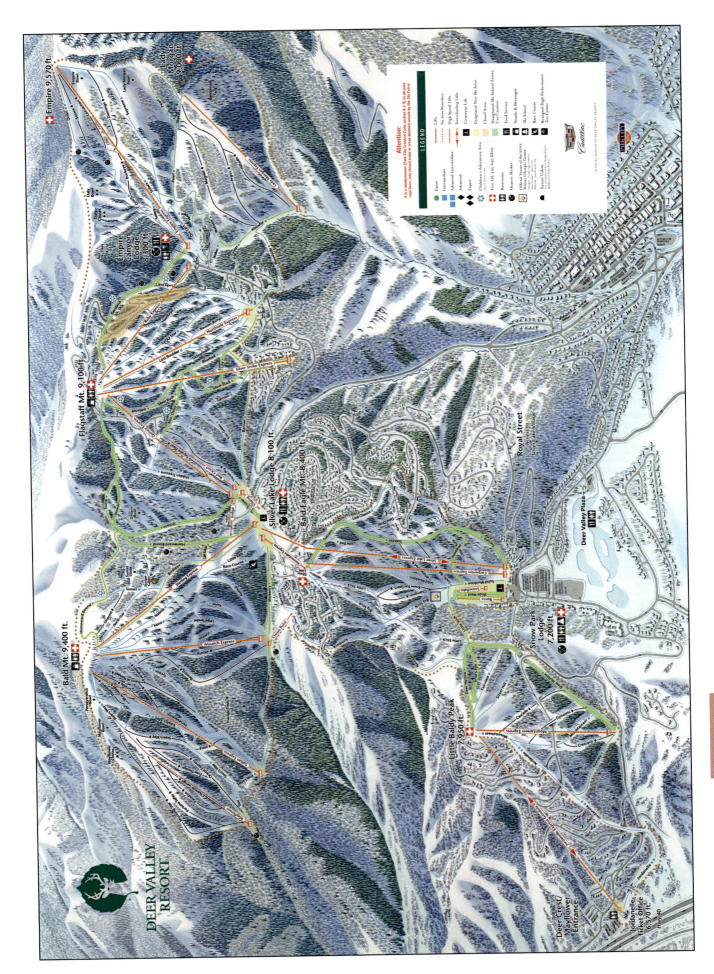

Solitude

Established: 1957	Acres: 1200	Vertical: 2030'	Annual Snowfall: 500"

Solitude is divided into two distinct areas from which to begin your mountain adventures—the Moonbeam and Village base areas. Moonbeam generally services day skiers and riders while the Village area is home to most of the resort's lodging guests.

From the Moonbeam base you'll have easy access to the Moonbeam and Eagle Express chairlifts. Moonbeam Express serves much of Solitude's beginner terrain, and you'll find little packs of smiling ski schoolers playing follow the leader. Eagle Express chairlift runs above a number of solid blue runs, some groomed and some left au natural, as well as a few steeper blacks.

From the Village base, the big show is the Apex Express chairlift. A new run from the top of Apex provides easy access to the realigned and upgraded Summit Express chairlift, which takes you literally to the top of the mountain. Summit Express opens up Solitude's most daunting and rugged terrain, the famed Honeycomb Canyon. On a powder day, Honeycomb's steep chutes and glorious tree runs feel more like backcountry than in-bound resort skiing. Sunrise chairlift also runs out of the Village base area and its easier blues are a great place for learners to work out the kinks in their form.

In addition to alpine skiing and snowboarding, Solitude also has 20 kilometers of Nordic skiing trails groomed for skate and classic styles, as well as a set of snowshoeing trails.

Solitude has ten restaurants, including two on-mountain establishments. For a unique experience, take a guided snowshoe adventure through a moon lit forest to a Mongolian yurt, where chefs prepare a memorable four-course dinner right before your eyes.

Solitude is part of the Ikon Pass.

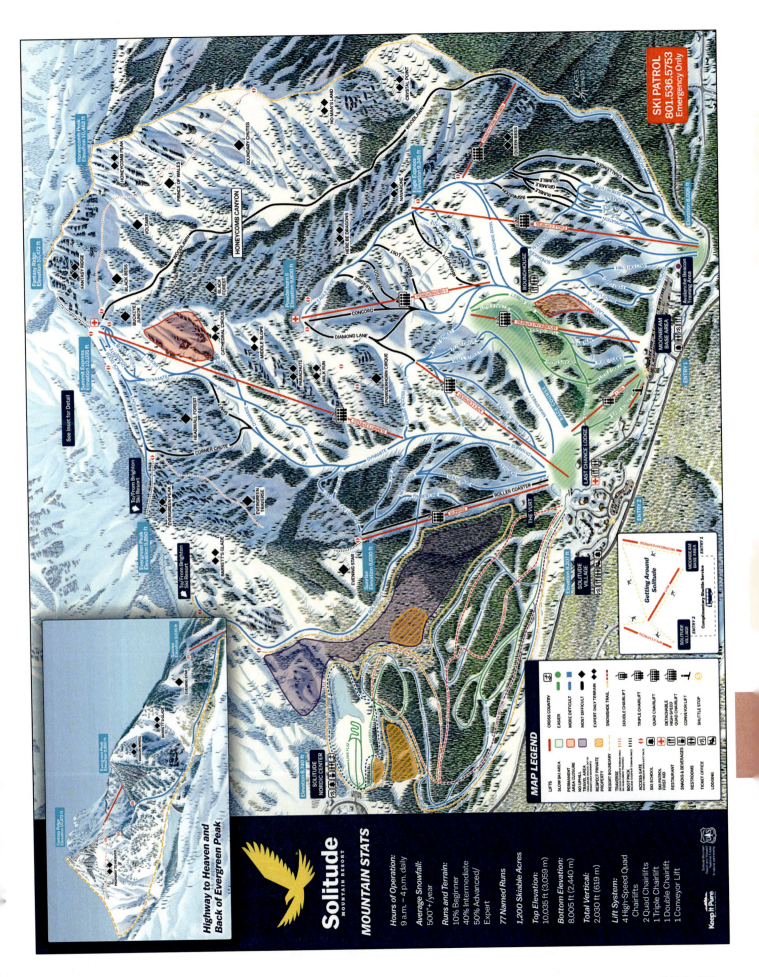

SKI PATROL
801.536.5753
Emergency Only

Highway to Heaven and
Back of Evergreen Peak

Solitude
MOUNTAIN RESORT

MOUNTAIN STATS

Hours of Operation:
9 a.m. – 4 p.m. daily

Average Snowfall:
500'+/year

Runs and Terrain:
10% Beginner
40% Intermediate
50% Advanced/
Expert

77 Named Runs

1,200 Skiable Acres

Top Elevation:
10,035 ft (3,059 m)

Bottom Elevation:
8,005 ft (2,440 m)

Total Vertical:
2,030 ft (619 m)

Lift System:
4 High-Speed Quad
    Chairlifts
2 Quad Chairlifts
1 Triple Chairlift
1 Double Chairlift
1 Conveyor Lift

MAP LEGEND

LIFTS

CROSS COUNTRY
EASIER
MORE DIFFICULT
MOST DIFFICULT
EXPERT ONLY TERRAIN
SNOWSHOE TRAIL
DOUBLE CHAIRLIFT
TRIPLE CHAIRLIFT
QUAD CHAIRLIFT
DETACHABLE
HIGH-SPEED
QUAD CHAIRLIFT
CONVEYOR LIFT
SHUTTLE STOP

SLOW SKI AREA
PERMANENT
AREA CLOSURE
NO UPHILL
TRAVEL AREA
RESPECT PRIVATE
PROPERTY
RESORT BOUNDARY
TRAVERSE
ACCESS GATE
SKI SCHOOL
SKI PATROL,
FIRST AID
RESTAURANT
SMOKES & BEVERAGES
RESTROOMS
TICKET OFFICE
LODGING

Getting Around Solitude

Complimentary Shuttle Service

Brighton

| Established: 1936 | Acres: 1050 | Vertical: 1745' | Annual Snowfall: 500" |

SNOW

The mountain averages 500 inches of snow a winter. The snow is traditionally light, fluffy and dry making it a paradise for riders and skiers. Brighton is located directly in the path of winter storms and it is also at the very top of Big Cottonwood Canyon so it gets the very best of the "greatest snow on earth," and lots of it.

The terrain park crew keeps moving the features around so what's here today might be gone tomorrow. The challenge keeps changing.

NIGHT SKIING

And there's Night skiing. They have the most night skiing terrain in Utah with 22 runs on over 200 lighted acres. Night skiing: 4 – 9 pm Monday through Saturday early December through March.

GROOMING

Brighton's grooming is five star. It is consistently top quality. Beginner runs are groomed nightly. Intermediate trails are groomed nightly, except for a few obscure trails which are groomed as needed. And for the experts, main runs are groomed, but most is left au naturale for those who like their powder deep without any fuss.

TERRAIN

Terrain is their trump card – and 100% of the terrain can be accessed by high speed quad. Perhaps it is the only mountain where friends or families can ride together on the same lift and then peel off onto different trails - beginner, intermediate, or expert– and all meet at the bottom to ride the lift together again. Most skiers and riders stick to the immaculately groomed trails, but there are trees and chutes, cliffs and natural terrain parks all within bounds for those who like white knuckle terrain. And they have Terrain Parks. Freestyle riders and skiers enjoy Brighton's four terrain parks for all abilities.

LEARNING

Brighton is famous for its Ski and Snowboard School. It is known as "The place where Utah learns to ski and ride and keeps on learning." It has earned that reputation because of its consistent dedication to the students. Brighton's Ski and Snowboard School has private lessons, daily group classes for every ability level of skiers and riders, and specialty series for kids, women, seniors, and much more.

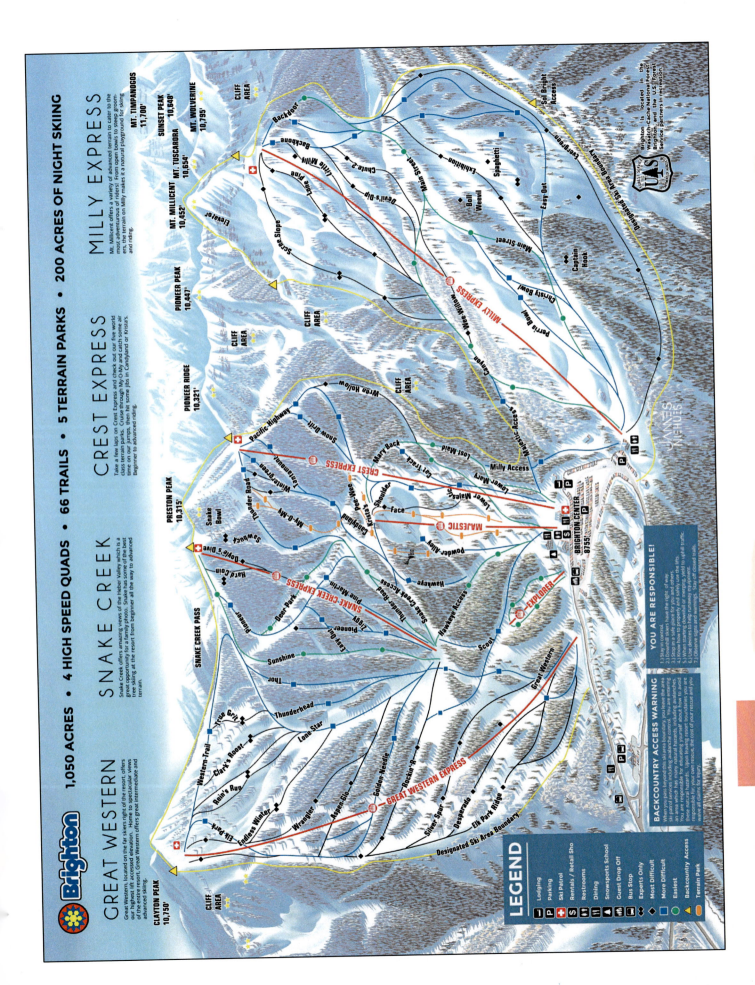

Brighton

1,050 ACRES · 4 HIGH SPEED QUADS · 66 TRAILS · 5 TERRAIN PARKS · 200 ACRES OF NIGHT SKIING

GREAT WESTERN

Great Western, located on the far skiers right of the resort, offers our highest lift accessed elevation. Home to spectacular views of the entire resort, Great Western offers great intermediate and advanced skiing.

CLAYTON PEAK
10,750'

SNAKE CREEK

Snake Creek offers amazing views of the Heber Valley which is a great opportunity for a family photo. Snake has some of the best tree skiing at the resort, from beginner all the way to advanced terrain.

CREST EXPRESS

Take a few laps on Crest Express and check out our five world class terrain parks. Cruise through My-O-My and catch some air time on our jumps, then hit some jibs in Candyland or Krista's. Beginner to advanced riding.

MILLY EXPRESS

Mt. Millicent offers a variety of advanced terrain to cater to the most adventurous of riders! From open bowls to steep groomers, the terrain on Milly makes it a natural playground for skiing and riding.

MT. TIMPANOGOS
11,700'

SUNSET PEAK
10,648'

MT. TUSCARORA
10,554'

MT. WOLVERINE
10,795'

MT. MILLICENT
10,452'

PIONEER PEAK
10,447'

PIONEER RIDGE
10,321'

PRESTON PEAK
10,315'

SNAKE CREEK PASS

BRIGHTON CENTER
8755'

Sol Bright Access

Brighton is located in the Wasatch-Cache National Forest. Brighton and the U.S. Forest Service are partners in recreation

MILLY EXPRESS

Backdoor · Backbone · Little Milly · Lone Pine · Devil's Dip · Chute 2 · Main Street · Exhibition · Spaghetti · Boll Weevil · Easy Out · Captain Hook · Christy Bowl · Perria Bowl · Wren Hollow · Scree Slope · Elevator · Majestic Access · Canyon

CREST EXPRESS

Pacific Highway · Snow Drift · Mary Back · Lost Maid · Milly Access · Gat Track · Vantagepoint · Wintergreen · Thunder Road · My-O-My · Lower Mary · Lower Majestic · Shoulder · Face · Landgrab · Powder Alley · Hawkeye · Snake Creek Access · Pine Marten · Hard Coin · Doyle's Dive · Sawbuck · Snake Bowl · Scout · Hawkeye Access · EXPLORER · MAJESTIC

SNAKE CREEK EXPRESS

Deer Park · Pioneer · Ziggy · Sunshine · Thor · Thunderhead · Lone Star · Tree Grit · Clark's Roost · Rein's Run · Western Trail · Easy Out · Great Western

GREAT WESTERN EXPRESS

Golden Needle · Rockin' R · Aspen Glo · Wrangler · Endless Winter · Elk Park · Silver Spur · Desperado · Elk Park Ridge · Great Western

CLIFF AREA

Designated Ski Area Boundary

JAMES NIEHUES

LEGEND

Lodging · Parking · Ski Patrol · Rentals / Retail Sho · Restrooms · Dining · Snowsports School · Guest Drop Off · Bus Stop · Experts Only · Most Difficult · More Difficult · Easiest · Backcountry Access · Terrain Park

Beaver Mountain

Established: 1938	Acres: 828	Vertical: 1600'	Annual Snowfall: 400"

Beaver Mountain ("The Beav") has 828 skiable acres containing well maintained slopes with northeastern exposure, perfect for catching morning rays. The mountain has a variety of terrain, perfect for every ability.

Beaver Mountain Ski Resort's excellent runs, friendly atmosphere and low prices make it a popular destination for locals - some say it is one of Utah's best-kept secrets. It has been family-owned and operated since 1939, making it the oldest continuously owned family ski area in the US. Downhill skiing and snowboarding are major winter activities but there are also excellent cross-country ski and snowmobile trails nearby.

Ski season generally runs from early December through the first week of April. The end of ski season is celebrated with the Beaver Bash. The resort builds a 90 foot pond for skiers and snowboarders to try to ride across. There are many fun races and competitions at the Beaver Bash.

The Beaver Mountain area is also a great summer destination with fishing, hiking, horseback riding, boating and other activities nearby. During summer months, families or other groups can rent the lodge and yurt facilities, or stay in the RV park or campground.

NIGHT SKIING

Beaver Mountain offers night skiing on the Little Beaver lift. It's a unique opportunity to rent the entire slope and lodge for your private group. Night skiing at Beaver is almost all private groups but there are a few "public" nights every season.

GETTING THERE

"The Beav" is located 27 miles northeast of Logan, just a mile off of US-89, the Logan Canyon Scenic Byway, a national scenic byway.

Brian Head Resort

| Established: 1965 | Acres: 650 | Vertical: 1320' | Annual Snowfall: 360" |

Brian Head Resort offers The Greatest Snow on Earth®, with annual average snowfall of over 360 inches, and Utah's highest base elevation. Covering over 650 acres, the Resort has two connected mountains, Giant Steps and Navajo, offering 71 runs and 8 chair lifts and 2 surface lifts.

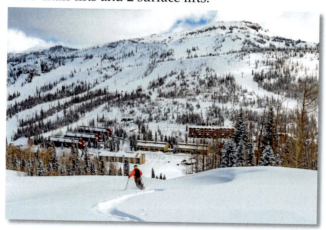

Being the highest ski resort in Utah (the base is 9,600 and the peak is 11,307 ft), the powder is light and fluffy, hence the Greatest Snow on Earth®. The high elevation also translates into a longer ski season (mid-November to mid-April). There is rarely a lift line so that you have plenty of room on the slopes.

On Friday and Saturday nights, night skiing allows one to extend the fun until 9 pm on the Blackfoot lift.

Brian Head has two day-lodges and numerous mountain-side lodging options.

TUBING PARK

Tubing is another exciting way to experience winter at Brian Head Resort. It's like sledding only easier, more fun, and you don't have to hike back up the hill! Tubing is the perfect group or family activity. Navajo Tube Hill is a 75' vertical drop with a 550' slope length. The Giant Steps Tube Hill is a 100' vertical drop with a 600' slope length.

GETTING THERE

Brian Head Resort is just minutes off of Interstate 15 near Parowan, Utah. Whether you are driving from Southern California, Las Vegas, or Utah the drive is easy with beautiful views. It's a 3 hour drive from Las Vegas, or 3.5 hours from Salt Lake City.

BRIAN HEAD PEAK
ELEVATION 11,307 FEET

BRIAN HEAD PEAK
Experts only.
Accessible through access gates.

EXPERT ONLY

TO DEVO'S PITCH

NAVAJO PEAK
ELEVATION 10,575 FEET

NAVAJO MOUNTAIN
Beginner and intermediate terrain for kids and adults of all ages and skill levels.

SHIVWITTS

TRAILS AT NAVAJO SUBDIVISION

SNOW TUBE PARK

TO 1-15, PAROWAN, CEDAR CITY, LAS VEGAS, & LOS ANGELES

NAVAJO LODGE & LEARNING CENTER
Tickets/Guest Services
Kids Camp
Ski Patrol/First Aid
Rental Shop
Winter Sports School
Restrooms
Navajo Lodge Grill
High Mountain Outfitters
ATM

FREE MOUNTAIN SHUTTLES
Complimentary ground transportation throughout Brian Head.

PIONEER CABINS LOOP

GIANT STEPS LODGE
Tickets/Guest Services
Ski Patrol/First Aid
Rentals/Demo Center
Lost Chair Saloon
Giant Steps Grill
ATM
High Mountain Outfitters

NAVAJO
MARYLAND PARKWAY
EASY TIME
BRAVE
FREMONT
GOLD GULCH
EASY TIME
THE STRIP
PARADISE
PARADISE
YOU'RE READY
FIRST TIME
FUN RUN
#6 PIONEER
#4 NAVAJO
NAVAJO LOOP
SUGAR LOAF
SUN DOG
UTE
APACHE PITCH
UTE
MOON BOGGLE
PAIUTE
KODACHROME BOWL
DINEH
MAMMOTH
LOWDIVE
CHANTRELLE
Ski Bridge
CEDAR BREAKS NATIONAL MONUMENT
WILDFLOWER

BRISTLECONE BOWL
LOBO VALLEY
THE WAVE
THE TUBE
OUT SKIRTS
THE PLUNGE
LAST CHANCE
SUNBURST
GEORG'S ROCK RUN
HUNTER'S RUN
PILLOWS
DOUBLE AUGHT
ED'S SHORTCUT
AUGHT
GIANT STEPS
BEAR PAW
LOOKOUT
ALL DAY
DOUBLE YUMPS
I LOVE IT
YARDSALE
DAY BREAK
THE DUNES
#7 THE DUNES
ENGENS
GIANT STEPS EXPRESS
#2 GIANT STEPS EXPRESS
POWDER RUN
RACE COURSE
#8 ALPEN GLOW
SNOW TUBE PARK
ALPEN WAY
BEAR PAW PITCH
OVERTIME
ALPEN WAY
YAZ
HEAVENLY DAZE
DESBAH
#3 BLACKFOOT
AREA BOUNDARY
DARK HOLLOW
STRAIGHT UP
#5 ROULETTE
NINJA
FIRST TRACKS
HARD TIMES
WILD RIDE
CHAIR LIFT SUMMIT 10,920 FT.

LEGEND

LIFTS	RESTAURANTS
SURFACE LIFTS	PARKING
	LOUNGE
EASIEST	X-COUNTRY
MORE DIFFICULT	FREESTYLE TERRAIN
MOST DIFFICULT	BC ACCESS GATES
EXPERT	SLOW ZONE
AREA BOUNDARY	

CHAIRLIFTS

1) **WILDFLOWER** – Triple Chair Lift
2,887 ft. long – 579 ft. vertical
2) **GIANT STEPS** – High Speed Quad
EXPRESS   4,934 ft. long –
1,161 ft. vertical
3) **BLACKFOOT** – Triple Chair Lift
2,300 ft. long – 439 ft. vertical
4) **NAVAJO** – Triple Chair Lift
3,895 ft. long – 604 ft. vertical
5) **ROULETTE** – Triple Chair Lift
3,075 ft. long – 762 ft. vertical
6) **PIONEER** – Double Chair Lift
919 ft. long – 139 ft. vertical
7) **THE DUNES** – Triple Chair Lift
2,618 ft. long – 570 ft. vertical
8) **ALPEN GLOW** – Triple Chair Lift
2,366 ft. long – 558 ft. vertical

Eagle Point

| Established: 1973 | Acres: 650 | Vertical: 1500' | Annual Snowfall: 350" |

Eagle Point Resort offers five lifts with access to over 650 skiable acres and 40 runs ranging from tree-lined groomers to the steepest, most challenging runs in southern Utah. Beyond the slopes, a progressive terrain park, snowshoeing trails and endless backcountry entertain the whole family.

Lift lines are nearly non-existent and the snow quality is some of the finest. These two reasons bring visitors coming back year after year. If you like to adventure beyond the resort boundaries, you will find some of Utah's best backcountry touring terrain surrounding Eagle Point. In cooperation with the National Forest Service, the resort offers several gates where skiers and riders can access the vast lands and peaks of Fishlake National Forest.

VILLAGE

Eagle Point Resort also has a village of it's own, complete with slope-side condos, cabins, and two lodges with dining. The Lookout is a European-style warming hut offering on-the-mountain dining with spectacular views.

MT. HOLLY 12,001 ft

LAKE PEAK 11,317 ft

ACCESS FROM LOOKOUT QUAD

COUNTRY ROAD

PAIUTE CROSSING

BLACK DIAMONDS PASS

TUSHAR PEAKS SURFACE LIFT

ACCESS TO ◆

Resort area boundary – not patrolled beyond this point. Enter through access gates only.

PUFFER LAKE

Resort area boundary – not patrolled beyond this point. Enter through access gates only.

RESORT AREA BOUNDARY

COUNTRY ROAD

BEAVER TAIL

RUNAWAY CARTER

MISSING LINC

DONNER'S DESCENT

SATISFACTION

DELANO DROP

VERTIGO

ANASAZI TREEFALL

RESORT AREA BOUNDARY

HIKE OUT ONLY

THE LOOKOUT

WHITEOUT

LOOKOUT QUAD CHAIR

MONI STEPS

HOODOOS

TUSHAR

THE NARROWS

WOLVERINE

CANYONSIDE POMA LIFT

SUBWAY BOWL

TUNNEL VISION

CANYONSIDE LODGE

RESORT AREA BOUNDARY

AVERY'S ALLEY

FALLING WATER

EDDIE'S MAZE

Resort area boundary – not patrolled beyond this point. Enter through access gates only.

TEDDY'S TWIST

FULL MOON

CASSIDY

SQUARE

MONARCH TRIPLE CHAIR

EASIER GLADE

TERRAIN PARK

BIG HORN

ELK MEADOWS

SKYLINE DOUBLE CHAIR

HUMMINGBIRD

ANNABEL WAY

BELKNAP FLOW

RESORT AREA BOUNDARY

SKYLINE LODGE

KEY

🎫 TICKET SALES		🅿️ PARKING AREA
🛍 RENTAL SHOP		👥 GROUP PROGRAMS
🛒 RETAIL		🚻 RESTROOMS
✚ SKI PATROL / FIRST AID		🛅 LODGING CHECK-IN
🎓 SNOWSPORTS SCHOOL		🔥 WARMING STATIONS
🍴 RESTAURANT		▮▮▮ TERRAIN PARK
🚌 SKYLINE-CANYONSIDE SHUTTLE		▮ EASIEST WAY DOWN
◢ ACCESS GATE		● EASIER
┄ SKI AREA BOUNDARY		● MORE DIFFICULT
		◆ MOST DIFFICULT
		◯ ASPEN CREST AT EAGLE POINT

EAGLE POINT
BEAVER
UTAH

EAGLEPOINTRESORT.COM f 🐦

Sundance

sundance
MOUNTAIN RESORT

Established: 1969	Acres: 450	Vertical: 2150'	Annual Snowfall: 300"

"To us, Sundance is and always will be a dream. What you see, smell, taste and feel here is a dream being carefully nurtured. It is an area whose pledge is to people. What we offer in the form of art and culture, spirit and service, is homegrown and available to all."

- Robert Redford

In 1969, Robert Redford bought the land now known as Sundance and envisioned the growth of a community committed to the balance of art, nature and community. Sundance offers an atmosphere steeped in cultural heritage, inspired by the Ute tribes that first inhabited this canyon and continuing through the early 20th century as the Stewart family homesteaded the area. The second generation of Stewarts developed the mountain into a small ski resort, Timp Haven.

Investors began eyeing the picturesque locale as a place to erect expansive condominiums, but Redford wanted to

preserve the land and "to develop a little and to preserve a great deal." Rejecting advice from New York investors to fill the canyon with an explosion of lucrative hotels and condominiums, Redford saw his newly acquired land as an ideal locale for environmental conservation and artistic experimentation.

Many writers, directors, actors and artists have been inspired by the beauty of this canyon. Years of experimentation and refinement have ultimately resulted in what is now call Sundance.

Today Sundance Mountain Resort is home to 5,000 acres of cultivated wilderness enjoyed by guests year-round. During the winter, four lifts give skiers access to 2,100 feet of vertical drop. Free host tours, a terrain park, senior ski groups and expansive night skiing allow guests of all ages and levels to enjoy the mountain.

In the summer, the mountain is home to 25+ miles of biking and hiking trails. The Sundance ZipTour goes from the top of the mountain, stretching nearly 2 miles, the 3rd longest in the nation and 1st in vertical drop. Visitors also enjoy artistic activities throughout the year, with theatre performances, concerts, live music, dining experiences and author events.

It's Sundance's ability to blend process and place that makes it dynamically unique and places it on uncharted waters on a steady course all of its own.

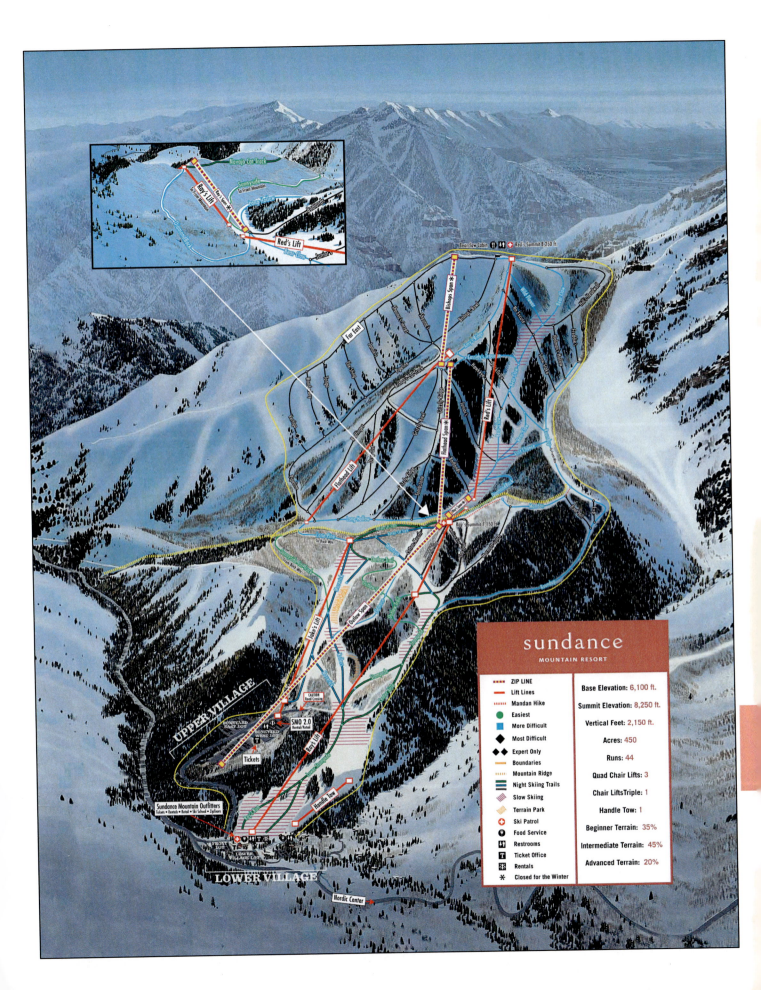

Cherry Peak

Established: 2015	Acres: 200	Vertical: 1265'	Annual Snowfall: 322"

Cherry Peak is one of the newest ski areas to the West. It is the local hill for the town of Logan (only 15 miles away), but offers more than just skiing. It has a two lane tubing hill (with moving sidewalk), Nordic trails, and a large night skiing operation every night it is open. The resort is ready for when Mother Nature comes up short by utilizing a state-of-the-art snow making system so you'll be sure of a great ski experience.

The new lodge was made to look like it has been there for 100 years, so it has all the charm of an old resort with all the modern touches. Inside you'll find the grill restaurant, ski rentals, ski school, and ski shop.

In the summer time, Cherry Peak converts to its summer activities. They have a Summer Concert Series, Horseback Riding, Disk Golf, two Redneck Waterslides, Mountain Biking Trails, Ultimate Bungee, and the Kiiking Swing. Enough activities for your whole family to enjoy!

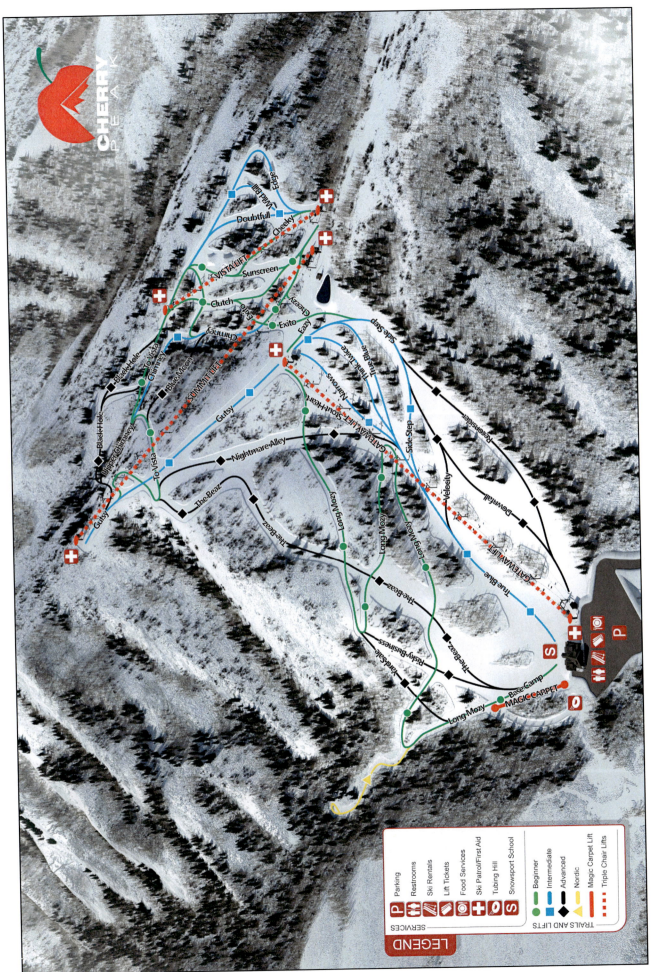

CHERRY PEAK

LEGEND

SERVICES

P	Parking
	Restrooms
	Ski Rentals
	Lift Tickets
	Food Services
+	Ski Patrol/First Aid
	Tubing Hill
S	Snowsport School

TRAILS AND LIFTS

- Beginner
- Intermediate
- Advanced
- Nordic
- Magic Carpet Lift
- Triple Chair Lifts

Trails: Wild Bill, Edge, Doubtfull, Cheeky, Sunscreen, VISTA LIFT, Clutch, Exito, Exito, Eazy, Greezy, Side Step, Black Hole, To Vista, Chimney, Blue Moon, SUMMIT LIFT, Gutsy, Think Twice, The Blue, Side Step, Narrows, GATEWAY LIFT, SouthHeart, Upper Chimney, To Vista, Nightmare Alley, Gutsy, The Beaz, Long Mozy, Long Mozy, Long Mozy, Velocity, Downfall, Recondside, GATEWAY LIFT, True Blue, The Beaz, The Beaz, The Beaz, Risky Business, Yard Sale, Long Mozy, Base Camp, MAGIC CARPET

UTAH 247

Nordic Valley

| Established: 1968 | Acres: 140 | Vertical: 960' | Annual Snowfall: 300" |

NORDIC VALLEY

In the year 1968, a small ski area in the heart of Utah's powder country was born –Nordic valley. Nordic Valley is nestled deep in the heart of the Wasatch Mountains, however, it is just a few short miles from the restaurants, entertainment and comforts of the booming town of Ogden. Named by Forbes magazine as the third best city in the country to raise a family, Nordic Valley is one of the most accessible, family and budget friendly ski areas, in the country.

Nordic Valley is famous for its ski school, intermediate and advanced slopes, and family friendly atmosphere. Nordic Valley was immortalized as one of the best downhill training ski areas for the 2002 Winter Olympics, which the Austrians discovered was worth pure Gold.

TERRAIN PARKS

Spend your day jumping, sliding, and grinding in their adventure-filled terrain park. The terrain park was designed with a wide variety of features for all riders and all abilities. The park has beginner, and intermediate features to help you push your shredding to the next level. There is an assortment of rails and box features, along with awesome rollers and kickers.

The park is groomed nightly from top-to-bottom to ensure that each feature has a smooth take-off and a better landing. All of the features are hand raked daily to add the finishing touch.

NIGHT SKIING

Enjoy Utah's largest night skiing with 100% of the mountain under lights. Open until 8 pm, Monday through Saturday.

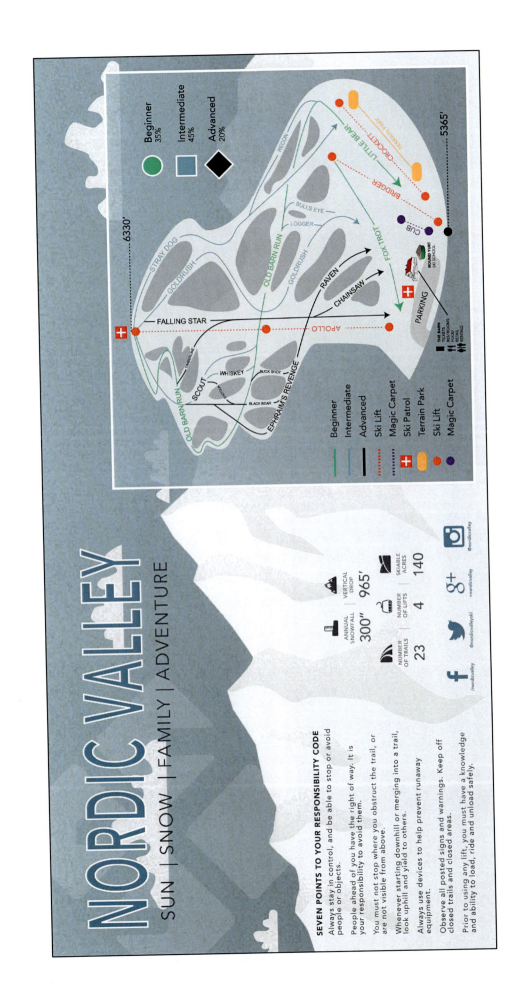

NORDIC VALLEY

SUN | SNOW | FAMILY | ADVENTURE

SEVEN POINTS TO YOUR RESPONSIBILITY CODE

Always stay in control, and be able to stop or avoid people or objects.

People ahead of you have the right of way. It is your responsibility to avoid them.

You must not stop where you obstruct the trail, or are not visible from above.

Whenever starting downhill or merging into a trail, look uphill and yield to others.

Always use devices to help prevent runaway equipment.

Observe all posted signs and warnings. Keep off closed trails and closed areas.

Prior to using any lift, you must have a knowledge and ability to load, ride and unload safely.

ANNUAL SNOWFALL 300"

VERTICAL DROP 965'

NUMBER OF TRAILS 23

NUMBER OF LIFTS 4

SKIABLE ACRES 140

f /nordicvalley
@nordicvalleyski
g+ +nordicvalley
@nordicvalley

Beginner 35%
Intermediate 45%
Advanced 20%

Beginner
Intermediate
Advanced
Ski Lift
Magic Carpet
Ski Patrol
Terrain Park
Ski Lift
Magic Carpet

6330'
5365'

RECON
STRAY DOG
BULLS EYE
LOGGER
GOLDRUSH
OLD BARN RUN
GOLDRUSH
RAVEN
CHAINSAW
FOX TROT
LITTLE BEAR
CROCKETT
TERRAIN PARK
BRIDGER
CUB
FALLING STAR
APOLLO
PARKING
ROUND YURT SKI SCHOOL
THE BARN TICKETS RESTROOMS FOOD RETAIL RENTALS
TIMBERLINE
SCOUT
WHISKEY
BUCK SHOT
BLACK BEAR
EPHRAIM'S REVENGE
OLD BARN RUN

TRAVEL TIP: SKI BAGS

If you plan to fly with your skis or snowboard, it is important to know the airline rules for your ski luggage. Almost all of the airlines will treat the combination of a ski bag AND a boot bag as a single piece of luggage when it comes time to check them in. However, the combination of the two bags must be under 50 lbs (check your specific airline to verify). This can be a problem if you are trying to pack two sets of skis into a bag or if you are using a heavy ski case.

Option 1: Simple ski bags. These can be found for $40 but those will have very little padding. You can wrap your skis and poles in towels or clothing, but there is always the risk that something is cut by the edges.

Option 2: Padded ski bags. These are more typical and aren't much more expensive. They have internal padding and thicker exterior material for better protection.

Option 3: Roller bags (hard or soft shell). These are the way to go if you are planning on traveling a lot with your equipment. Trying to transport a carry-on bag, boot bag, and ski bag through an airport is no easy task. If you have a roller bag, that's one less thing to lug on your shoulder. The Dakine Fall Line Ski Roller Bag can fit two sets of skis, poles, and your boots all in one bag.

Airlines can be particular about the quantity of skis in your bag. The official rules say one pair of skis, poles, and boots. However, it is rare that they check the inside of your bag to see if you have two pairs. If the ski bag and boot bag can be kept under the weight allowance, you'll most likely be fine.

If you do not want to purchase a real boot bag, any boot-sized luggage will do. For example, the American Tourist iLite Max Spinner carry-on (19") can hold a pair of boots but also has room for some clothing. Strictly speaking, the airlines do not want clothing in the ski or boot bag. I haven't had any issues packing coats, gloves, ski pants in the bags with my skis and boots. The benefit of a dedicated boot bag is that it often can be carried on your back (like a backpack) which makes life easier.

Washington

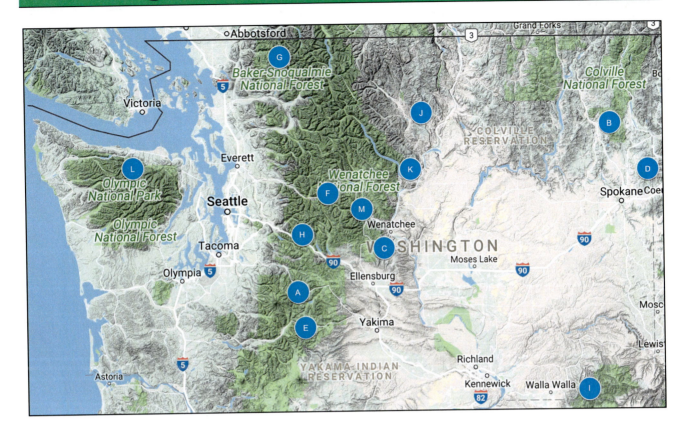

		Page
A.	Crystal Mountain	252
B.	49° North	254
C.	Mission Ridge	256
D.	Mt. Spokane	258
E.	White Pass	260
F.	Stevens Pass	262
G.	Mt. Baker	264
H.	The Summit at Snoqualmie	266
I.	Bluewood	274
J.	Loup Loup	276
K.	Echo Valley	277
L.	Hurricane Ridge	278
M.	Leavenworth Ski Hill	279

Crystal Mountain

Established: 1962	Acres: 2600	Vertical: 3100'	Annual Snowfall: 486"

Crystal Mountain is the largest ski resort in Washington State with a total of 2,600 acres and over 50 named runs. You'll find acres of gentle groomed runs for beginners to challenging steeps, glades, chutes, bowls and expansive backcountry for the more adventurous skiers and snowboarders. Crystal Mountain averages 486 inches of snowfall annually which gives powder enthusiasts plenty to smile about.

Puget Sound skiers and riders flock to the slopes during the winter months to enjoy breath-taking views of Mt. Rainier and to ride some of the best terrain in Washington State, only 2 hours away from Seattle in the heart of the Cascade Mountains.

Guests can enjoy the breathtaking scenery of Mt. Rainier while dining at the Summit House Restaurant at the top of the Mt. Rainier Gondola or take a break from skiing at the mid-mountain and base area lodges. Guests can extend their stay at Crystal Mountain at any of the slopeside accommodations. More info on lodging can be found at www.staycrystal.com

BACKCOUNTRY

If untracked terrain is your desire, there are plenty of choices of backcountry access points. All backcountry users leaving the ski area boundary must observe the signage and exit through official exit points. It's important that all guests looking to travel outside the ski area boundary have proper avalanche education, equipment, experience and local knowledge.

GONDOLA

Guests can enjoy the beautiful views of Mt. Rainier all year long. The Mt. Rainier Gondola gives everyone the opportunity to dine at the Summit House Restaurant and enjoy the wonderful view of Mt. Rainier in the winter and summer. Seasons may change, but your destination doesn't have to!

Crystal Mountain is part of the Ikon Pass.

MT. RAINIER
14,410'

SUMMIT HOUSE
RESTAURANT

SILVER QUEEN
7,002'

SILVER KING
7,012'

THE THRONE
6,600'

MORNING
GLORY PEAK

NORTHWAY PEAK
6,778'

NORTHWAY
NOTCH

ELK PASS
6,521'

GREEN VALLEY EXPRESS

CHINOOK EXPRESS

RAINIER EXPRESS

FOREST QUEEN EXPRESS

MT RAINIER GONDOLA

DISCOVERY

GOLD HILLS

QUICKSILVER

CAMPBELL BASIN

A-BASIN

SILVER BASIN

POWDER PASS
6,600'

BULLWHEEL BAR & RESTAURANT
CHINOOK GRILL
CASCADE GRILL
FIRESIDE CAFÉ & SUN DECK
RIGHT ANGLE SPORTS SHOP
EQUIPMENT CENTER

ALPINE INN RESTAURANT & HOTEL
SNORTING ELK CELLAR

MAINTENANCE

EMPLOYEE
HOUSING

VILLAGE INN
QUICKSILVER LODGE
CRYSTAL CHALETS
SILVER SKIS CHALET

CRYSTAL MOUNTAIN BLVD.

SOUTHBACK BOUNDARY

49° North

Established: 1935	Acres: 2325	Vertical: 1851'	Annual Snowfall: 301"

Washington's best kept secret, 49° North Mountain Resort truly offers adventures for everyone. This traditional Northwest resort is blessed with wide open groomed runs, moguls, and hundreds of acres of legendary tree skiing. As the second largest ski area in the state, it boasts of 82 named runs on two summits in three basins served by seven lifts and 2,325 skiable acres (primarily north-facing).

For freestyle adventure, the Terrain Park offers fun and excitement for all levels of skiers and riders. Features include rails, boxes, hits and more. The hardworking Park Crew at 49º North puts their collective "heart and soul" into creating an environment for the best park experience possible.

49° North several dining options – Quick Turn Café is at the base lodge and Cy's Café is located mid-mountain in a cozy yurt. After a long day of carving on world-class corduroy or ripping fresh tracks through bone-dry powder, stop by the Boomtown Lounge and enjoy the company of your fellow skiers and riders. The Boomtown Lounge has a full bar and a large selection of beers on tap, full service lunch menu and appetizers.

MOUNTAIN HOSTS

The Mountain Host Program leads guests around the slopes whether they are new to the area, or veteran 49ers looking for a fresh perspective. Mountain Hosts can provide the history of the mountain, explanations of the trails, and can also help with information on après skiing entertainment. When you are in line, their friendly hosts might be that single rider that you ride with up the hill. They can point you towards superbly groomed runs or where a nice powder stash might be hiding.

NORDIC CENTER

Located adjacent to the 49° North Alpine Area sits the 49° North Cross Country Center. The Nordic Center invites families to enjoy a variety of winter activities all at one location. There is a warm and cozy yurt located at the trail head of the Nordic Center. A spacious deck overlooks the teaching area and the beautiful front acres of the Nordic Trail System. The Nordic Trails roll off into the forest where hundred year-old trees tower above the expansive corridors. Nordic skiers can enjoy 25 km of groomed trails with track and skate decks. Additional ungroomed snowshoe trails lace the Nordic Center, and Fatbikes are always welcome.

Mission Ridge

| Established: 1966 | Acres: 2000 | Vertical: 2250' | Annual Snowfall: 200" |

Light powder. Tons of sun. Amazing views. Terrain that fits everyone in the family. Only 12 miles from Wenatchee, the ski area is built into a 2,000 acre basin on the eastern side of the Cascade Mountains. Mission Ridge is a little higher, a little drier, and quite a bit sunnier (300 days annually) than other mountains in the area. That means when storms come in, they drop a different kind of snow at Mission Ridge: light, dry powder.

Mission Ridge has more than 36 designated runs spread over 2,000 spectacular acres of trails, chutes, and bowls, with a 2,250 foot vertical drop.

TERRAIN PARKS

Mission Ridge has garnered regional and national attention for its innovative terrain parks. The 100LAPS Terrain Park is the only dedicated rope tow serviced park in the Pacific Northwest and can be found off of Chair 1. True to its name, you can spin laps in this park all day. Not quite ready to ride in the 100LAPS park? Develop your skills in the Lil' Bombers Park on Mimi first and progress you skill

and style. For a unique park experience visit the top of the mountain and the Bomber Bowl Park. Developed as the nation's first season long "bowl park" the Bomber Bowl Park consists of all snow features that open up creative possibilities and lines for skier and riders of all abilities.

DINING

Mission Ridge offers on-mountain dining at both the base area and mid-mountain lodges. Ka-Wham Cafe' offers one stop, cafeteria style dining at the Hampton Lodge (base area). Next to Ka-Wham is the Chair 5 Pub, a full service restaurant accompanied with a full bar. If you want to stay on the mountain, hit the Midway Lodge, located at the base of Chair 2. Relax, recharge, and warm up inside the lodge at their cafeteria style seating area, or enjoy slopeside dining out on the deck while watching the action of the skiers and riders.

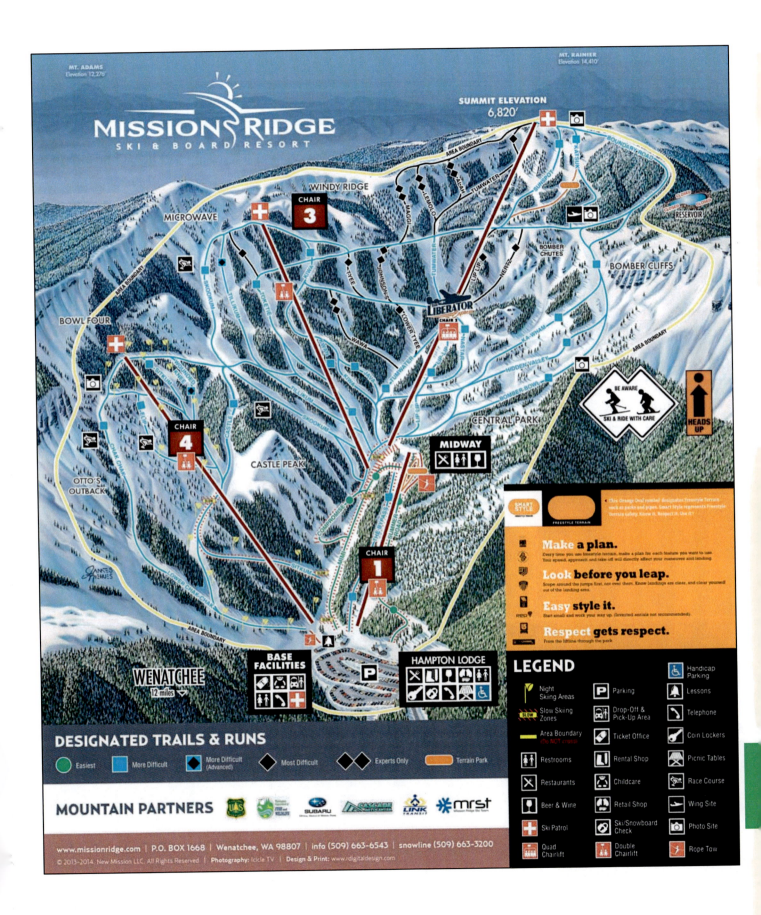

Mt. Spokane

Established: 1932	Acres: 1425	Vertical: 2000'	Annual Snowfall: 300"

Mt. Spokane Ski & Snowboard Park is all about serving it's community of skiers and boarders. As a non-profit chartiable organization, it exists to provide a family-friendly ski area where customer service is a priority in part by returning all profits to the recreation area. Mt. Spokane Ski & Snowboard Park has been a fixture in the local Spokane community since the 1930's, when members of the Spokane Ski Club formed the first organized skiing on the mountain. In 1997, community volunteers again joined to incorporate the ski area as a 501(c)3 non-profit organization. Since then, Mt. Spokane has been very proud to remain closely involved with many community organizations, donating services, man hours, and in-kind gifts towards education, community programs, at-risk youth, health agencies, and countless other non-profit groups.

Mt. Spokane has three day lodges, including the historic Vista House from 1933, built by the Civilian Conservation Corps (CCC).

NIGHT SKIING

Mt. Spokane is typically open for night skiing Wednesday through Saturday night during the main season (mid-December through mid-March).

Night skiing begins at 3:30pm and runs until 9:30pm. That's a total of six hours of skiing & riding under the lights! Enjoy the Foggy Bottom Lounge and full-service cafeteria until close. Live bands play on most Saturday nights.

TERRAIN PARKS

Mt. Spokane has three large terrain parks: Half Hitch, Gnarwood Forest, and Progression Park. The parks have features for all levels from beginner to expert (such as 15-30 foot jumps). And all parks are kept fresh with biweekly changes.

CHAIR 4

White Pass

Established: 1952	Acres: 1402	Vertical: 2050'	Annual Snowfall: 450"

White Pass is known as the laid back, friendly ski area amongst those who frequent the Washington Cascades. With eight lifts (3 quads), over 2,000 vertical feet and nearly 1,500 acres White Pass offers terrain that suits everyone. Be sure to check out some of the best tree skiing in the Northwest. Or for the freestylers, check out the terrain park with a variety of jumps, jibs, and rails.

There is slopeside lodging at the White Pass Village Inn. There is no shortage of dining options with seven choices on the slope or at the base to cover everything from breakfast, lunch, and dinner. Try the After Dark Café for fine dining or the Sitzmark Pub for aprés drinks.

NIGHT SKIING

See White Pass under the stars by extending your visit with night skiing. Available around Christmas from 4 to 9 pm.

NORDIC CENTER

White Pass maintains 18 kilometers of trail that provide a variety of terrain suitable for beginning through expert cross country skiers. They offer rental equipment for cross country skiing, skate skiing and snowshoeing. There's even a yurt which is the perfect spot to relax, grab a snack and catch up with friends and family upon your return to the trail head.

TUBING HILL

The three-lane tubing hill provides a fun experience for the non-skier on weekends and holidays.

Stevens Pass

| Established: 1937 | Acres: 1125 | Vertical: 1800' | Annual Snowfall: 460" |

Stevens Pass provides the best terrain closest to Seattle for both day and night skiing. At a base elevation of 4061 feet, it will be snowing when it's raining in the city. Three high speed and 7 fixed-grip lifts whisk you up the mountain so that you can pack in the laps on a variety of terrain including glades, bowls, and faces or groomed runs. In fact, the grooming is some of the finest around. Operating 11 snowcats each night, the grooming crew is meticulous, ensuring that 20 to 30+ runs are groomed by the morning every day.

Being in the Cascades, Stevens Pass is known for large quantities of snow. A typical year will bring 460" of snowfall which translates to an average base that is easily 105" or more.

When you need a break, the base area has three day lodges with numerous dining choices.

TERRAIN PARKS

Stevens Pass has the largest terrain park in the state as well as three smaller parks for a range in ability. The far right side of the mountain is nearly entirely terrain park, serviced by it's own lift (Brooks). If you are looking to get some air, this is the place to do it.

NIGHT SKIING

Stevens Pass offers a great night experience up to five nights a week (Wednesday through Sunday). Bright white lights illuminate everything on the slope making it easy to ski even during a blizzard. And best of all, six lifts are running allowing you access to the largest night skiing operation in the state.

Stevens Pass is part of the Epic Pass.

STEVENS PASS

MILL VALLEY

Mt. Baker

| Established: 1953 | Acres: 1000 | Vertical: 1500' | Annual Snowfall: 663" |

Mt. Baker Ski Area makes sure that when people visit, they feel like they have arrived AT Mt. Baker, not just another city in the mountains. They forego a significant amount of potential "advertising" monies and do not accept corporate sponsorships for permanent signage or logo placement. Adding to the community feel, Mt. Baker remains one of only a few originally owned ski areas in the U.S. and is predominately owned by people residing in the local community

Mt. Baker also has a long history associated with the sport of snowboarding and people often ask "when" did Mt. Baker first "allow" snowboarding. In fact, Mt. Baker never did NOT allow snowboarding. Baker is considered one of the first in the world to officially support snowboarding. The Mt. Baker Legendary Banked Slalom and the U.S. Open are the two longest running snowboarding events in the world, and the Banked

Slalom is the longest running snowboarding event in the world held on the same course location!

RECORD SNOWFALL

Mt. Baker receives the highest (as in #1) annual average snowfall of more than 740 ski areas in North America, with the 15-year average of 663-inches of average annual snowfall. In 1998-99 they set the World Record for the most snow to fall in one winter anywhere on Earth - 1,140 inches. While the tremendous snowfall that Baker typically receives and the consolidated amount of challenging terrain of the area draws people to Baker, it is the community feel and friendly atmosphere that helps keep them coming back.

MOUNT BAKER
• 10,781 FT

MOUNT SHUKSAN
• 9,131 FT

HEMISPHERES
• 5,550 FT

MT·BAKER
2017 TRAIL MAP 2018

Mount Baker Wilderness

PANORAMA DOME

North Cascades National Park

Mount Baker Wilderness

OUT OF SKI AREA
BACKCOUNTRY
AVALANCHE DANGER

OUT OF SKI AREA
BACKCOUNTRY
AVALANCHE DANGER

CHAIR 8 / SHUKSAN SIDE

Mt. Baker-Snoqualmie National Forest

OUT OF SKI AREA
BACKCOUNTRY
AVALANCHE DANGER

HEATHER MEADOWS
BASE AREA

HEATHER MEADOWS
DAY LODGE
OPEN WEEKENDS & HOLIDAYS

Mountain Shop

FIRST AID

WHITE SALMON
BASE AREA

WHITE SALMON DAY LODGE
OPEN DAILY

FIRST AID

RAVEN HUT LODGE
OPEN DAILY

SKI AREA BOUNDARY

SKI AREA BOUNDARY

SKI AREA BOUNDARY • NO RETURN TO SKI AREA

SKI AREA BOUNDARY • NO RETURN TO SKI AREA

Extreme Danger Zone

Extreme Danger Zone

DANGER! CLIFFS

DANGER! CLIFFS

EXPERTS ONLY LIFT

Gunner's Zone
DANGER! CLIFFS

Gunner's Zone

Canyon Gate

The Chute

North Face

Blueberry Cat Track

Austin

Pan-Face

Home Run

Chair 5 lift

Rainbow

Border

Mitch's

Big Creek

Bard Klause

Holiday

Upper Canuck's

The Canyon

Lower Canuck's

Canuck's Delux

Cat Track

Cat

Track

SLOW ZONE

SLOW ZONE

SLOW ZONE

SLOW ZONE

SLOW ZONE

SLOW ZONE

SLOW ZONE

SLOW ZONE

SLOW ZONE

SLOW ZONE

Gabl's

Natural Halfpipe

Nose Dive

White Salmon

Easy Money

Easy Money

Diehl's

White Salmon

Oh Zone

Daytona

Big Hemi'

Espresso

Espresso

Octo-Bahn

Blroked

Flat Cat Track • 15 Min Wait

DANGER! CLIFFS

Extreme Danger Zone

C-1
C-2
C-3
C-4
C-5
C-6
C-7
C-8

The Summit at Snoqualmie: Alpental

THE SUMMIT AT SNOQUALMIE

| Established: 1967 | Acres: 818 | Vertical: 2280' | Annual Snowfall: 428" |

Alpental was built in 1967 by two Tacoma businessmen, Bob Mickelson and Jim Griffin. Before making the commitment to build a brand new ski area, noted mountaineers Jim and Lou Whittaker hiked up the proposed runs to see if the terrain was suitable for skiing. Their conclusion was a surprise - they thought the terrain was too steep! Those steeps and back bowls are still home to the most challenging, adrenaline charged and breathtaking terrain in North America.

BACK BOWLS

Accessed via two gates, an expert adventurers off-piste playground, the Alpental Back Bowls feature legendary terrain. The Alpental Back Bowls can be the highlight of your day, but it can quickly become just the opposite. Preparing yourself for skiing or snowboarding in this wild terrain is essential to your safety, and the safety of others.

MOUNTAIN SAFETY CLASSES

The David Pettigrew Memorial Foundation operates out of the mid-mountain David Pettigrew Mountain Safety & Education building, conducting general mountain safety classes, companion rescue classes, and avalanche awareness classes. Once you are ready for the back bowls, hone your skills with your avalanche transceiver at the Transceiver Training Park in the parking lot.

NIGHT SKIING

A large portion of the lower mountain is open until 10 pm for night skiing Tuesday through Saturdays.

4 SKI AREAS – ONE PASS

Alpental is only one of the four ski areas accessible with a lift ticket to The Summit at Snoqualmie. All four areas (Alpental, West, Central, East) can be visited by a quick eco-friendly shuttle bus ride that is powered by biodiesel.

The Summit at Snoqualmie is part of the Ikon Pass.

Alpental

Alpental's Legend

Easiest Trail ●
More Difficult ■
Most Difficult ◆
Experts Only ◆◆

⊙ High-Speed Quad	Ⓖ Guest Services
☒ Double Chairlift	Ⓐ Access Gate
☐ Magic Carpet	— Night Skiing Area
ⓘ Information	···· Ski Area Boundary

Ⓗ Restrooms	Ⓗ Food
$ ATM	Ⓔ Espresso
☒ Rentals	Ⓑ Bar
Sport Shop	Ⓛ Lift Tickets

⊕ Ski Patrol	
Ⓢ Shuttle Bus Stop	
Ⓟ Parking	
SnowSports School	

❄ B.A.R.K. Transceiver Training Park

Alpental Back Bowls

DENNY MOUNTAIN 5,610ft.

No designated trails or runs in the Back Bowls

CLIFF AREA

NASH GATE

UPPER INTERNATIONAL

ADRENALIN

ELEVATOR GATE

SNAKE DANCE

FELSEN

BACKBOWL BOUNDARY

BACK BOWL BOUNDARY

TOP STATION 5,420ft.

CLOSED CLIFF AREA

PERMANENTLY CLOSED

LOWER INTERNATIONAL

St. BERNARD

ST. BERNARD

SESSEL

SESSEL

SHOT-SIX

DOM

EISFALLEN

CASCADE TRAVERSE

MEISTER

DEBBIE'S GOLD

EDELWEISS

ARMSTRONG EXPRESS

AREA BOUNDARY

INGRID'S INSPIRATION

MIDWAY 4,400ft.

MOUNT RAINIER 14,410ft.

HUMPBACK MTN. 5,174ft.

Return Route from Back Bowls

Upper Lot Ⓟ

Ⓟ Lot 3

Shot 10 Lot Ⓟ

BASE ELEV. 3,140ft.

To Summit East, Central, West

To Summit East, Central, West

Exit 52

90

B.A.R.K. BEACON PARK

Lower Lot Ⓟ

Main Lot Ⓟ

Main Lot

Edelweiss Bowl

CHAIR PEAK 6,238ft.

THE TOOTH 5,604ft.

DENNY MOUNTAIN 5,610ft.

CHAIR PEAK

LOWER INTERNATIONAL

NASH GATE

INTERNATIONAL

Behind Cliff

BACK BOWL BOUNDARY

PERMANENTLY CLOSED

CLOSED CLIFF AREA

SHOT-SIX

SHOT SIX

TO INTERNATIONAL

KANTE

SCHLUCT

ROLLEN

GUNMOUNT

EDELWEISS BOWL

AREA BOUNDARY

POWDER BOWL

PERMANENTLY CLOSED

BREAKOVER

THE FAN

EDELWEISS

MIDWAY 4,400ft.

TOP OF CHAIR 1

ARMSTRONG EXPRESS

PERMANENTLY CLOSED

The Summit at Snoqualmie: Central

THE SUMMIT AT SNOQUALMIE

Established: 1948	Acres: 539	Vertical: 1025'	Annual Snowfall: 428"

The Summit at Snoqualmie (Central) offers up diverse terrain for every ability level. From an award-winning terrain park to black diamond and beginner runs. Summit Central also has the majority of ski schools, a separate bunny slope with two Magic Carpets, and a dedicated lift for the beginner terrain.

Enjoy the new lodge at the base of the Silver Fir Express lift where there is a new cafeteria, bar, outdoor fire pits, and a rental shop below.

TERRAIN PARKS

Known as one of the best Terrain Parks in the Northwest, Central Park offers small to large jumps and utilizes a fleet of over 70 features. Terrain parks are also built at the other areas at different times of the season.

NIGHT SKIING

The Summit at Snoqualmie has some of the latest and largest night skiing in the Western USA. Extend your ski day into the night until 10 pm!

TUBING PARK

Located at the base of Summit Central, The Summit Tubing Park is perfect for anyone looking to play in the snow! Enjoy 550 feet of groomed tubing lanes (20+) that drop 40 ft, then ride the magic carpet back to the top.

4 SKI AREAS – ONE PASS

Summit Central is only one of the four ski areas accessible with a lift ticket to The Summit at Snoqualmie. All four areas (Alpental, West, Central, East) can be visited by a quick shuttle bus. Or ski over to East or West via the InterSummit crossover trails.

The Summit at Snoqualmie is part of the Ikon Pass.

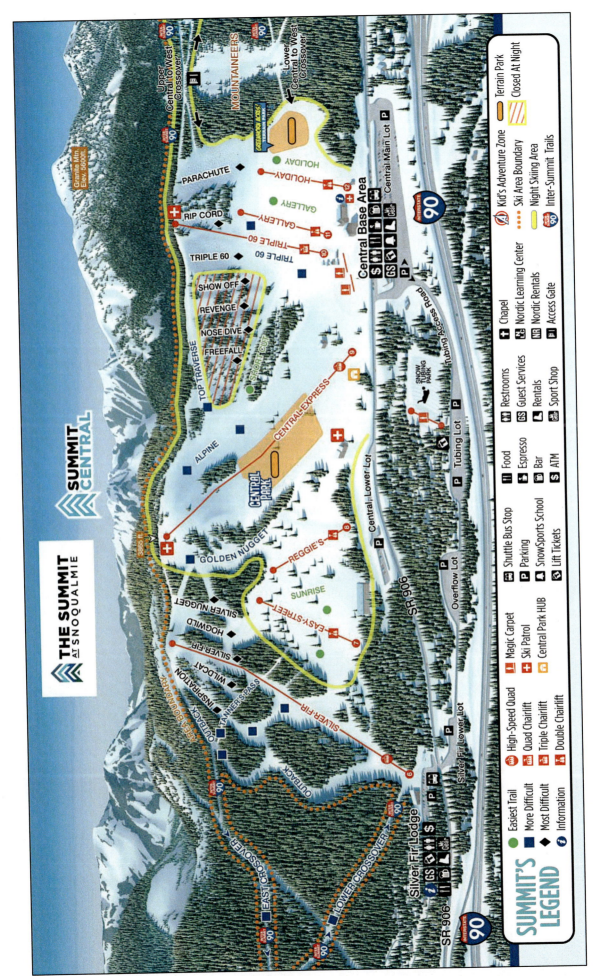

The Summit at Snoqualmie: East

Established: 1930s	Acres: 340	Vertical: 1100'	Annual Snowfall: 428"

Summit East is an adventurer's paradise. Tons of terrain from mellow cruisers all the way up to steep black diamonds, and everything between. Summit East is also home to some of the best tree skiing at The Summit. Unlike the other Summit ski areas, Summit East has a backside that takes you away to your own set of trails away from the rest of the world.

Once you've exhausted all 20 trails, ski the InterSummit 90 Lower Crossover which takes you to the Silver Fir lifts at Summit Central.

NORDIC CENTER

Summit East is home to the The Summit Nordic Center. Based out of the Old Milwaukee Lodge, the Nordic Center offers snowshoe and cross country rental equipment, lessons, and tours for all ages and ability levels. The Summit Nordic Center is at the base of Summit East, next to the start of 50 km of groomed cross-country trails.

Once you are on the trails, try one of the two warming huts. The Jim Brooks warming hut is located just over Windy Pass (on the west side). It is usually in place between late December and late March. There is also a hut at Grand Junction that has room for a few skiers at a time.

4 SKI AREAS – ONE PASS

Summit East is only one of the four ski areas accessible with a lift ticket to The Summit at Snoqualmie. All four areas (Alpental, West, Central, East) can be visited by a quick eco-friendly shuttle bus ride that is powered by biodiesel or simply ski between areas by using the InterSummit crossover trails.

The Summit at Snoqualmie is part of the Ikon Pass.

THE SUMMIT AT SNOQUALMIE

HIDDEN VALLEY - East Backside

MT. HYAK 3710 ft.

EAST PEAK

SOLUTION

REVELATION

HIDDEN VALLEY

ECLIPSE

Squirrel's Forest

SOLITUDE

SUMMIT EAST

MT. CATHERINE 5052 ft.

SILVER PEAK 5605 ft.

MT. HYAK 3710 ft.

MILWAUKEE RIDGE

VIC'S

SISSY'S

BLOWDOWN

KENDALL

CUTOFF

CREEK RUN

CHICKAMIN

SARRAH'S RUN

RAMPART

CREEK RUN

EAST CROSSOVER

EAST PEAK

DINO'S REVENGE

HYAK FACE

ROZ'S

EAST PEAK

LOWER CROSSOVER

Power Lines

NORDIC CENTER

East Base Area

P Upper Lots

P

EXIT 54

SR 906

Lower Lot

INTERSTATE 90

SUMMIT'S LEGEND

🟢 Easiest Trail	🚡 High-Speed Quad	🟧 Magic Carpet	🚌 Shuttle Bus Stop	🍴 Food		
🟦 More Difficult	🚡 Quad Chairlift	➕ Ski Patrol	🅿 Parking	☕ Espresso		
◆ Most Difficult	🚡 Triple Chairlift	🟧 Central Park HUB	🏠 SnowSports School	🍺 Bar		
ℹ Information	🚡 Double Chairlift		🎟 Lift Tickets	💲 ATM		

🚻 Restrooms   ✝ Chapel   Ⓐ Kid's Adventure Zone   🟧 Terrain Park

GS Guest Services   🅰 Access Gate   •••• Ski Area Boundary   Closed At Night

🎿 Rentals   NR Nordic Rentals   🟨 Night Skiing Area

🏔 Sport Shop   NLC Nordic Learning Center   Inter-Summit Trails

The Summit at Snoqualmie: West

THE SUMMIT AT SNOQUALMIE

| Established: 1933 | Acres: 299 | Vertical: 765' | Annual Snowfall: 428" |

Summit West is where Seattle learns to ski and snowboard – known for its convenient family fun and great learning terrain by day, West truly comes to life at night. Whether it's fresh corduroy or fresh pow, West is the place to catch first tracks for night skiing, as it opens later in the day. West is open for day skiing only on weekends and holidays.

NIGHT SKIING

Summit West has one of the best night skiing schedules because the slopes are not used during the day (Monday-Wednesday), then Wednesday night the slopes are opened to night skiers. Nowhere else can you find night skiing that offers fresh tracks. The slopes are also groomed just for night skiers on Wednesday through Friday. Stay up as late as you can, the skiing doesn't end until 10 pm.

DINING

Summit West has a variety of dining options for any tastebud. Timberwolf Bar & Grill for apres drinks, pizza and pasta. Big Air BBQ offers platters & ribs.

Rosita's has Mexican burritos, tacos, nachos, and more. Or for fine dining, try Webb's Restaurant – the Summit's finest.

LESSONS

Summit West has some of the best beginner terrain that allows for one to easily progress into intermediate runs. Ski and snowboard lessons are available several times a day through the Summit SnowSports School. Besides having three dedicated Magic Carpets, there is also the Little Thunder quad that accesses beginner terrain.

4 SKI AREAS – ONE PASS

Summit East is only one of the four ski areas accessible with a lift ticket to The Summit at Snoqualmie. All four areas (Alpental, West, Central, East) can be visited by a quick eco-friendly shuttle bus ride that is powered by biodiesel or simply ski between areas by using the InterSummit crossover trails.

The Summit at Snoqualmie is part of the Ikon Pass.

THE SUMMIT AT SNOQUALMIE

SUMMIT WEST

Denny Mtn. Elev. 5,610ft.

Upper Central to West Crossover

INTER-SUMMIT 90

MAIN CHUTE

BEAVER LAKE

3765 ft.

FREERIDERS

360 BOWL

BIG BILL

WILDSIDE

THUNDERBOLT

THUNDERBIRD

MOUNTAINEERS

INTER-SUMMIT 90

EASY RIDER

EASY RIDER

WILDSIDE

THUNDERBIRD

DODGE RIDGE

DODGE RIDGE

PACIFIC CREST

JULIES

JULIES

Main Parking

Lower Central to West Crossover

15

16

LITTLE THUNDER

LITTLE THUNDER

17

18

19

20

West Base Area

SR 906

GS

EXIT 53

To Alpental

EXIT 52

INTERSTATE 90

SUMMIT'S LEGEND

- 🟢 Easiest Trail
- 🟦 More Difficult
- ♦ Most Difficult
- ℹ Information

- High-Speed Quad
- Quad Chairlift
- Triple Chairlift
- Double Chairlift

- Magic Carpet
- Ski Patrol
- Central Park HUB

- Shuttle Bus Stop
- Parking
- SnowSports School
- Lift Tickets

- Food
- Espresso
- Bar
- ATM

- Restrooms
- Guest Services
- Rentals
- Sport Shop

- Chapel
- Access Gate
- Nordic Rentals
- Nordic Learning Center

- Kid's Adventure Zone
- •••• Ski Area Boundary
- Night Skiing Area

- Terrain Park
- Closed At Night
- Inter-Summit Trails

Bluewood

Established: 1979	Acres: 400	Vertical: 1125'	Annual Snowfall: 300"

Perched high atop the Blue Mountains, just 52 miles northeast of Walla Walla, Bluewood occupies the second-highest base elevation (4,545 feet) in Washington State. The Blue Mountains rise out of a high-desert region, which provides clear skies and some of the lightest, fluffiest, smoke-dry powder in the state.

The mountain offers 400+ skiable acres of lift-serviced terrain for every ability level. With three lifts, 24+ trails, epic tree skiing, a terrain park and world-class grooming, Bluewood is the place to make memories skiing and snowboarding.

In the lodge, discover their rental and repair shop. Whether you need to rent a ski package, snowboard package, boots, or poles, they'll get you fitted correctly. Stop by the repair shop for minor fixes, tunes and hot waxing needs. In the retail shop, you'll find t-shirts, sweatshirts, gloves, goggles, hats and more. Before or after shredding the slopes, fuel up with an energizing breakfast, quick snack, leisurely lunch or pub fare.

Bluewood employees are well-known for friendliness, and guests love the family-friendly vibe. Bring a friend, the kids or a whole group and experience a mountain of fun at Bluewood!

VINTNER'S RIDGE SNOWCAT

Explore the "other side" of Bluewood via Vintner's Ridge. This amazing side-country terrain is ungroomed and ready for wonderful off-piste experiences. On many days (typically most Saturdays and Sundays, holidays, and select other times), when conditions allow, Bluewood offers snow-cat transportation to the top of the ridge for a small fee. Hiking access is allowed daily whenever Vintner's Ridge is open. This expert area opens up to more than 200 acres of amazing terrain.

LESSONS

Whether you're a first-timer or looking to hone your skills, expert instructors help you have fun learning to ski or snowboard at Bluewood. There are several lesson options for adults and kids starting as young as 4 years, including:

- Group lessons—any day Bluewood is open.
- One-on-one instruction—either for an hour or all day.
- Specially priced packages for beginners and for those who want to explore the mountain at the next level.

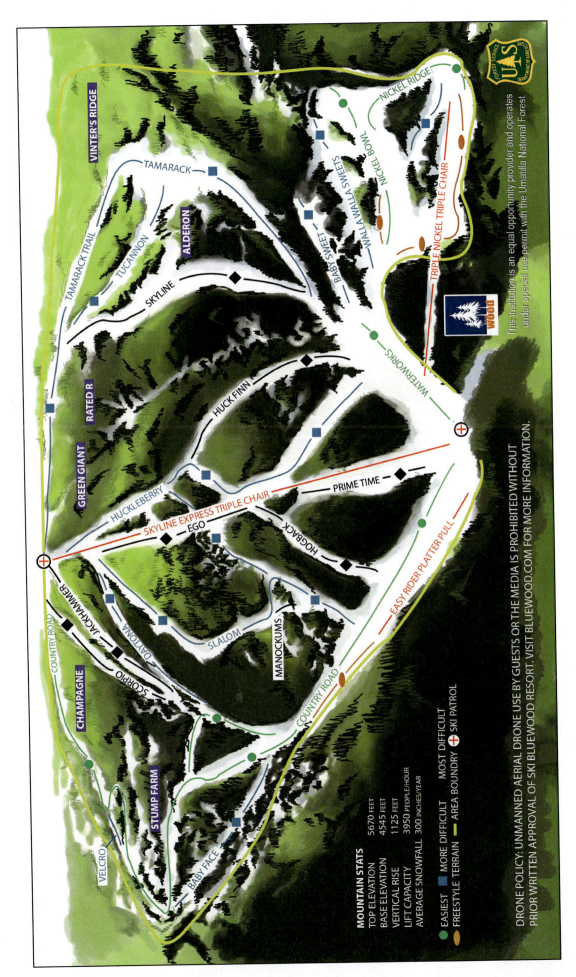

MOUNTAIN STATS

TOP ELEVATION	5670 FEET
BASE ELEVATION	4545 FEET
VERTICAL RISE	1125 FEET
LIFT CAPACITY	3950 PEOPLE/HOUR
AVERAGE SNOWFALL	300 INCHES/YEAR

● EASIEST   ◆ MORE DIFFICULT   ◆ MOST DIFFICULT
● FREESTYLE TERRAIN   — AREA BOUNDRY   ✛ SKI PATROL

VINTER'S RIDGE

TAMARACK

ALDERON

TAMARACK TRAIL

TUCANNON

SKYLINE

RATED R

GREEN GIANT

HUCK FINN

BABY SWEET

WALLA WALLA SWEETS

NICKEL BOWL

NICKEL RIDGE

TRIPLE NICKEL TRIPLE CHAIR

WATERWORKS

WOOD

HUCKLEBERRY

PRIME TIME

SKYLINE EXPRESS TRIPLE CHAIR

EGO

HOGBACK

EASY RIDER PLATTER PULL

CHAMPAGNE

JACKHAMMER

DAYTONA

SCORPIO

COUNTRY ROAD

SLALOM

MANOCKUMS

COUNTRY ROAD

STUMP FARM

VELCRO

BABY FACE

DRONE POLICY: UNMANNED AERIAL DRONE USE BY GUESTS OR THE MEDIA IS PROHIBITED WITHOUT PRIOR WRITTEN APPROVAL OF SKI BLUEWOOD RESORT. VISIT BLUEWOOD.COM FOR MORE INFORMATION.

This institution is an equal opportunity provider and operates under special use permit with the Umatilla National Forest.

Loup Loup

| Established: 1958 | Acres: 300 | Vertical: 1240' | Annual Snowfall: 150" |

Experience dry Okanogan powder and perfectly groomed runs — with little or no wait time — on 300 acres of diverse terrain. The Mountain has a lot to offer beginner through advanced alpine skiers, nordic skiers and boarders alike. Open on Wednesday through Sunday, 9:00 a.m. to 3:45 p.m. During Christmas and February Presidents' Day holidays Loup Loup is also open every weekday except Christmas Day.

The Rental Shop stocks alpine skis and snowboards, kids' rental equipment & helmets, and other rental gear. Forgot something? Purchase poles, goggles, gloves, socks & other items from their Retail Shop. PSIA-certified Ski School Instructors offer all levels of Alpine and Snowboarding Lessons.

Loup Loup is the first Western ski area to offer luge sledding. A snowcat transports the sledders to the dedicated luge sledding trails, giving the sledders a 1200 foot gain in elevation. Snowcats leave four times per day on weekends and holidays. There are over 12 km of groomed trails just for the luge sledders.

The Little Buck Cafe is a rustic day lodge, featuring a rock fireplace, food, beer and wine services. Open 8:30 a.m. – 4:00 p.m. on all lift-operation days.

Loup Loup also features a terrain park, Wild Wolf Tubing Hill, and 30 km of Nordic trails at the Loup Loup South Summit Sno Park.

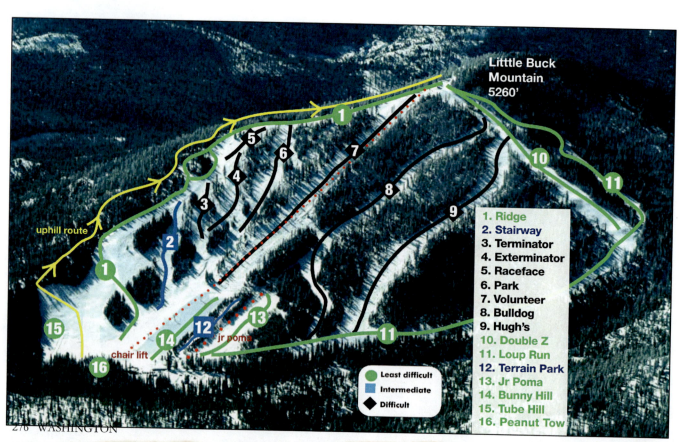

Litttle Buck Mountain 5260'

1. Ridge
2. Stairway
3. Terminator
4. Exterminator
5. Raceface
6. Park
7. Volunteer
8. Bulldog
9. Hugh's
10. Double Z
11. Loup Run
12. Terrain Park
13. Jr Poma
14. Bunny Hill
15. Tube Hill
16. Peanut Tow

uphill route

jr poma

chair lift

● Least difficult
■ Intermediate
◆ Difficult

Echo Valley

| Established: 1955 | Acres: 70 | Vertical: 900' | Annual Snowfall: 39" |

Echo Valley is the place for winter recreation in the Lake Chelan Valley. Families have been skiing at Echo Valley for several generations and visitors to the Valley love the friendly family atmosphere. From skiing to snow tubing, it's all here at Echo Valley. Echo Valley Ski Area is run by an all-volunteer non-profit group.

Facilities include three rope tows, a 1,400 foot Poma Lift and a 4-lane tubing hill. They offer ski/snowboard instruction & rentals for all ages & abilities. The base area has a day lodge & eatery with a roaring log-sized fireplace to warm the toes while enjoying the food concession, Terri's Treats! Piping hot breakfast & lunch with lots of variety to please the entire family.

Echo Valley Area Map

□ EASY
○ INTERMEDIATE
◆ MORE DIFFICULT

Echo Mountain

RIDGE RUN □

BOWL □

CANYON □

FACE ◆

PTARMIGAN ◆

Tubing Hill

#1 Rope Tow

#3 Rope Tow

#2 Rope Tow

LODGE

POMA-LIFT

Hurricane Ridge

| Established: 1958 | Acres: 50 | Vertical: 800' | Annual Snowfall: 400" |

Hurricane Ridge Ski and Snowboard Area is located in the Olympic National Park, 17 miles south of Port Angeles, Washington, one of only two remaining lift operations in the National Parks. Rising a mile high, Hurricane Ridge offers winter recreation and activities and features winter vistas unmatched anywhere in the Pacific Northwest. It is a small, family oriented ski area, offering to residents and visitors alike a quality winter sports experience, without the high cost or congestion of most ski areas.

The Ridge boasts some groomed areas, but for the accomplished skier or snowboarder the steeps, bowls and glades are well worth the effort it takes to get there. Check out the terrain park and tubing area, too.

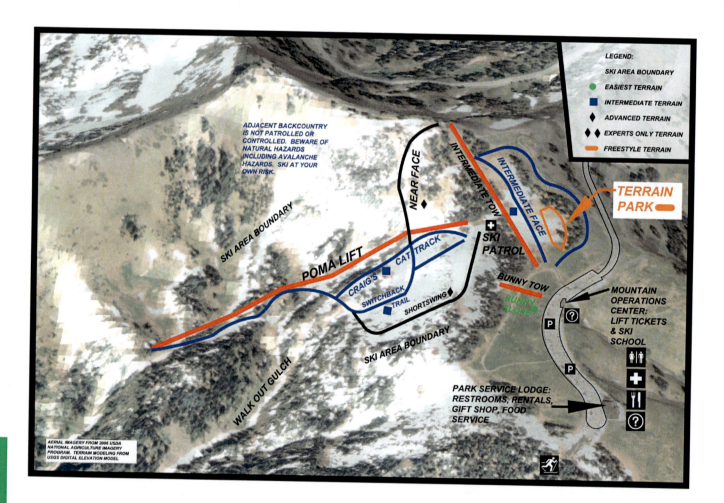

Leavenworth Ski Hill

Established: 1928	Acres: 17	Vertical: 200'	Annual Snowfall: 100"

The Leavenworth Ski Hill is less than two miles from downtown Leavenworth (a town modeled after a Bavarian village). Since 1928, the non-profit Leavenworth Winter Sports Club (LWSC) or some early form of it has been facilitating winter recreation in the Leavenworth area. Traditionally the "base" of operations has been the "Ski Hill" where today they offer two rope tows, an Alpine jumping hill, a tubing hill and 8 km of Nordic trails of which 5 are illuminated for night skiing. (Check schedule for alpine night skiing.)

The Ski Hill hosts free events throughout the winter such as a snowshoe demo and spectators are always welcome at the Alpine races, Nordic races and ski jumping tournaments. Food, beverages and warmth are available at the historic Ski Hill Lodge.

- Downhill Skiing & Snowboarding - Two groomed hills serviced by rope tows.
- Lt Michael Adams Tubing Park - Tubing fun for the whole family!
- Ski Jumping - The only ski jump on the West coast!
- Nordic Skiing - 5 km lit for night skiing until 10 PM
- Snowshoeing - 7 km of trails
- Fat Bike - Trails groomed and lit!
- The Historic Ski Hill Lodge - Watch the kids ski, warm up around the fireplace and take a hot cocoa break.

NORDIC TRAILS AND SNOWSHOE ROUTES

START HERE

N

MAP KEY					
S TRAILS START	**3**	TRISH'S LOOP	**T**	TICKET BOOTH
1 RACE START	**4**	LOOP B	**P**	PARKING
2 LIGHTED TRAILS	**5**	LOOP C	**L**	LODGE
♦ EASY LOOP	**6**	LOWER CUTOFF	→	ONE WAY TRAIL
♦ MODERATE LOOP	**7**	UPPER CUTOFF	⊘	NO DOGS ALLOWED

TRISH'S LOOP

SKI JUMP HILL

MODERATE

BIG TOW

LITTLE TOW

LOOP C

ALPINE HILL

EASY

LOOP B

YOU ARE HERE

TUBING AREA **T**

P

TRAVEL TIPS: ALTITUDE SICKNESS

Most of the ski areas in the West are at a high enough elevation (8,000 ft) to cause some symptoms of altitude sickness, such as headaches, dizziness, muscle aches, and nausea. This is also referred to as Acute Mountain Sickness (AMS). If you have worse symptoms, like trouble breathing – then you'll need to see a doctor and/or get to a lower elevation. Staying hydrated will help as well as deep breathing can help since the main reason you are experiencing such symptoms is lack of oxygen. After a day or so, you should be feeling better as your body acclimates. Know your body and whether you do well at altitude because you may not want to plan to ski on the day you arrive.

One trick to staying hydrated on the mountain is to carry a small 8 oz flask filled with water. Flasks are designed to fit in your pocket so they are a natural container choice when you don't have a backpack. Just be sure to select a flask with a top that is tethered to the flask – you don't want to lose the cap on the ski lift.

Wyoming

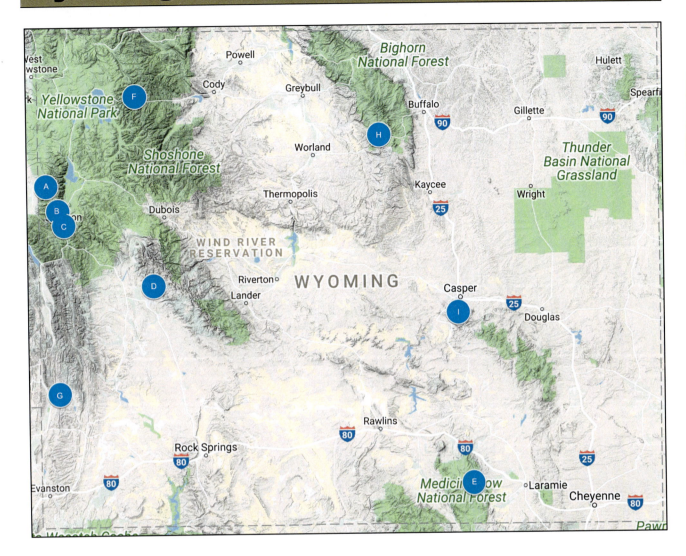

		Page
A.	Grand Targhee	282
B.	Jackson Hole Mountain Resort	284
C.	Snow King Mountain	286
D.	White Pine	288
E.	Snowy Range	290
F.	Sleeping Giant	292
G.	Pine Creek	294
H.	Meadowlark Ski Lodge	295
I.	Hogadon Basin	296

Grand Targhee

GRAND TARGHEE RESORT

Established: 1969	Acres: 2602	Vertical: 2030'	Annual Snowfall: 500"

Grand Targhee Resort is a year round mountain resort situated in the Western slope of the Tetons in Alta, Wyoming. Located in the Caribou-Targhee National Forest, the abundance of light powder snow (more than 500 inches annually) and lack of lift lines amid spectacular views creates an adventure-lover's paradise. Grand Targhee Resort is continually recognized for its great snow, unparalleled mountain biking, genuine Western hospitality, scenic beauty, excellent value, and commitment to sustainability.

Grand Targhee is a full-service resort with on-mountain dining, slopeside lodging, rental shop, ski school, and a range of activities including early tracks, tubing park, snowmobile backcountry tours, fat biking, snowshoeing, cross-country skiing, and sleigh-ride dinners.

MOUNTAIN TOURS

Learn the mountain and its numerous runs with the Ski & Snowboard instructor-led complimentary daily mountain tours. Get inside tips on hidden powder stashes, learn the mountain, short cuts to lifts, explore the vast terrain, and enjoy incredible views of the Grand Tetons, Teton Valley, Wyoming, Idaho, and Montana. Guests get inside tips on après activities at Grand Targhee Resort. Daily from 10:30am to noon. Meet at the base of Dreamcatcher beside the Mountain Tour Flag.

SNOWCAT SKIING & BOARDING

Only with Grand Targhee Snowcat Adventures can you access 602 acres of untracked powder, expertise from professional guides, and the powder experience of a lifetime. Up to 12 skiers and boarders will experience up to 18,000 vertical feet in just one day of unbelievable deep, dry Teton powder in the vast terrain only accessible to Snowcat Adventures. Cruise through open bowls, endless glades, and steep tree pitches with Wyoming's only cat skiing.

KIDS ADVENTURE ZONE

Kids Adventure Zone has terrain dedicated to families, first time skiers or riders, lessons, and children. The terrain was developed based learning features that build skills, balance, and confidence in a safe environment. For kids that are too young to ski, Grand Targhee also has a licensed child care center for children ages 2 months to 12 years.

GRAND TARGHEE RESORT
ALTA, WYOMING

PEAKED MOUNTAIN
South View

GrandTarghee.com

GRANDTARGHEE.COM

MOUNT MORAN
12,605'

MOUNT OWEN
12,928'

GRAND TETON
13,770'

MIDDLE TETON
12,804'

SOUTH TETON
12,514'

FRED'S MOUNTAIN
9,862'

MARY'S NIPPLE
9,920'

PEAKED MOUNTAIN
9,830'

DREAMCATCHER

Papoose

Palmer's Raceway

PAPOOSE

SHOSHONE

Big Horn

Rainbow Road

Lower Exhibition

Upper Exhibition

Little Big Horn

The Meadows

Pie Highway

Fred's Chute

Alley Oop Alley

Outback

LITTLE BEAVER TRAVERSE

Bobsled

North Pole

KIDS FUN ZONE

SKI AREA BOUNDARY

SLEIGH RIDE
DINNER YURT

GRAND TARGHEE
NORDIC TRAILS

BLACKFOOT

RESPONSIBILITY CODE

TARGHEE MAIN PLAZA

RESORT FACILITIES
Base Elevation 7,860 ft.

MAP LEGEND

Jackson Hole Mountain Resort

| Established: 1965 | Acres: 2500 | Vertical: 4139' | Annual Snowfall: 450" |

THE TRAM

"Arguably the best lift in North America, the Jackson Hole Tram has a well-justified reputation. Not because the tram ops play rad music on the way up, even though they do. Not because this new tram, built in 2008 to replace the old one, can operate in 70 mph winds, which it does. No, this lift rules simply because of the terrain it serves, and especially its backcountry access. From steep north-facing powder shots, aesthetic couloirs with mandatory airs, silent tree glades, wide open bowls, ass-puckering ridge hikes and long tours, the skiing off the tram is reason enough to forget all the other crap going on in your life, and get to Jackson as soon as you can."

Matt Hansen, Powder Magazine

Photo courtesy of JHMR

TETON VILLAGE

Home to the Jackson Hole Mountain Resort's Aerial Tram and Grand Adventure Park, Teton Village is a playground for young and old. Teton Village offers shopping, dining and fun for the entire family. Located 1 mile from the southern entrance to Grand Teton National Park on the Moose to Wilson Road, Teton Village is a great jump off point for any adventure in Jackson Hole.

THE TERRAIN

Jackson Hole is known for some of the best steeps and chutes in the lower 48, but if you've ever spent a day on the groomers, you know they're nothing short of amazing. From mellow-pitched green runs to intermediate blues and advanced black diamond groomed runs, skiers and riders will find plenty of carving terrain to explore in Jackson Hole.

Photo courtesy of JHMR

While Jackson Hole is known for offering terrain for skiers/snowboarders of all ability levels, no discussion of the terrain at Jackson Hole Mountain Resort is complete without talking about the legendary Corbet's Couloir. The tram cruises right by Corbet's on its way to the top, offering skiers/riders a glimpse of the famed run.

Photo courtesy of JHMR

While Jackson Hole is known as being a natural playground of terrain, the natural features are complemented by two terrain parks, four Burton Stash parks and a halfpipe. Regardless of your style (or level) of riding or skiing, there is a park for you.

Jackson Hole is part of the Ikon Pass.

Snow King Mountain

SNOW KING
MOUNTAIN RESORT since 1939

| Established: 1939 | Acres: 400 | Vertical: 1571' | Annual Snowfall: 167" |

Welcome to Snow King Mountain, Jackson Hole's hometown hill. Wyoming's very first ski resort is still a great place to ski and snowboard 80 seasons later. The King is just steps from Jackson's Town Square with terrain from beginner to expert, and great views of the town of Jackson and the Tetons. With 400 skiable acres, 3 lifts and 32 named runs, Snow King is a world-class ski resort right in the heart of Jackson.

Snow King is "the local's mountain" with a long history of recreational skiing, racing, and a full-service mountain sports school. There are two terrain parks, two restaurants, and a full-service rental facility. For non-skiers and snowboarders, King Tubes, the Cowboy Coaster, and the scenic chairlift provide alternatives for people of all ages and abilities to enjoy the thrills of winter, and breathtaking views of downtown Jackson and the Teton Range. Snow King is your affordable ticket to outdoor fun both summer and winter. In summer, Snow King offers a range of activities for all ages from the Treetop Adventure high ropes course and zip-lines to the classic Alpine Slide.

Parking is free at both bases, and there's also a START bus that can bring you to both Snow King base areas.

DINING

Whether you are looking for an afternoon meal with the family or just a quick bite after a hike up Snow King, King's Grill and Lodge Room Cafe are perfect options. Stop by in the morning for a coffee and breakfast sandwich or swing in for lunch, après or dinner.

LESSONS

Elevate your skiing and riding to a higher level with their Mountain Sports School for adults and kids of all abilities. Whether you want to sharpen your existing techniques or try skiing for the first time, their qualified staff will provide you with an unforgettable learning experience that will make you want to come back for more!

SNOW KING
MOUNTAIN
JACKSON HOLE • WY

7808 FT
PANORAMA HOUSE

BEAR CAVE

BEAR CLAW GLADES

UPPER EXHIBITION

EXHIBITION

HOLY LAND

SUMMIT CHAIRLIFT

COUGAR

BELLY ROLL

BIGHORN

COUGAR TRIPLE CHAIRLIFT

SADDLE CORRIDOR

SLOW TRAIL

BISON

OLD LADY'S FLAGS

JUMP RUN

LOWER ELK

ELK

OLD MAN'S FLAGS

SLOW TRAIL

DUMPIKE

WEBB'S CHUTE

SLOW TRAIL

GRIZZLY

LOWER GRIZZLY

KAREN'S WAY

UPPER KELLY'S

SLOW TRAIL

CUB RUN

KELLY'S ALLEY

EAST'S CHUTE

MOOSE

TOWERS

SNAKE RIVER RUN I

FLYING SQUIRREL

CUBS

CUBS TRAIL

RAFFERTY CHAIRLIFT

RAFFERTY CENTER
MOUNTAIN SPORTS CENTER
KINGS GRILL
COWBOY COASTER

MAGIC CARPET

KING TUBES TOW
KING TUBES

PHILBAUX PARK

KIM'S CAFE &
LODGE ROOM
SKATING RINK

LITTLE MARE

SNOW KING
MOUNTAIN SPORTS

VistaMap

White Pine

| Established: 1938 | Acres: 370 | Vertical: 1100' | Annual Snowfall: 150" |

White Pine (originally named Surveyor Park Ski Area) opened to skiers on January 5, 1940. One of Wyoming's first cable tows had been installed the previous Fall consisting of a ½ inch cable run around 2 drums powered by a gas fired Chevy motor. In 1961 the US Forest Service issued a 20 year lease covering 76 acres on Fortification Mountain. Stocks were sold to cover the purchase of a lift which was purchased and shipped from France. The White Pine lift was the longest in Wyoming at the time, starting at 8,500 feet elevation and taking skiers an additional 900 feet to the top of Fortification Mountain.

Currently, White Pine Ski Area has 25 runs for downhill skiing and snowboarding and is adjacent to 35K of looping Nordic ski trails for all skill levels. Two lifts service groomed downhill runs and the terrain park offers jumps and slides. Fortification Mountain rises to an elevation of 9,500 feet and offers spectacular views of the Continental Divide, Wind River Mountains, the Bridger-Teton National Forest, Fremont Lake, as well as the nearby Wyoming Mountain Range.

Year-round recreation at White Pine includes downhill & Nordic skiing, snowboarding, horseback adventures, downhill mountain biking, cross country mountain biking, scenic chairlift rides, hiking, camping and fishing. Additionally, White Pine hosts special events such as weddings, retirement parties, birthday parties, outdoor retreats and company parties. They have an assortment of facilities for rental including cabin accommodations, a tent village with fresh water bathrooms and showers, fully staffed lodge, meeting rooms, bar, and grill.

LODGING

Get the real mountain experience and stay in one of their rustic cabins, walking distance to the lifts. Cozy fireplace included.

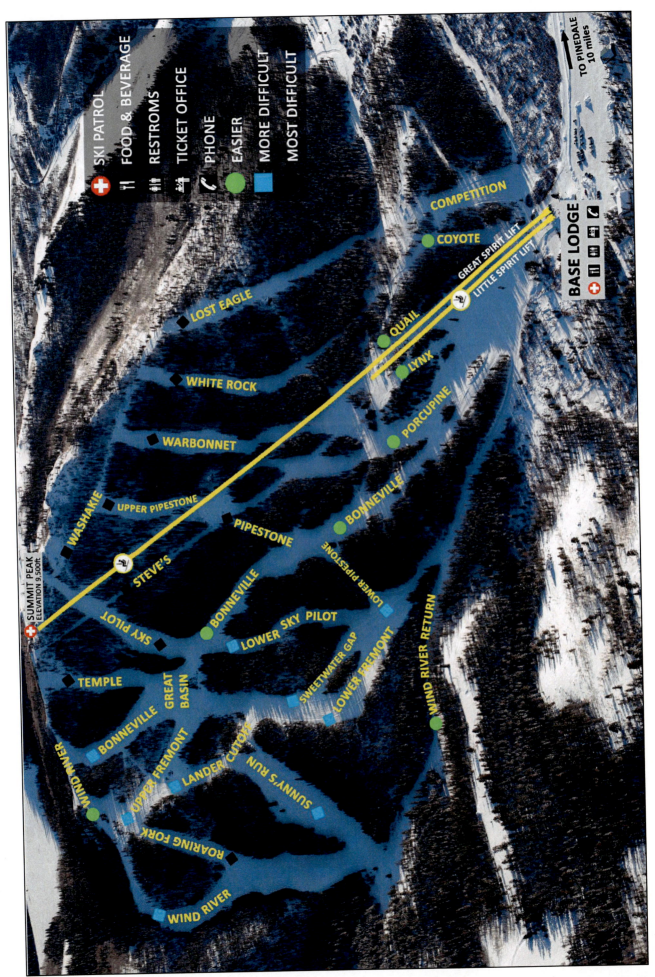

SKI PATROL

FOOD & BEVERAGE

RESTROMS

TICKET OFFICE

PHONE

EASIER

MORE DIFFICULT

MOST DIFFICULT

TO PINEDALE
10 miles

COMPETITION

COYOTE

GREAT SPIRIT LIFT

LITTLE SPIRIT LIFT

BASE LODGE

QUAIL

LYNX

LOST EAGLE

WHITE ROCK

PORCUPINE

WARBONNET

BONNEVILLE

WASHAKIE

UPPER PIPESTONE

PIPESTONE

LOWER PIPESTONE

STEVE'S

SUMMIT PEAK
ELEVATION 9,500ft

SKY PILOT

BONNEVILLE

LOWER SKY PILOT

WIND RIVER RETURN

SWEETWATER GAP

LOWER FREMONT

TEMPLE

GREAT BASIN

BONNEVILLE

UPPER FREMONT

LANDER CUTOFF

WIND RIVER

SUNNY'S RUN

ROARING FORK

WIND RIVER

Snowy Range

Established: 1960	Acres: 250	Vertical: 990'	Annual Snowfall: 245"

Snowy Range is nestled in the stunningly beautiful Medicine Bow-Routt National Forest. This pristine setting is the perfect backdrop for a winter break.

Beginner, intermediate, expert. Regardless of your personal level of proficiency, you'll find the perfect ski or snowboard run, whether it's a downhill screamer or a casual glide through tree-lined forests. 27 trails serve all skiing abilities from beginner to expert. The four chairlifts - Sundance, Virginian, Pioneer, Chute and the Magic Carpet Surface Lift will move you up the mountain quickly and keep you skiing instead of standing.

The Snowy Range Mountain Sports School is home to snowboarding and skiing lessons for first-timers and accomplished individuals of all ages. Available in 2-hour and full day group lessons, as well as private lessons, the Mountain Sports School has a lesson perfect for everyone. Take your skills to the next level.

The Snowy Range day lodge is home to the Happy Jack Café and the Libby Creek Bar & Grill. The lodge also has the gift shop, rental shop, and ski school complete with a childcare center, Kids' Corner. Warm, safe and comfortable, your child will have a blast in this interactive environment, while under the attentive care of their experienced and State of Wyoming licensed staff. Kids' Corner at Snowy Range is open all weekends and holidays.

MEDICINE BOW TERRAIN PARK

Designed with all ages and abilities in mind, Snowy Range has built one of the best terrain parks around. Over the season the park will be rebuilt and completely redesigned multiple times in order to bring the local riders a continuously changing and ever challenging park. With rails, jumps and features for riders of all abilities Snowy Range is investing in a new direction for all of their guests.

MAP KEY

- ● Easiest
- ● More Difficult
- ◆ Most Difficult
- ⸺ Lift
- ⸺ Ski Area Boundry

?	Tickets & Information
✚	Ski Patrol
	Phones and Lockers
	Restrooms
	Rentals & Accessories
	Ski School
	Cafe/Lounge
	Gifts & Accessories

All lodge services and amenities located at the base area.

Medicine Bow – Routt National Forest
The Snowy Range Ski and Recreation Area is an equal opportunity service provider. The Snowy Range Ski and Recreation Area is a permitee of the Medicine Bow – Routt National Forests.

Caution:
Ski area vehicles may be encountered at any time.

Map Illustration by Matt Scharf
Matt Scharf ©

Medicine Bow Peak: 12,013 feet

Centennial, Wyoming

Laramie: 32 miles
Centennial: 5 miles

Sleeping Giant

Established: 1938	Acres: 184	Vertical: 810'	Annual Snowfall: 310"

Only 3½ miles from Yellowstone National Park, is Sleeping Giant which is one of Wyoming's longest running ski areas. SG is all about steep tree skiing and cliffs for the experts, Terrain parks to test your ability, really fun rolling intermediate terrain, and a perfect pitch for the beginner. Inexpensive adult day tickets and private lessons. Sleeping Giant is a locally owned nonprofit ski area dedicated to bringing a positive outdoor experience to the school kids in the surrounding communities with a package that gives the child rentals, lesson, ticket and bus ride.

Open Fridays through Sundays and some holidays.

The base lodge has a rental shop, ski school, and two dining options:

Betty's Grill: The cafe has cool and hot drinks to quench your thirst. Entrees range from $3.00 – $7.25 include soups, chilis, quesadillas, burgers, pizza, nachos, burritos, taco salad, brats and dogs and are available 10 am-3 pm .

T-Bar: Upstairs tucked in the attic is Wyoming's smallest bar- don't be shy to ring the beer bell! They carry beer and wine. So go ahead ring the bell (it does not mean you have to buy everyone a round- but if you wish, wink wink).

NORDIC SKIING

The all-volunteer non-profit Park County Nordic Ski Association (PCNSA) features over 12 miles (19.3 kilometers) of groomed trails at Pahaska Tepee, the Eastern gateway of Yellowstone National Park, west of Cody, Wyoming. These trails are leased through a special use permit from the U.S.F.S. – Shoshone National Forest and come right through Sleeping Giant. So head to the teepee and skate to the Giant for some snacks or to grab a beer!

SLEEPING**GIANT** *ski area*

EASIEST ●
INTERMEDIATE ■
EXPERT ◆
BOUNDARY LINE
OUT of BOUNDARY ACCESS ▲
LIFT ▬

Red Cross/Ski Patrol ✚
Freestyle Terrain Park ▬
Slow Zone
Chapel Area ✚
Ski School
Snowmaking ✳
Cross Country Path

Upper Far West

Pucker

Yellowstone Traverse

Grizzly Glades

Gunbarrel

Hawkeye

North Fork Traverse

Stagecoach

Drano

Huckleberry

Reg/Ridge

T-bar

Twigg's Trail

First Face

Second Face

Pine Pitch

Little Snake

Twigg's Trail

The Slot

Freddy's Run

Lower Far West

Wapiti

Shoshone Steeps

Last Chance

Moose Drool

Silvertip Traverse

Midway Unload

Puff-n-Stuff

SHEEPEATER

Lobo

Colter

Third Face

Catch Pen

Pipeline

AVALANCHE AREA

Short Shot

Squirrly

Wild Bill

Husky Hollow

Hops

Bottleneck

Cubby

WONDERCARPET

Bobby's Headwall

BIGHORN

Lazy JD

Dolo's Run

Meadow

Red Star

Calamity

National Park

Terrain Park

Upper Homebound Traverse

Lower Homebound Traverse

Canfield Traverse

Gulch

SLEEPING GIANT *ski area*

Sleeping Giant Ski Area operates under a special use permit with the Shoshone National Forest.

Pine Creek

Established: 1952	Acres: 640	Vertical: 1400'	Annual Snowfall: 300"

Pine Creek Ski Resort is centrally located just east of Cokeville in western Wyoming. Getting there is easy from Kemmerer, Evanston, Star Valley, and Bear Lake Valley in Idaho. The mountain is a part of the Tunp Range –it rises to 8,225 feet at the summit and features more than 1,400 vertical feet of skiing.

The mountain has 30 runs and the the shortest lines around. The runs vary in difficulty, for all types of skiers. Whether you are just beginning or have been skiing for several years Pine Creek has a run for you. Only open for Friday through Sunday, 9:30 am to 4 pm.

The day lodge was recently renovated and contains the retail/rental shop and snack bar. Outside you can soak up the views from the warmth of the fire pits.

Meadowlark Ski Lodge

Established: 2010	Acres: 300	Vertical: 1000'	Annual Snowfall: 300"

Meadowlark Ski Lodge in the Big Horn Mountains offers skiing, boarding and snowmobiling. The rental shop has boards, skis, boots, helmet and pole rentals. The gift shop has goggles, snow pants, coats, hats, gloves, boarding pants sweatshirts and t-shirts. Great gift ideas! After hitting the slopes, warm up in the dining area with warm soup and hot chocolate or grab a bite to eat from their buffet line. Cozy up to the fireplace or enjoy the full service bar.

Snowmobile rentals, snowshoe, cross-country ski rentals are available at the Lake lodge across the lake from the ski hill. Meadowlark Lake Lodge provides lodging, a restaurant and full bar.

The beauty of the Big Horn mountains is breathtaking. Come and enjoy the winter!

Hogadon Basin

| Established: 1958 | Acres: 60 | Vertical: 600' | Annual Snowfall: 80" |

As part of the City of Casper Parks system Hogadon Basin Ski Area is a place like no other in Wyoming. Located just south of the City of Casper atop Casper Mountain, offering scenic panoramic views of downtown Casper and a stunning vista of the Big Horn Mountains.

Hogadon Basin offers skiers and snowboarders trails for beginners to experts. Group and private lessons are available along with access to all of the rental equipment you will need. This is a one stop shop where you will be able to get a lift ticket, rental equipment, and a ski lesson all in one place.

Not only is Hogadon Basin is a family-oriented winter destination, it also has hiking / mountain biking trails for summer adventures.

Hogadon Basin is a unique ski area in that guests park at the top and ski to the lift at the bottom. This allows everyone that one extra run! With very few ski areas like this in the United States Hogadon Basin is a must ski!

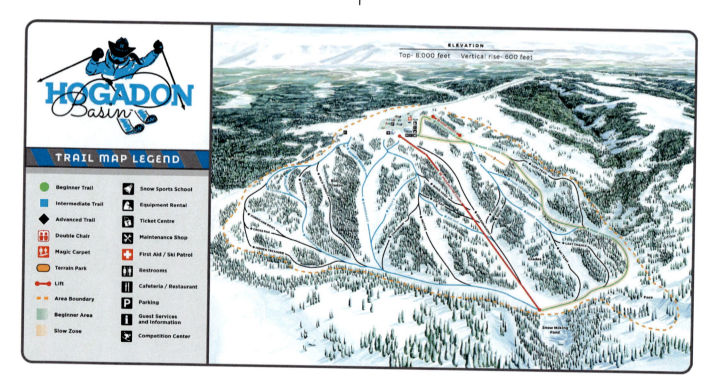

PHOTO CREDITS

Photos are courtesy of the individual ski areas unless otherwise stated here or in the ski area write-up. Photo credits are listed clockwise on the page starting in the upper left corner.

Alpine Meadows: Grant Kaye Ben Arnst, Tom Zikas, Grant Kaye, Jeff Engerbretsen
Arapahoe Basin Ski Area: Dave Camara/Arapahoe Basin Ski Area
Beaver Creek: Jack Affleck
Big Sky: Glenniss Indreland, Jeff Engerbretson, Cody Whitmer, Michel Tallichet, Jeff Engerbretson
Breckenridge: Jack Affleck (upper left & right), Andrew Maguire
Brian's Head: Mike Saemisch
Bridger Bowl: Austin Larson, Jennie Milton, Rob Wales
Copper Mountain Resort: Tripp Fay
Crystal Mountain: Rory Robison, Jeff Wolff, Jason Anglin, Kyle Coxen
Northstar: Chris Bartkowski, Jocelyn Little, Corey Rich
Keystone: Daniel Milchev, Jack Affleck, Sean Boggs, Tom Cohen
Kirkwood: Corey Rich
Park City: Mike Madsen, Dan Campbell, Jack Affleck
Snowbird: Matt Crawley
Squaw Valley: Grant Kaye, Trevor Clark, Jeff Engerbretsen (2)
Steamboat: Larry Pierce/Steamboat Ski Resort
Summit at Snoqualmie (Alpental): Jeff Hawe (upper left & lower right)
Summit at Snoqualmie (Central): Jeff Hawe (upper left)
Tamarack Resort: Reid Morth
Willamette Pass: Larry Turner, Jeff Kraemer (lodge)

Cover is courtesy of Bogus Basin with layout by Jim Boydston, Boydo Graphics of Portland Oregon

Maps are courtesy of Google

SKI AREA CONTACT INFORMATION

State	Ski Area Name	Phone #	Website
AZ	Arizona Snowbowl	928-779-1951	https://www.arizonasnowbowl.com
AZ	Sunrise Park Resort	855-735-SNOW	http://sunriseskiparkaz.com
CA	Alpine Meadows	800-403-0206	http://squawalpine.com
CA	Bear Mountain	909-866-5766	http://www.bigbearmountainresort.com
CA	Bear Valley	209-753-2301	https://www.bearvalley.com
CA	Boreal Mountain	530-426-3666	http://www.rideboreal.com
CA	China Peak	559-233-2500	http://www.skichinapeak.com
CA	Dodge Ridge	209-965-3474	http://www.dodgeridge.com
CA	Donner Ski Ranch	530-426-3635	https://www.donnerskiranch.com
CA	Granlibakken	800-543-3221	http://granlibakken.com
CA	Heavenly	775-586-7000	http://www.skiheavenly.com
CA	Homewood Mountain Resort	530-525-2992	http://www.skihomewood.com
CA	June Mountain	888-856-3686	https://www.junemountain.com
CA	Kirkwood	209-258-6000	http://www.kirkwood.com
CA	Mammoth Mountain	800-626-6684	https://www.mammothmountain.com
CA	Mountain High	888-754-7878	http://www.mthigh.com
CA	Mt. Baldy	909-982-0800	https://mtbaldyresort.com
CA	Mt. Shasta Ski Park	530-926-8610	https://www.skipark.com
CA	Mt. Waterman	619-708-6595	http://www.mtwaterman.org
CA	Northstar	800-466-6784	http://www.northstarcalifornia.com
CA	Sierra-at-Tahoe	530-659-7453	https://www.sierraattahoe.com
CA	Snow Summit	909-866-5766	http://www.bigbearmountainresort.com
CA	Snow Valley	909-867-2751	http://www.snow-valley.com
CA	Soda Springs	530-426-3901	http://www.skisodasprings.com
CA	Squaw Valley	800-403-0206	http://squawalpine.com
CA	Sugar Bowl	530-426-9000	http://www.sugarbowl.com
CA	Tahoe Donner	530-587-9444	http://www.tahoedonner.com
CA	Yosemite Ski & Snowboard Area	209-372-8430	http://www.travelyosemite.com
CO	Arapahoe Basin	888-ARAPAHOE	http://arapahoebasin.com
CO	Aspen	800-525-6200	https://www.aspensnowmass.com
CO	Beaver Creek	866-348-9028	http://www.beavercreek.com
CO	Breckenridge	800-985-9842	http://www.breckenridge.com
CO	Cooper	800-707-6114	http://skicooper.com
CO	Copper Mountain	866-841-2481	http://www.coppercolorado.com
CO	Crested Butte	844-993-9545	http://www.skicb.com

State	Ski Area Name	Phone #	Website
CO	Echo Mountain	970-531-5038	https://www.echomountainresort.com
CO	Eldora	303-440-8700	https://www.eldora.com
CO	Granby Ranch	888-850-4615	http://www.granbyranch.com
CO	Hesperus	970-259-3711	https://www.ski-hesperus.com
CO	Howelsen Hill	970-879-8499	http://steamboatsprings.net/ski
CO	Keystone	800-238-1323	http://www.keystoneresort.com
CO	Loveland	800-736-3SKI	http://skiloveland.com
CO	Monarch Mountain	719-530-5000	http://www.skimonarch.com
CO	Powderhorn	970-268-5700	http://www.powderhorn.com
CO	Purgatory	970-247-9000	https://www.purgatoryresort.com
CO	Silverton Mountain	970-387-5706	http://silvertonmountain.com
CO	Steamboat	877-783-2628	https://www.steamboat.com
CO	Sunlight Mountain Resort	800-445-7931	http://sunlightmtn.com
CO	Telluride	877-935-5021	http://www.tellurideskiresort.com
CO	Vail	970-754-8245	http://www.vail.com
CO	Winter Park	800-979-0332	https://www.winterparkresort.com
CO	Wolf Creek	800-754-9653	https://wolfcreekski.com
ID	Bald Mountain	208-464-2311	http://skibaldmountain.com
ID	Bogus Basin	208-332-5100	http://bogusbasin.org
ID	Brundage Mountain	208-634-4151	https://brundage.com
ID	Kelly Canyon	208-538-6251	http://www.skikelly.com
ID	Little Ski Hill	208-634-5691	http://www.littleskihill.org
ID	Lookout Pass	208-744-1301	https://skilookout.com
ID	Magic Mountain	208-736-7669	http://www.magicmountainresort.com
ID	Pebble Creek	208-775-4452	http://pebblecreekskiarea.com
ID	Pomerelle	208-673-5599	http://www.pomerelle.com
ID	Schweitzer Mountain	208-263-9555	http://www.schweitzer.com
ID	Silver Mountain	888-344-6275	http://www.silvermt.com
ID	Snowhaven	208-983-3866	http://grangeville.us (select Snowhaven)
ID	Soldier Mountain	208-764-2526	http://www.soldiermountain.com
ID	Sun Valley	888-490-5950	https://www.sunvalley.com
ID	Tamarack	208-325-1000	http://tamarackidaho.com
MT	Bear Paw Ski Bowl	406-265-8404	http://www.skibearpaw.com
MT	Big Sky Resort	800-548-4486	http://bigskyresort.com
MT	Blacktail Mountain	406-844-0999	http://www.blacktailmountain.com
MT	Bridger Bowl	800-223-9609	https://bridgerbowl.com
MT	Discovery Ski Area	406-563-2184	http://www.skidiscovery.com

State	Ski Area Name	Phone #	Website
MT	Great Divide	406-449-3746	http://skigd.com
MT	Lost Trail Powder Mountain	406-821-3742	https://losttrail.com
MT	Maverick Mountain	406-834-3454	http://www.skimaverick.com
MT	Red Lodge Mountain	800-444-8977	http://www.redlodgemountain.com
MT	Showdown Montana	800-433-0022	http://www.showdownmontana.com
MT	Snowbowl	406-549-9777	http://www.montanasnowbowl.com
MT	Turner Mountain	406-293-2468	http://www.skiturner.com
MT	Whitefish	877-SKI-FISH	https://skiwhitefish.com
NV	Diamond Peak	775-832-1177	http://www.diamondpeak.com
NV	Elko Snobowl	775-777-7260	https://www.facebook.com/snobowl
NV	Lee Canyon	702-385-2754	http://www.leecanyonlv.com
NV	Mt. Rose - Ski Tahoe	800-SKI-ROSE	http://skirose.com
NM	Angel Fire	844-218-4107	https://www.angelfireresort.com
NM	Pajarito Mountain	505-662-5725	https://skipajarito.com
NM	Red River	575-754-2223	http://www.redriverskiarea.com
NM	Sandia Peak	505-242-9052	http://www.sandiapeak.com
NM	Sipapu	800-587-2240	https://www.sipapunm.com
NM	Ski Apache	800-545-9011	http://www.skiapache.com
NM	Ski Cloudcroft	575-682-2333	http://skicloudcroft.net
NM	Ski Santa Fe	505-982-4429	https://skisantafe.com
NM	Taos	800-776-1111	https://www.skitaos.com
OR	Anthony Lakes	541-856-3277	http://anthonylakes.com
OR	Cooper Spur	541-352-6692	http://cooperspur.com
OR	Hoodoo	541-822-3799	http://skihoodoo.com
OR	Mt. Ashland	541-482-2897	http://www.mtashland.com
OR	Mt. Bachelor	800-829-2442	http://www.mtbachelor.com
OR	Mt. Hood Meadows	503-337-2222	https://www.skihood.com
OR	Mt. Hood Skibowl	503-272-3206	http://www.skibowl.com
OR	Timberline	503-272-3311	http://www.timberlinelodge.com
OR	Warner Canyon Ski Area	541-947-5001	http://warnercanyon.org
OR	Willamette Pass	541-345-SNOW	http://www.willamettepass.com
UT	Alta	801-359-1078	http://www.alta.com
UT	Beaver Mountain	435-946-3610	http://www.skithebeav.com
UT	Brian Head Resort	435-677-2035	http://www.brianhead.com
UT	Brighton	855-201-SNOW	http://www.brightonresort.com
UT	Cherry Peak	435-200-5050	http://www.skicherrypeak.com
UT	Deer Valley	800-424-3337	http://www.deervalley.com

State	Ski Area Name	Phone #	Website
UT	Eagle Point	855-EAGLE-PT	https://www.eaglepointresort.com
UT	Nordic Valley	801-745-3511	http://nordicvalley.com
UT	Park City	435-649-8111	http://www.parkcitymountain.com
UT	Powder Mountain	801-745-3772	http://www.powdermountain.com
UT	Snowbasin	888-437-5488	https://www.snowbasin.com
UT	Snowbird	800-232-9542	http://www.snowbird.com
UT	Solitude	801-534-1400	https://solitudemountain.com
UT	Sundance	866-259-7468	https://www.sundanceresort.com
WA	49° North	509-935-6649	http://www.ski49n.com
WA	Bluewood	509-382-4725	http://bluewood.com
WA	Crystal Mountain	888-754-6199	https://crystalmountainresort.com
WA	Hurricane Ridge	848-667-7669	https://hurricaneridge.com
WA	Leavenworth Ski Hill	509-548-6975	https://www.skileavenworth.com
WA	Loup Loup	509-557-3401	https://skitheloup.com
WA	Mission Ridge	509-665-6543	https://www.missionridge.com
WA	Mt. Baker	360-734-6771	http://mtbaker.us
WA	Mt. Spokane	509-238-2220	http://www.mtspokane.com
WA	Stevens Pass	206-812-4510	https://www.stevenspass.com
WA	The Summit at Snoqualmie	425-434-7669	http://www.summitatsnoqualmie.com
WA	White Pass	509-672-3101	http://skiwhitepass.com
WY	Grand Targhee	800-TARGHEE	http://www.grandtarghee.com
WY	Hogadon Basin	307-235-8499	http://www.hogadon.net
WY	Jackson Hole Mountain Resort	888-DEEP-SNO	https://www.jacksonhole.com
WY	Meadowlark Ski Lodge	307-267-2609	http://www.lodgesofthebighorns.com
WY	Pine Creek	307-279-3201	http://www.pinecreekskiresort.com
WY	Sleeping Giant	307-587-3125	http://www.skisg.com
WY	Snow King Mountain	307-201-KING	https://snowkingmountain.com
WY	Snowy Range	877-I-SKI-WYO	https://www.snowyrangeski.com
WY	White Pine	307-367-6606	http://www.whitepineski.com

ABOUT THE AUTHOR

I grew up in a family of cross-country skiers. Going downhill was avoided since it often resulted in awkward poses on the ground with skis pointed in all directions. This made for great photo opportunities for my dad. At that time, skiing was still known for broken legs so I had no desire to take up such a costly and dangerous sport. Eventually at the age of 40, I figured I should at least try it since it seemed like many people (especially coworkers) enjoyed it so much. I took my first lesson in 2010 at Stevens Pass. After taking the advice of the instructor to "point your knees the direction you want to go," I made enough turns to fall in love with the sport.

Now I am addicted so much that when I can't be skiing, I enjoy making functional ski art from old skis. Skis are built with such durable materials that they will take thousands of years to decompose in a landfill, therefore I started a local recycling program at a few ski shops and Stevens Pass. I usually have more skis than I need, so I give away the excess skis to other craftsmen and people building ski fences. My creations are available on Etsy or just visit SkiArtistry.com and it will take you there.

Fortunately, my lovely bride (Joan) and my daughters (Julia and Natalie) are very supportive of my hobbies.

Ski Artistry.com

Made in the USA
San Bernardino, CA
31 October 2018